# Praise for *Discovering Jesus in the Old Testament*

*Discovering Jesus in the Old Testament* is an insightful and relevant guide for understanding full revelation in Jesus Christ. Pam, Jean, and Karla are quite the team! They creatively draw out important theological truths from Genesis through the prophets and offer practical ways to apply these truths to our lives today.

**Sean McDowell**, PhD, author, speaker, professor

Sometimes we act like our picture of Jesus is limited to the text of the Gospels. But as Jones, Farrel, and Dornacher show, the entire Old Testament is a rich source of knowledge about Jesus that has the same power to impact our lives. I'm delighted in the Old Testament passages they chose to dig into: ones that will satisfy your mind, challenge your spirit, and make your heart sing. Simply put, this is a beautiful book. It is beautiful in its layout and artwork, and beautiful in the full and vibrant ways it illustrates the person, the work, and the glory of the Savior.

**Craig Hazen**, PhD, Biola University apologetics program director, author of *Fearless Prayer*

This book is desperately needed in the realm of Bible studies. Understanding how the Old Testament consistently points to Jesus is extremely important; yet, it's admittedly a complex subject. I love how *Discovering Jesus in the Old Testament* makes the richness of the subject understandable for anyone and is structured in such a memorable way. I'll be recommending this for years to come.

**Natasha Crain**, author of *Keeping Your Kids on God's Side* and *Talking with Your Kids About God*

*Discovering Jesus in the Old Testament* is a theologically rich yet accessible and attractive study—a rare gem! It will appeal to a wide range of readers, from novices to seasoned students of Scripture. I will recommend it frequently.

**Melissa Cain Travis**, PhD, assistant professor, Houston Baptist University

*Discovering Jesus in the Old Testament* is a fun and insightful Bible study that I recommend to women everywhere. If you want to engage your creativity while gaining seminary-level knowledge, this study is for you!

**Alisa Childers**, host of *The Alisa Childers* podcast and contributor to *Mama Bear Apologetics*

Jean, Pam, and Karla have done it again! *Discovering Jesus in the Old Testament* is a Bible study you'll devour. As a Bible teacher and pastor's wife, I know how hard it is to find compelling studies that grip you with insight, draw you closer to Jesus, and leave you breathless at the wonders of God. This study delivers the goods!

**Donna Jones**, national speaker, pastor's wife, and author

*Discovering Jesus in the Old Testament* is a tour de force, masterfully showing how the person of Jesus Christ is woven throughout the pages of the Bible from Genesis to Revelation.

**Hillary Morgan Ferrer**, Mama Bear Apologetics director, editor of *Mama Bear Apologetics*

Studying the Old Testament is important to understand God's pursuit of us from the very beginning. *Discovering Jesus in the Old Testament* is a powerful tool to examine how Jesus's coming to earth was not Plan B...or even Plan E. This Bible study is not only a creative outlet and expression but also a solid study by the strong Farrel-Jones-Dornacher team. I can't wait to share this with the women at my church.

**Janet Holm McHenry**, author of 24 books, including the bestselling *PrayerWalk*

Pam, Jean, and Karla have done it again! *Discovering Jesus in the Old Testament* is an eye-opening study that dusts for Jesus' fingerprints and discovers Jesus' footprints all through the Old Testament.

**Sharon Jaynes**, author of *Enough: Silencing the Lies that Steal Your Confidence*

*Discovering Jesus in the Old Testament* allows you to fully see and experience Jesus. He is the one who defines you and brings full meaning to your life. Through this insightful study coupled with empowering life application, you will discover a Savior who not only came to rescue you, but who offers to change you, bringing new life and meaning into anything you are facing.

**Erica Wiggenhorn**, author of *Unexplainable Jesus*

Do you want to have a clearer picture of who Jesus is? Often we think about simply exploring the New Testament to learn more about Jesus, but the Old Testament is filled with portraits of our Savior. In *Discovering Jesus in the Old Testament*, you will have the perfect opportunity to study the Son of God who was and is and always will be. Your love for Jesus is sure to grow as you get to know him from the perspective of the Old Testament.

**Karol Ladd**, author of *Becoming a Woman of the Word*

Just as God created the cosmos to be an orderly arrangement of parts, each working in harmony with the whole, so the Word of God is flawlessly congruent. All its parts speak the same message, each enhancing it and unveiling its mysteries. This trifecta of amazing women has merged their gifts for unpacking the truths of God's Word and has produced an amazing and essential resource showing that Jesus is the one and only message.

**Jennifer Kennedy Dean**, author of *Live a Praying Life®* and numerous books

*Discovering Jesus in the Old Testament* is the most unique Bible study I've ever seen. It combines the depth of rich biblical teaching, the practical application of how the main points matter to us today, and stunning artistry that catches the eye, emphasizes the subject of each week's teaching, and gives a fun activity that reinforces learning. If you're looking for a study that will help you get to know Jesus more personally and increase your understanding of Scripture, look no further. I love the format and the depth of meaningful content in this study. Don't miss it!

**Carol Kent**, speaker and author of *He Holds My Hand: Experiencing God's Presence & Provision*

What a wonderful resource for small groups and individuals alike! Designed to help readers experience Bible study in a fresh, new, and interactive way, *Discovering Jesus in the Old Testament* sheds biblical light on the relentless and eternal love of God expressed in the person of Jesus Christ and revealed consistently throughout both the Old and the New Testaments. Buckle up and enjoy the ride! You're in for a life-changing adventure in the Word!

**Stephanie Shott**, pastor's wife, Bible teacher, author, and founder of The MOM Initiative

All of Scripture points to the centrality of Jesus Christ! If you want to dive in and discover Jesus in the Old Testament, this is your study! Beautifully written and illustrated, Pam Farrel, Jean E. Jones, and Karla Dornacher have delivered an amazing and powerful Bible study! I highly recommend!

**Becky Harling**, speaker, author of *Who Do You Say That I Am?*, podcast host of Beyond Beautiful

Once again this dynamic team has made Scripture sing in a deep and engaging way. *Discovering Jesus in the Old Testament* brings the promises of God to life. I can't wait to share it with everyone I know... it's that good.

**Gari Meacham**, author of *Watershed Moments*, *Truly Fed*, and *Be Free*; president of The Vine Uganda

In *Discovering Jesus in the Old Testament*, Pam, Karla, and Jean capture the great mercy of the Lord in redeeming his children, a plan he devised from before the foundation of the world—a plan unveiled through the earliest pages of Scripture, his mighty prophets, and even the psalmists. They remind us the God of the Bible does not change, and his purposes and promises cannot be foiled.

**Dawn M. Wilson**, founder of Heart Choices Today

# DISCOVERING JESUS IN THE OLD TESTAMENT

## PAM FARREL & JEAN E. JONES
author & illustrator **KARLA DORNACHER**

**HARVEST HOUSE PUBLISHERS**
EUGENE, OREGON

Cover design by Dugan Design Group

**Discovering Jesus in the Old Testament**

Copyright © 2019 text by Pam Farrel, Jean E. Jones, and Karla Dornacher. Illustrations © Karla Dornacher
Published by Harvest House Publishers
Eugene, Oregon 97408
www.harvesthousepublishers.com

ISBN 978-0-7369-7520-9 (pbk.)

Library of Congress Cataloging-in-Publication Data is on file at the Library of Congress, Washington, DC.

**Printed in the United States of America**

21  22  23  24  25  26  27  / CM-JC /  10  9  8  7  6  5  4  3  2

## Dedication

To all those who love the deep richness and life-forming truth of God's Word and thrive on learning more of the Christ who gave it all for you:

[We] pray...that Christ may dwell in your hearts through faith. And [we] pray that you, being rooted and established in love, may have power, together with all the Lord's holy people, to grasp how wide and long and high and deep is the love of Christ, and to know this love that surpasses knowledge—that you may be filled to the measure of all the fullness of God (Ephesians 3:16-19 NIV).
~ All of us

To Jesus, my life-giving, heart-transforming, wisdom-teaching, wonderful Savior who "redeemed my life from the pit" and brought me to the pulpit—I am forever grateful! To my husband, Bill: my pastor, best friend, life companion, and the best Bible teacher I know—thank you for pouring love and wisdom into me.
~ Pam

To my Lord and Savior, your love for people and your plan to bring us to dwell with you astonishes me. To Clay, your love, kindness, humor, and wisdom fill me with joy.
~ Jean E.

To Jesus...discovering you is the best thing that ever happened to me! To my dear friend and mentor, Sandi Phillips: thank you for inspiring me to love God's Word as passionately as you do.
~ Karla

# Contents

## Do You Want to See Jesus in the Old Testament?

Welcome to *Discovering Jesus in the Old Testament*. This is a 12-week study designed to help you learn from God's Word, apply what you've learned, and rejoice in God's amazing plan for us.

The Old Testament reveals that God created humans to dwell with him. But something happened to separate people from God. Through the ages, God revealed his plan to reunite people with himself so that they could again dwell with him.

The New Testament reveals that Jesus "was foreknown before the foundation of the world but was made manifest in the last times" (1 Peter 1:20). That amazes me! I (Jean) love looking at the Old Testament from the vantage point of how God revealed his eternal plan. His great love, care, and patience are on display, along with his compassion for those who suffer, his righteous anger with those who mistreat others, and his mercy toward those who seek forgiveness.

As we see God's plan unveil, we'll also discover lessons we can apply to our lives. The Old Testament abounds in examples of how to walk with God. After all, these are the Scriptures from which Jesus and the New Testament writers taught.

Many of God's revelations about Jesus occur in the prophetic books. The New Testament explains how Jesus fulfilled numerous prophecies in his first coming. It teaches that he'll fulfill the rest in his second coming. We'll concentrate on the former and touch on the latter. Conservative Christian scholars differ in their interpretations of passages about his second coming, so we'll not take a position on those. After all, the main things are the plain things, and the plain things are the main things. The important thing is Jesus is coming to take us to our eternal dwelling place with the Lord our God.

### Why We Wrote this Discovery Book for You

Pam, Karla, and I (Jean), with our different paths and gifts, have connected over our love for interacting with God's Word and encouraging others to experience the hope of his promises and faithfulness.

All of us grew up without a Christian influence in the home and know what it's like to encounter the Old Testament for the first time when older. Many women tell us they would love to know more about the Old Testament. Others have expressed confusion over atheist claims that "the God of the Old Testament" is not a God of love. Our hearts break when we hear this because nothing could be farther from the truth! God never changes (James 1:17). God is love, and he has always been love (1 John 4:8). Just like us, he's angry when people intentionally wrong others and commit horrific crimes. But unlike us, he's quick to offer mercy and a way to be washed clean from sins, no matter how bad. His plan to save is also a plan to end evil.

With love,

Jean F., Pam, Karla

## The Treasures in Each Chapter

We collaborated on this book to inspire *you*. Here's what you'll find in every chapter.

### Daily Lessons—Jean

You'll hear from me throughout this journey. In each chapter, I share an introduction to one key hope that the Old Testament reveals about Jesus. The chapters have five daily lessons that will take 20–25 minutes to finish. Each Day 5 lesson concludes by guiding you in a private time of worship and prayer. The lessons use these icons:

♥ This is a personal question designed to help you apply what you're learning to your life and to possibly spark a rich discussion with others.

This activity guides you in prayer and worship.

An activity marked with this has further instructions on www.DiscoveringTheBibleSeries.com.

### The Little Details—Jean

Along the way, you'll see sidebars titled The Little Details. These are extra insights for both seasoned Christians and seekers who thrive on details.

### A Walk with Christ—Pam

Pam's A Walk with Christ devotionals invite you to rest in God's strength and love. She shares some of her go-to ways for remembering and holding on to the promises of Jesus. She'll take you forward with faith and hope.

### The Heart and Art of Worship—Karla

You'll hear from Karla at the end of each chapter. She'll encourage you to connect creatively with God and others as you delight in God's eternal plan throughout this study.

### Illustrations—Karla

The bookmarks and coloring pages will help you connect with God's Word as you spend time coloring and meditating on each verse. You can also slip designs under a page in your Bible, sketchbook, or journal for tracing.

### Creative Ideas—All of Us

The Creative Ideas appendix offers fresh ways to express, experience, and meditate on passages. Discover your favorites! What a gift it is to have God's eternal plan to save us etched on your mind, heart, and spirit.

## Discover More on www.DiscoveringTheBibleSeries.com

Here are the extras you'll find on our website.

- Instructions for how to use this discovery book for both small groups and individual study
- A small group leader's guide
- Timelines
- Action steps from this book summarized and illustrated for you to download and color
- Links to worship music to go with each chapter
- Links to Karla's art instructions
- Links to articles that go deeper into chapter topics
- More inspiring ideas

## Chapter 1

# Genesis 3
## Jesus the Serpent Crusher

The hope of evil's end

He will crush your head, and you will strike his heel.

genesis 3:15 niv

### Day 1

## How It All Began

For my seventeenth birthday, my then-boyfriend Clay gave me (Jean) a white leather Bible containing both the Old and New Testaments. Until then, I'd had only a paperback New Testament. Not having been raised in a Christian home, I was excited to finally be able to read the rest of the Bible and see what it said.

As I read through Genesis, I thought, *So that's what happened! God created people good, and that was Plan A. But they blew it and disobeyed, so God had to go with Plan B, a flood.* Later, I read about God calling Israel to be a nation and giving them commandments. But the Israelites blew it and disobeyed God too. I thought, *Israel was Plan C, and Jesus was Plan D! God had to keep starting over because people kept messing up his plans.*

I was wrong.

I had missed the significance of 1 Peter 1:20, which says Jesus "was foreknown before the foundation of the world but was made manifest in the last times." Revelation 13:8 (NIV) reads similarly: Jesus is "the Lamb who was slain from the creation of the world." And there's 2 Timothy 1:8-10, which reads, "God...saved us and called us...because of his own purpose and grace, which he gave us in Christ Jesus before the ages began, and which now has been manifested through the appearing of our Savior Christ Jesus."

In other words, God knew before he created the world and the first humans that Jesus would one day die for the sins of the world. He knew Satan would deceive Adam and Eve, and he had a plan in place to rescue humankind. There was always just one plan. This book will show how he revealed that plan over time, beginning in Eve's lifetime.

### The Reveal

*Eve's Day*

"In the beginning, God." Those are the first four words of the Bible. They introduce the story of how God created the heavens and the earth and then populated the earth with birds, fish, and animals.

### God's Word to Us

Take a moment to pray for insight as you read God's Word.

## The Little Details
### Genesis

Genesis is a book of beginnings: the beginning of creation, of humans, of sin on earth, and of the reveal of God's plan to bring people back into relationship with him. It's the first book of the Bible and the first of the five books of Moses. Together the five books are called the Pentateuch. Professor Albert H. Baylis writes that Moses knew the people were going to a land whose inhabitants worshiped gods that were "like most people—and worse! They play and drink, and drink too much. They fight, deceive, and engage in licentious behavior."[1] Since "people become like the gods they worship,"[2] Moses's challenge was to show in Genesis what the true God was like.

In Genesis 1, Moses shows that "God is the transcendent, sovereign ruler of the creation. He is in complete control. He is not a part of it. Nor does it control him. It came into existence at his command...The surrounding gods are nonentities."[3] People thought humanity's purpose was to serve the pagan gods, but the true God created humankind for fellowship.

1. ♥ Read Genesis 1:26-31; 2:5-17; and all of chapter 3. What stands out to you from your initial reading of these passages? Why?

Quite a story, isn't it? Let's look at some of the pertinent details.

2. (a) When God looked over his creation, what did he see it was (Genesis 1:25)? (b) In whose image did he create the man and woman (verse 27)? (c) What blessing did he give them (verse 28)?

The man and woman were God's image-bearers. God blessed them and told them to fill the earth with more image-bearers, subduing the earth and ruling over all its creatures.

3. When God looked over his creation, what did he see it was (Genesis 1:31)?

God placed them in a garden with a river and fruit trees. God walked with them and talked with them. The garden was a sanctuary where he could dwell with his people. He created the first couple not just to rule, but to fellowship with him.

4. (a) What two special trees were in the middle of the garden (Genesis 2:9)? (b) What did God command the man not to eat (verses 16-17)? (c) What would happen if they ate (verse 17)?

And that's where things go wrong.

5. ♥ Describe a time you learned the hard way that a prohibition was in your best interest. Or describe a time your children learned the hard way that something you told them not to do was in their best interest.

# A Walk with Christ—Kick Satan to the Curb

Has the unwelcome, unwanted, unbearable, and unbelievably difficult entered your life? Maybe you said a little prayer when you picked up this book, hoping this study would help you become stronger, braver, and wiser. It is human to feel overwhelmed, exhausted, and undone. We all have those "desert days." I have been to this desert described in Matthew 4:1-11, where Christ walked. It is hot, rugged, rocky, and desolate.

Jesus went to the desert to fast, pray, and commune with God. When he was weary and hungry, Satan tried to trip him up so the triumph of the cross would not happen. Three times, Satan tempted Jesus. Three times, Christ answered by quoting the Word out loud. At the end of the 40 desert days then on through the cross and resurrection, the victory was secured by Christ! How did Jesus defeat Satan? Truth! God's Word is the power to overcome. Dr. Tim Muehlhoff, author of *Defending Your Marriage: The Reality of Spiritual Battle* shares that 25 percent of what Christ talked about in the Bible is about the battle we are in.

Satan uses the same devious tactics on us as he did on Christ. And to conquer him, God has equipped us with armor, described in Ephesians 6:13-17:

> Put on the full armor of God, so that when the day of evil comes, you may be able to stand your ground, and after you have done everything, to stand. Stand firm then, with the belt of truth buckled around your waist, with the breastplate of righteousness in place, and with your feet fitted with the readiness that comes from the gospel of peace. In addition to all this, take up the shield of faith, with which you can extinguish all the flaming arrows of the evil one. Take the helmet of salvation and the sword of the Spirit, which is the word of God (NIV).

## The power is in the Word.

Satan cannot read our minds; only God knows our thoughts. A solid defense against the attacks of Satan is to do what Jesus did: Speak out the truths of Scripture aloud over your life—and live like you believe in the victory God faithfully executes over evil. James 4:7 reminds us, "Submit yourselves, then, to God. Resist the devil, and he will flee from you (NIV)." If I gave you a backstage pass to my life, you would hear me proclaim something like this:

> Dear Lord Jesus, I proclaim your victory on the cross through your blood shed to redeem and rescue. I acknowledge your power to take back territory and move me from darkness to light. Satan has no power here to discourage, disrupt, disillusion, or depress me in any way. God, I stand in Your power, provision, peace, and protection affirming Romans 16:20 (NIV): "The God of peace will soon crush Satan under your feet."

God's crushing of Satan is a complete shattering into dust. Sometimes, I symbolically stomp my spiked high heel or beat my flip-flop on the ground as evidence God has kicked the evil out. Give it a try sometime. It is a power moment of trust and faith. This study will teach you more about Christ and the power of specific scriptures in the living Word to vanquish the devil.

Go to www.DiscoveringTheBibleSeries.com for resources to help you walk closer with Christ, including an *In the Savior's Sandals* devotional for each chapter based on places Christ walked in the Holy Land.

*Pam*

# The Promise to Eve

The opening pages of Genesis—the first book of the Bible—give us our first glimpses of Jesus in the Old Testament. Some hint at what later revelations expand upon. But there's also a promise of his coming that we don't want to miss. Let's dig in.

## The Garden

In the last lesson, we read that God commanded the man and woman to rule over the creatures of the earth. But when a serpent entered the garden, that's not what happened. This serpent "was more crafty than any of the wild animals the Lᴏʀᴅ God had made" (Genesis 3:1 ɴɪᴠ). The New Testament links the serpent to Satan (Revelation 12:9). Albert Baylis, in his book *From Creation to the Cross,* notes that in the garden came an "already fallen intelligence" (see sidebar).

Here's what God commanded: "You may surely eat of every tree of the garden, but of the tree of the knowledge of good and evil you shall not eat, for in the day that you eat of it you shall surely die" (Genesis 2:16-17).

> 6.  Compare Genesis 2:16-17 above with Genesis 3:1. How did the serpent's representation of God's command differ from God's actual command?

When the serpent asked, "Did God actually say?" it may have been the first time Eve had experienced a creature doubting God. The serpent exaggerated the Lord's command and emphasized the only thing the couple had been denied in the abundance of the garden.

> 7.  (a) In what way did the serpent say God had lied (Genesis 3:4)? (b) What did the serpent say was God's true motivation for denying the fruit (3:5)?

The woman had a choice: She could believe God, or she could believe the serpent. God had never given her reason to doubt his character or his word, but now the serpent told her God was denying her something that would benefit her. In other words, God wasn't acting in her best interest. Suddenly, the fruit was attractive. It looked good, would taste good, and would make her wise like God (Genesis 3:6). The desire to be like God, to be his equal even, enticed her, and she believed the serpent.

She reached out her hand, seized the fruit, ate, and gave some to her husband. Then their eyes opened, and the couple who had never known shame for the first time ever felt humiliation and guilt. They knew that they were naked and wanted to hide.

They tried to cover up their nakedness with fig leaves. When they heard God walking in the garden, they hid. This divine manifestation is called a *theophany* (see sidebar). When God called out, "Where are you?" the man replied, "I heard the sound of you in the garden, and I was afraid, because I was naked, and I hid myself" (Genesis 3:10). Fellowship was broken.

## The Little Details

### *Baylis on the Serpent:*

We are forbidden by the passage to make the scene mythical. We seem forbidden by the conversation to make the serpent one of God's good creatures and nothing more. It is clear from the narrative that a sinister mind is at work in the serpent. The ancient Israelite readers were aware of the use of the serpent as a god. They also recognized that false gods were demonic (Deut. 32:17). All of this agrees with the view of New Testament writers who identify the serpent with Satan (see John 8:44; Rev. 12:9; Rom. 16:20; 1 Cor. 10:20). Our account of the entrance of sin into human experience assumes an already fallen intelligence—devilishly so![4]

The woman had a choice: She could believe God, or she could believe the serpent.

God asked the man if he had eaten the forbidden fruit. God knew the answer but gave him a chance to confess.

8.  (a) What two beings did the man blame for his transgression (Genesis 3:12)? (b) Whom did the woman blame (Genesis 3:13)? (c) Does blaming others remove guilt? Why or why not?

Shifting blame started in the garden and continues today.

9.  ♥ (a) How does focusing on what we can't have instead of on what we do have affect our relationship with God? (b) Why is it important to remember God's intentions for us are good when we're tempted to disobey his commands?

## Hope Within Judgment

God judged the three beings, but in the judgment, he gave the man and woman hope. When he cursed the serpent, he said, "I will put enmity between you and the woman, and between your offspring and hers; he will crush your head, and you will strike his heel" (Genesis 3:15 NIV).

He pronounced judgment, but he didn't curse the couple. Instead, he promised a serpent crusher would one day come. The serpent would bruise his heel, but the woman's off-spring—literally her *seed*—would deal him a mortal blow.

Genesis 3:15 is called the *Protoevangelium* because it is the first announcement of the gospel: the good news that a seed of the woman will crush the serpent. The serpent will cause that seed to suffer, but the suffering seed will destroy the serpent.

God's judgment on the woman was that through painful labor she would bring forth children. Within the judgment lived the hope of bearing life. God's judgment on the man was that through painful toil he would bring forth food. Within the judgment lived the hope of sustaining life. Though they would eventually die, humans would continue.

God cursed the ground: It would bear thorns and thistles and was bound to decay (Genesis 3:17-19; Romans 8:21). Professor Clay Jones says, "Natural evil entered the world because God cursed the earth in response to Adam's sin. In fact, what pestilence—mold, decay, cancer, and so on—can't have ensued from God looking at planet Earth and saying, 'I curse you'?"[6]

When the man heard God's judgment coupled with hope, he in faith "named his wife Eve, because she would become the mother of all the living" (Genesis 3:20 NIV). *Eve* sounds like the Hebrew word for *living*. The man continued to be called by the Hebrew word for *man, 'ādām* or Adam. In compassion, God clothed Adam and Eve, covering their nakedness and protecting them from the elements.

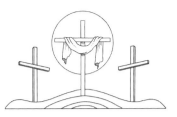

## The Little Details
### *Theophany*

Throughout the Old Testament, God reveals himself to some people in a way that is tangible to human senses; for instance, a human form or a physical manifestation such as a burning bush. This type of divine revelation is called a *theophany*. The first mention of a theophany in Scripture is Genesis 3:8, where the man and woman hear God walking in the garden.

Prophets such as Abraham and Moses experienced quite a few theophanies. In fact, the Lord regularly spoke with Moses "face-to-face, as one speaks to a friend" (Exodus 33:11). However, God did not fully reveal himself to even Moses. When Moses asked to see God's glory, God refused and said Moses couldn't see his face and live (Exodus 33:20). *The New Dictionary of Biblical Theology* explains: "Apparently God's 'glory' and 'face' refer in 33:18-23 to the full splendor of his majesty, which he was not willing to reveal."[5]

---

God judged the three beings, but in the judgment, he gave the man and woman hope.

---

**The Little Details**

*T. Desmond Alexander on God's Dwelling Place:*

The opening chapters of Genesis assume that the earth will be God's dwelling place. This expectation, however, is swiftly shattered when Adam and Eve disobey God and are expelled from his presence. From there he occasionally descends to meet with selected individuals, although these encounters are always relatively brief and sometimes unexpected. When God reveals himself, it is always for a particular purpose. This pattern is found throughout almost all of Genesis and the first half of Exodus.[7]

---

By eating the fruit of the knowledge of good and evil, Adam and Eve plunged humankind into knowing evil, but also into knowing good.

---

10. (a) What would humans now know (Genesis 3:22)? (b) Why did God banish them from the Garden of Eden (3:22-24)?

11. ♥ (a) Why wouldn't God want creatures who had chosen to rebel to be able to live forever? (b) What hope did God give in letting people know a tree of life exists?

God placed cherubim (winged heavenly creatures) on the east side of the garden to block the way to the tree of life. Without access to this tree, Adam, Eve, and their offspring would eventually die.

By eating the fruit of the knowledge of good and evil, Adam and Eve plunged humankind into knowing evil, but also into knowing good. Evil lets virtues such as self-sacrifice, courage, and mercy arise. None of these are humanly possible without the risk of personal loss or harm. The greater the loss or harm, the more heroic is the virtue that counters it.

12. God had commanded Adam and Eve to fill the earth and subdue it. With what did they fill the earth (Genesis 6:11)?

The story has just begun. In the next chapter we meet the family through which the seed of the serpent crusher will be traced.

## Day 3

# God's Plan Unfolds

Let's summarize how the Lord God dwelt with people in Eve's day and then look at God's continuing revelation about how he'll fulfill his promise to Eve.

### God with Us Then

At first, Eve lived in a flourishing garden with Adam. They enjoyed God's company. He told them to subdue and rule the earth and to fill it with descendants. But when Eve took of the forbidden fruit and shared it with Adam, everything changed. God expelled them from the garden.

The Bible describes God briefly visiting certain people outside the garden. It looked like the serpent had defeated God's goal of an earth filled with people with whom he could dwell. But God's promise that a seed of the woman would crush the serpent remained.

## The Reveal Continued

This discovery book divides time into nine important eras: six Old Testament eras and three New Testament eras. Let's discover what else God revealed about the garden and God's promise to Eve during the six Old Testament eras. Later, we'll jump ahead to see what God revealed in three New Testament eras: Jesus's day, today, and forever.

### Eve's Day

In Eve's day, God announced that the woman's seed—or offspring—would crush the serpent's head. He showed mercy and grace. God prevented access to the tree of life, but he gave Eve the ability to produce life and Adam the ability to sustain life.

### Abraham's Day

Around 2100 BC, God called a man named Abraham to move to a distant land. He told him of his plan to create a nation there from Abraham's descendants. He announced that Abraham's seed—offspring—would be a blessing to all nations.

Another man who lived around that time was Job.[8] The book of Job tells us important things about God and Satan. It tells us that Satan accused Job of being righteous only because God blessed him in return. Satan wanted to test Job's righteousness to see if it was true righteousness or simply self-interest. God permitted the test.

### Moses's Day

Eventually, Egypt enslaved Abraham's descendants, the Israelites. Around 1450 BC, God called Moses to free them from slavery and lead them to the land he promised Abraham. On the way to their new home, he made a covenant with the people (a covenant is like a contract). The covenant stated that they could live in the land if they obeyed God's commands. But if they broke the covenant, God would expel them from the land just like he expelled Adam and Eve from the garden. The people agreed to it.

God showed Moses how to make a tabernacle in which God could place his presence so that he could dwell with them. It was filled with garden motifs, including a curtain embroidered with cherubim that barred the way to the Most Holy Place. After Moses set up the tabernacle and consecrated it, the glory of the Lord filled the tabernacle's Most Holy Place.

### David's Day

Around 1000 BC, God gave Israel a king to shepherd his people in justice and righteousness. David and kings descended from him were called the Lord's *anointed*, from the Hebrew *māshîah*, from which we get the word *messiah*.[9] God announced he would establish the throne of David's offspring—literally *seed*—forever.

King David loved the Lord God and wanted to build a house for him to replace the tabernacle. God gave him the plans for a temple but told him his son Solomon would build it. Like the tabernacle, garden motifs adorned it. A curtain embroidered with cherubim barred the way to the temple's Most Holy Place. When Solomon dedicated the temple, the glory of the Lord filled it.

## The Little Details
### The Major and Minor Prophets

The Old Testament divides the prophetic books by author and then by size. Lamentations is attributed to Jeremiah, so it follows Jeremiah even though it's short. The Major Prophets consists of Isaiah, Jeremiah, Lamentations, Ezekiel, and Daniel.

These four prophets wrote their books over the two centuries from the beginning of the exile of the northern territories to the end of the exile of the southern territories: about 740 to 530 BC. They call the people to return to God, warn of impending exile, and offer future hope.

The 12 shorter prophetic books are called the Minor Prophets. They date from about 800 BC to 430 BC. They are invaluable for understanding social conditions, injustices, and changing attitudes.

----

God prevented access to the tree of life, but he gave Eve the ability to produce life and Adam the ability to sustain life.

----

## The Little Details

### G.K. Beale and Sean M. McDonough on Satan as the Accuser:

The ancient foe of God's people here in [Revelation] 12:9 is also "called devil and Satan," meaning, respectively, "slanderer" and "adversary." He is a slanderous adversary in two ways. Genesis 3 attributes to him the two functions of slanderer and deceiver. After the fall, the serpent and his agents do on a worldwide scale what he began in the garden...Here in 12:9 he is called "the one deceiving the whole inhabited earth" and in 12:10 "the accuser" of God's people.

On the basis of this description and the description of Satan in Job 1:6-11; 2:1-6; Zech. 3:1-2, it can be concluded that the devil was permitted by God to come before him in heaven and "accuse" his people of sin. The OT texts portray Satan accusing saints of unfaithfulness, with the implication that they did not deserve God's salvation and gracious blessings (Zech. 3:1-5,9; cf. *Midr. Rab.* Num. 18:21). Implicit also in the accusations was the charge that God's own character was corrupt.[11]

----------------------------

Just as God gave Eve hope within her judgment, so he gave the exiles hope within their judgment.

----------------------------

### The Major Prophets' Day

Over time, Abraham's descendants drifted farther and farther from God. They stopped obeying the covenant commands. God sent prophets to call them back to him, but few Israelites listened to them.

By 722 BC,[10] evil and corruption were so bad that God exiled many people. A century later, God's presence left the temple. Finally, in 586 BC, foreigners destroyed the temple and exiled the rest of the people.

But just as God gave Eve hope within her judgment, so he gave the exiles hope within their judgment. The prophets announced that their exile would be temporary. They foretold more about God's promise to Eve. They said that God's "plans formed of old, faithful and sure" included that he would "swallow up death forever" (Isaiah 25:1,8). The Lord would slay the serpent (Isaiah 27:1). The future would hold an Eden-like garden with trees that healed and a river that brought life (Ezekiel 47). And the Lord himself would dwell again with humans (Isaiah 60:19-20). These prophecies assured the exiles that God's promise to Eve still stood.

### The Second Temple's Day

Thankfully, what seemed impossible to the exiles happened. They began returning to the promised land in 538 BC. They built a new temple. But unlike what happened with the tabernacle and the first temple, they did not see the glory of the Lord descend on it. They lived under foreign rule, awaiting an offspring of David to rule them—a messiah.

---

**13.** Read Zechariah 3:1-5. (a) What does Satan do to the high priest (verse 1)? (b) What happened to the priest's filthy clothes, which symbolize iniquity (verse 4)?

---

The prophet Zechariah described Satan as an accuser, but God as merciful and able to remove iniquity from the accused (Zechariah 3:1-5).

---

**14.** ♥ Which of the previous revelations encourages you the most? Why?

---

### Jesus's Day

God promised Eve a serpent-crushing descendant. The Bible usually talks about children being the offspring (literally, *seed*) of a man, but in Genesis 3:15, the promise is about a seed of the woman.

---

**15.** Read Luke 1:29-35. (a) Why was Jesus called "the Son of God" (verse 35)? (b) Jesus had only one human birth parent; who was it (verse 30)?

---

Jesus was the seed of a woman, but not the seed of a human man. That is our first hint that he is the serpent crusher promised to Eve.

When the adult Jesus began teaching, he explained more about what happened when Adam and Eve fell. Remember how God created Adam and Eve to reign over the earth?

**16.** (a) What did Satan do in John 13:2? (b) What did Satan do in John 13:27? (c) Judas left to procure soldiers to arrest Jesus. Who did Jesus say was coming in John 14:30?

When Adam and Eve believed Satan over God, Satan became ruler of the earth.

**17.** In whose power is the whole world (1 John 5:19)?

Jesus's followers "wrestle...against the rulers, against the authorities, against the cosmic powers over this present darkness, against the spiritual forces of evil in the heavenly places" (Ephesians 6:12).

When Satan entered Judas, things were dark. But the woman's seed had arrived.

## *Day 4*

# The Woman's Seed

Back in Genesis, the devil tested Eve's obedience to God by telling her the forbidden fruit wasn't fatal but would make her like God. Thinking God denied her something beneficial—something good to eat, pleasing to behold, and exalting to have—she stretched out her hand, tugged, and ate.

Satan also tempted Jesus. After being baptized, Jesus followed the Spirit into the wilderness. There he fasted 40 days and nights. When he was hungry and physically weak, the devil came to test him.

### The Temptations

The first test called on Jesus to use his supernatural powers to turn stones into bread to satisfy his extreme hunger.

**18.** Read Matthew 4:1-4. How did Jesus respond to the first temptation?

The devil had convinced Eve that the forbidden fruit was good to eat. But although Jesus knew bread would take away his hunger, he resisted. He would not use his powers to give

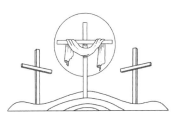

**The Little Details**
*The First Temptation, the Israelites, and Jesus*
Moses led the Israelites through the wilderness on the way to fulfilling God's mission for them. They faced temptations that foreshadowed the temptations Jesus faced. In fact, all the scriptures that Jesus quotes address the Israelites' wilderness experience.

First, the Israelites craved food, doubted God's promises, and demanded bread. Every morning, God gave them a miraculous food called manna.

When Jesus craved food after fasting, he responded to the first temptation by quoting Deuteronomy 8:3. It reads that God told the Israelites that he fed them "with manna...that he might make you know that man does not live by bread alone, but man lives by every word that comes from the mouth of the LORD."

***Lesson:*** We must know the Scripture and live by its words rather than what we crave.

## The Little Details

### The Second Temptation, the Israelites, and Jesus

After the failure with manna (see previous sidebar), the Israelites came to a place called Massah that lacked water (Exodus 17). They quarreled with God and demanded a miracle to prove God's care. They were testing God and revealing a proud sense of entitlement.

In Jesus's second temptation, Satan told Jesus to prove God's care as promised in Psalm 91:11-12. But Jesus wasn't fooled. He quoted a portion of Deuteronomy 6:16, which in full reads: "You shall not put the LORD your God to the test, as you tested him at Massah." He recognized that demanding proof of God's care was testing God.

*Lesson:* We should trust God's promises without demanding proof that he'll come through for us. After all, on the cross, he already has.

---

He would not use his powers to give himself an advantage against temptation that no other human had.

---

himself an advantage against temptation that no other human had. He put living by his Father's words above his bodily needs.

Jesus had said he lived by the Father's words. For the second test, the devil quoted Scripture. He stood Jesus on the highest point of the temple and told him to throw himself down, for Scripture promised angels would protect him.

> **19.** Read Matthew 4:5-7. How did Jesus respond to the second temptation?

Jesus recognized that putting one's life in danger to try to force God to prove his care was testing God. Though Satan had tried to plant doubt in God's good care (as he had done with Eve), Jesus trusted the Father completely and refused to test him.

In the third test, the devil offered Jesus the glorious kingdoms of the world. All Jesus needed to do was to bow and worship the devil—a seemingly easier path than the Father offered and something he could have immediately.

> **20.** Read Matthew 4:8-10. How did Jesus respond to the third temptation?

The devil deceived Eve into thinking the path to exaltation was through eating the fruit of the tree of the knowledge of good and evil. If she did so, he promised, she would be like God. Deceived, she succumbed.

But Jesus did not. He knew the path the Father put before him was a path of suffering. He also knew it was the only way to true exaltation.

> **21.** Read Matthew 4:11. (a) When Jesus ordered Satan to leave him, what did the devil do? (b) What else happened?

The angels delayed until after Jesus successfully resisted the devil's temptations. Where Eve and all humankind failed, Jesus prevailed.

> **22.** ♥ How can you imitate Jesus when resisting temptation?

### Jesus's Power over Satan

Afterward, Jesus began proclaiming, "The kingdom of God is at hand; repent and believe in the gospel" (Mark 1:13,15). *Gospel* means "good news." One Sabbath as he taught in a synagogue (a Jewish place of worship), a demon-possessed man cried out to him.

**23.** Read Mark 1:23-27. (a) Who did the impure spirit know Jesus was (verse 24)? (b) What did Jesus command the spirit (verse 25)? (c) What happened to the spirit (verse 26)? (d) How did the people react (verse 27)?

Thus, Jesus showed he had power and authority over the spiritual forces that opposed him. People began to wonder if he was the long-expected king—the Messiah.

Toward the end of his three-year ministry on earth, "Satan entered into" Judas Iscariot, one of Jesus's disciples (John 13:27). When Judas left to betray Jesus, Jesus told the remaining disciples that he would soon leave the world and go back to the Father (John 16:28). He said, "The ruler of this world is coming. He has no claim on me, but I do as the Father has commanded me, so that the world may know that I love the Father" (John 14:30-31).

Judas betrayed Jesus into the hands of people who opposed him. They arrested him and condemned him to death on a cross.

The serpent bruised Jesus's heel by putting him to death. But death was the penalty for sin and had no hold on the sinless Jesus. On that glorious Sunday morning, God raised him from the dead.

## Three Ways to Discover Jesus in the Old Testament

We've seen the start of how Jesus will defeat the serpent. Before we continue with that, let's discover three ways that the Old Testament points to Jesus.

### Promises

In Genesis 3:15, God promised Eve that one of her descendants would crush the head of the serpent who deceived her. This was a *promise* that pointed to Jesus. In this book, we'll see many such promises. Some will take the form of a covenant, which is a formal, binding agreement.

### Prophecies

In the Bible, God sometimes revealed things to people that they could not see or understand through natural means. These revelations are *prophecies*. Most prophecies called people to repent to avoid judgment. But sometimes they predicted a significant future event. That is the case in Genesis 3:15. God revealed that the serpent would bruise the heel of Eve's offspring, but the offspring would crush the serpent's head. At the cross, Satan bruised Jesus's heel. Shortly, we'll read how the cross brings Satan's final demise.

### Portents

A *portent* is something that foreshadows something in the future. Some Old Testament people, institutions, and events foreshadow either Jesus or something significant in Jesus's service or life. Bible translations use a variety of words to describe people and things that foreshadow the future, including *portents*, *patterns*, *copies*, *shadows*, and *types*. The fulfillment is always greater than the type. Jesus and the apostles frequently identified Old Testament types that Jesus fulfilled. They show us the amazing way that God directed history so that people could see his redemptive plan unfolding throughout the ages.

## The Little Details
### *Cherubim*

A cherub is a heavenly creature with multiple sets of wings. Cherubim are sometimes described as having four faces, one of which is humanlike. They have straight legs with feet like a calf's foot. Humanlike hands are under their wings. They're described in Ezekiel 1:4-25 and 10, where they bear the throne of God.

In the tabernacle built in Moses's day, solid gold cherubim perched above the mercy seat (Exodus 25:18-22). In the temple built in David's son's day, two 15' cherubim covered the ark of the covenant in the Most Holy Place (1 Kings 6:23-28). Both the tabernacle and temple had cherubim decorations.

Both also had a curtain embroidered with cherubim barring the way to the Most Holy Place (Exodus 26:1; 2 Chronicles 3:14).

- - - - - - - - - - - - - - - - - - - - - -

Just as Jesus resisted the devil and the devil fled, so we can resist temptation and the devil will flee.

- - - - - - - - - - - - - - - - - - - - - -

We'll see lots of portents in the chapters ahead. Here's one from Genesis. Romans 5:14 says "Adam...was a *type* of the one who was to come [Jesus]." First Corinthians 15:45-49 explains:

> "The first man Adam became a living being"; the last Adam became a life-giving spirit...The first man was from the earth, a man of dust; the second man is from heaven. As was the man of dust, so also are those who are of the dust, and as is the man of heaven, so also are those who are of heaven. Just as we have borne the image of the man of dust, we shall also bear the image of the man of heaven.

There you have it. Adam was a type of Jesus. Adam was a man of dust, but Jesus is the man of heaven. Remember, the fulfillment is always greater than the type. We all were born in the image of Adam, but when we become God's child, we're assured that we will bear the image of Jesus.

## Day 5

# The Serpent's End

Let's discover Satan's final defeat.

### The Serpent Crusher in Hebrews

The New Testament letter of Hebrews addressed a group of Jewish Christians. Persecution had caused some to doubt the truth of Christianity. They were thinking about going back to plain Judaism without Jesus as Messiah (*Christ* is from the Greek for *Messiah*). One of the problems was they had expected the Messiah to rule on earth in place of Rome, but Jesus said his kingdom was not of this earth. The author of Hebrews carefully showed how Jesus fulfilled Old Testament promises. Let's look at one.

> **24.** Read Hebrews 2:14-15. (a) Why did Jesus the Son of God take on "flesh and blood" (beginning of verse 14)? (b) What did he accomplish by his death (verse 14)? (c) From what does he deliver people (verse 15)?

In the garden, the devil brought death on humans and gained control over death.[12] Fear of death enslaved humans. But Jesus's death defeated the devil's power and brought Satan's certain demise.

### God with Us Still

*God with Us Today*

Fear of death isn't the only slavery from which Jesus releases us. Jesus said, "Everyone who practices sin is a slave to sin" (John 8:34). Jesus's death set us "free from sin" (Romans 6:18).

Other New Testament letters tell us how to live confidently as Christ followers who know that Jesus has defeated death and Satan.

**25.** In James 4:7 below, circle to whom we should submit. Box what we should do when tempted. Underline the result that will come.

> Submit yourselves therefore to God. Resist the devil, and he will flee from you.

Just as Jesus resisted the devil and the devil fled, so we can resist temptation and the devil will flee.

**26.** What does Romans 16:20 promise?

God's promise to Eve is ultimately fulfilled in Jesus, the serpent crusher. Because believers are in Jesus (John 17:21), God crushes Satan under their feet too.

**27.** ♥ Think of a difficult situation you face. What's one thing you can do to resist the devil?

### God with Us Forever

The last book in the New Testament is called Revelation. The name comes from the first few words: "The revelation of Jesus Christ." The word *revelation* comes from the Greek word *apokalypsis,* which is where we get our English word *apocalypse* that describes this genre. Apocalypses are writings that feature highly symbolic visions. Sometimes a supernatural being interprets the symbols and metaphors. Interpretations of Revelation differ, but we'll stay in straightforward passages.

In chapter 1, the risen Jesus appears to John. He says, "I died, and behold I am alive forevermore, and I have the keys of Death" (Revelation 1:18). Although Adam and Eve sinned and brought death to humans, now Jesus holds Death's keys. That's good news.

**28.** What will Jesus give to conquerors (Revelation 2:7)?

Adam and Eve lost access to the tree of life, but Jesus grants access. He reversed the work of the serpent in the garden and brought eternal life.

**29.** ♥ Read Revelation 12 for a big-picture view of the conflict between God's people and Satan. The woman symbolizes God's people. The iron scepter belongs to Jesus (Psalm 2:9; Revelation 19:15). The fallen stars are either the angels that fell with Satan (Revelation 12:9) or martyrs (Daniel 8:10). What encourages you the most?

There's still more. In Genesis 3:15 (NIV), God told the serpent, "You will strike his heel." When Satan prompted wicked humans to crucify Jesus, he wanted to destroy Jesus. But Jesus rose from the dead, making Satan's attempt no more than a strike to his heel.

### The Little Details
### *Types and Antitypes*

Bible translations use words such as *portents, patterns, copies, shadows,* and *types* to describe people, institutions, and events that foreshadow the future. Academic works tend to use the word *type,* which comes from the Greek word *typos* (pronounced TOO-poss).

The formal name for what the type foreshadows is *antitype.* In the Bible, an antitype (or fulfillment) is always greater than the type. For instance, the type may be imperfect (Adam), while the antitype is perfect (Jesus).

The New Testament identifies types by either directly quoting the Old Testament or alluding to well-known stories. The New Testament authors wrote in Greek and often quoted the Greek translation of the Old Testament called the Septuagint (abbreviated LXX). Of course, something translated from Hebrew to Greek to English will differ slightly from something translated from Hebrew to English.

------

He reversed the work of the serpent in the garden and brought eternal life.

------

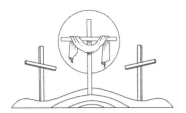

## The Little Details
### *Prophecy Versus Prophesy*

A prophet prophesies prophecy. An easy way to remember the spelling is that *prophecy* ends in a "cee" sound and is spelled with a *c*, while *prophesy* ends in a "sigh" sound and is spelled with an *s*. *Prophecy* is the noun and *prophesy* is the verb.

**30.** According to Revelation 20:10, what will happen to Satan?

Satan's end is sure. The woman's seed—Jesus—is the serpent crusher.

### *God with Me Now*

Psalms 113–118 are called the Hallel psalms because they frequently use the Hebrew word for praise (*hll*). They were part of the Passover celebration of the Israelites' escape from Egypt. Jesus's last supper with his disciples was during Passover, so they probably sang these psalms during the meal. We'll pray the first one today.

 Turn to Psalm 113 and read it. **Pray** the psalm to the Lord in worship.

 **Praise** God for something you saw of his character this week. **Confess** anything that convicted you. **Ask** for help to do something God's Word calls you to do. **Thank** God for something you learned this week.

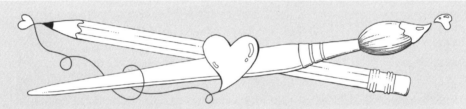

# The Heart and Art of Worship

We learned in this week's study that, just like Eve, we were created with a plan and purpose, but also, just like Eve, we have an enemy who seeks to distort our understanding of who God really is, who we really are in him, and how we see and relate to the people in our lives. I love that we wrapped up the week with a good dose of praise in Psalm 113 because worship, whatever form it takes, is God's way of aligning our hearts and minds with his...upward, inward, and outward...in order to bring the greatest glory to himself and the greatest blessing to us and to others.

When we talk about worship, most of us think about the time we gather together with other believers on Sunday morning and, using either a hymnal or overhead projector, we sing out our songs of praise to God in unity. And as important as this time of corporate praise is to our spiritual journey, we were reminded in Psalm 113 that God's desire for us is to praise him from sunrise to sunset—all day, every day. This tells me that the worship God is looking for goes far beyond the walls of the church and is more about creatively expressing our faith through how we live our lives and the activities we pursue.

For me personally, I find that expressing my faith through visual arts is as much an act of worship as when I sing. Creating art with lines, texture, and color reminds me of the One who created me in his image and for his glory. With this week's lesson I wanted to create an image that expressed the hope of evil's end through Jesus, the serpent crusher, and make us long for heaven where the tree of life awaits us in eternity. As you color this week's illustration and meditate on this truth, worship God for his victory over sin and death, and let his mercy and kindness fill your heart!

He
will crush your head,
and you will strike his heel.

genesis 3:15 niv

## Chapter 2

# Genesis 22
## Jesus the Sacrificed Son

The hope of the Father and Son's sacrifice

I WILL SURELY MULTIPLY your offSPRING as the STARS of heaven...

and in your offSPRING SHALL ALL the NATIONS of the eaRth be bLeSSed.

Genesis 22:16-18

## Day 1

## A Father's Sacrifice

**M**ovie catchphrases are part of our culture. "You had me at hello." "I'll be back." "Show me the money." When those who've seen the movies hear them, they instantly know the context and backstory.

Many New Testament references to the Old Testament directly quote it. But others allude to it with a catchphrase or reference that those familiar with the Old Testament would recognize, just as we recognize movie catchphrases and references. We'll discover a catchphrase in this chapter.

### The Reveal

Let's pick up the story where we left off and trace what happened between Eve's day and the time of a man named Abram, whom God would later rename Abraham.

### Eve's Day

God promised Eve that one of her descendants would crush the serpent who deceived her. Her first two sons were Cain and Abel. When grown, Cain murdered Abel, and God exiled him from his presence. The promised offspring could not come from either child. But Eve bore a third son, Seth, as well as other children.

### Abraham's Day

Adam lived nearly 1000 years, like most of the people born in that time. As the number of people increased, so did the amount of violence. Eventually, "the LORD saw that the wickedness of man was great in the earth, and that every intention of the thoughts of his heart was only evil continually" (Genesis 6:5). His good creation had become corrupt and filled with violence (Genesis 6:11).

The Lord acted to end the corruption. First, he sent a flood to cleanse the earth of violence. He preserved only the righteous man Noah, his family, and the animals they took into a huge ark that Noah built. Noah descended from Seth, Eve's third son.

Second, the Lord gradually shortened human lives after the flood: "His days shall be 120 years" (Genesis 6:3).[1] In this way, he limited the evil any one person could commit, and the evil any one person had to endure.

## The Little Details
### The Morality of Human Sacrifice

The people of Abraham's day thought human sacrifices were pious, not immoral. Archaeologist Laerke Recht writes that we should check our assumptions because "we may see a creature being sacrificed as a 'victim', while others could see it as honoured, sacred or some other aspect not immediately clear to us."[3]

Additionally, in cultures that believed in gods that give blessings in return for sacrifices, sacrificing offspring would be considered a moral good. Imagine living in such a culture during a time of catastrophic drought: Children will die if no rain comes. In such a culture, it would be morally obligatory to do all you can to appease the gods and save your village. Oxford professor John Day writes, "Desperate circumstances required desperate measures...and the offering of human sacrifice was thought to possess especially strong apotropaic power."[4]

**apotropaic:** intended to ward off evil

1. ♥ (a) According to Isaiah 57:1-2, why does a righteous person die? (b) Think of those who have been enslaved or unjustly imprisoned. What would be different if they lived 1000 years? (c) Think of a violent, corrupt ruler from history. What would be different if that person could live 1000 years?

After the flood, Noah's descendants spread over the earth. As time passed, people again rejected God's way for their own. They surmised that nature's forces were whims of gods whose attention they must seek through sacrifice and ritual. They made images of gods out of wood and metal, and they bowed and sacrificed to them. If the gods didn't respond, they increased the value of their sacrifices. In cities like Ur, human sacrifice became a means of manipulating capricious gods into providing rain and protection.[2]

Abram and his family lived in Ur during that era. They worshiped deaf and dumb idols (Joshua 24:2). Eventually, they moved to Haran. There, God spoke to Abram.

### God's Word to Us

Today's reading may unsettle you. But hang in there. It's meant to unsettle. As you read, imagine what it was like living in a culture in which priests and priestesses taught that unpredictable gods were behind weather, natural disasters, and fertility.

 Take a moment to pray for insight as you read God's Word.

2. ♥ Read Genesis 15:1-6; 17:1-19; 21:1-7; and 22:1-18. What stands out to you? Why?

Because this chapter's reading is challenging, let's take a brief glimpse ahead. In the last chapter, we talked about biblical portents: people, institutions, and events that foreshadow something significant in Jesus's life. In the Bible, God periodically asked prophets to act out future events so that people would recognize the event's significance when it happened. Abraham and Isaac were both prophets.

3. ♥ Read John 3:16 below. (a) What event in Jesus's life do you think Abraham and his son might have acted out? (b) How do your reactions to the story of Abraham and Isaac affect your appreciation of the verse below?

For God so loved the world, that he gave his only Son.

# A Walk with Christ—Watershed Belief

When an invitation to a free marriage retreat arrived from Forest Home Christian Conference Center, I was quite pregnant and Bill was a busy youth pastor. We leapt at the opportunity. There we experienced a God-ordained watershed moment listening to the story of God giving the covenant promise in Genesis 15:5-6:

> "Look up at the sky and count the stars—if indeed you can count them." Then he said to him, "So shall your offspring be." Abram believed the LORD (NIV).

In this chapter, we explore how Abram's watershed moment of faith—fueled by his belief in the faithful and loving character of God, brought him to the point when he was willing to sacrifice his dear son Isaac. Abram's trust and faith pleased God. And God kept his promises to Abram because of that faith.

Bill and I were not asked to sacrifice our child, but we were and *are* called to live out our faith in Jesus, the sacrificed Son of God. We intensely felt this in our watershed moment as we sat in the chapel at that retreat years ago. We recommitted ourselves to be used, as a couple, to share God's love and equip people to love wisely. We made the decision to present our faithfulness on the altars of our lives. We wanted to seek and please God together and for all of our days.

> And without faith it is impossible to please God, because anyone who comes to him must believe that he exists and that he rewards those who earnestly seek him (Hebrews 11:6 NIV).

Many others have had watershed moments at Forest Home. The founder, Henrietta Mears, brought young leaders to the mountain. One of her famous quotes is, "There is no magic in small plans. When I consider my ministry, I think of the world. Anything less than that would not be worthy of Christ nor of his will for my life."[5] Billy Graham had his watershed moment while a speaker at Forest Home at the start of his evangelistic ministry. During a walk, he stopped and laid down his Bible on a stump, and prayed, "Father...I will believe this to be Your inspired Word." He reflected on this moment in his autobiography: "I sensed the presence and power of God as I had not sensed it in months."[6] Weeks later, Graham preached the gospel at the Los Angeles Crusades to over 300,000, sparking the crusades that defined his ministry.

Christ brings each of us to a watershed moment to make a choice to believe in him, his Word, and his ability to keep his promises. He brought the disciples to Caesarea Philippi, where worship of false gods was taking place. Jesus asked, "Who do people say the son of man is?...Who do you say that I am?" It was their watershed moment. Peter replied, "You are the Messiah, the Son of the living God" (Matthew 16:13-18 NIV). Hebrews 11:1 calls us to this decision point: "Now faith is the assurance of things hoped for, the conviction of things not seen." I think of it this way: *Faith* is to have a solid conviction, and *assurance* is like having a land deed. So, faith is like the legal title to hope. When writing *Discovering Hope in the Psalms,* I defined hope as "to wait expectantly for God to show up and show off for your good and His glory." Hope believes God keeps his promises—even in the waiting.

In a journal or in the space below, write your watershed prayer to proclaim that Christ is your Savior, and God's Word and promises are true.

*Pam*

## The Little Details
### Isaac's Age at the Binding

The story of Abraham binding Isaac is in Genesis 22. The prior chapter brought Isaac to adolescence. In the following chapter, he is 37.

The ESV translates the Hebrew word *na'ar* as "boy" in Genesis 22:5,12, but elsewhere translates it "young man." The word is used of the trained men who went with Abraham to rescue Lot (Genesis 14:24); of men who attempted to rape angels (Genesis 19:4); of Joseph at age 28 (Genesis 41:12); of the spies whom Rahab hid (Joshua 6:23); of trained soldiers (2 Samuel 2:14); and of Absalom when he tried to overthrow David's throne (2 Samuel 18:32).

So, it is safe to estimate Isaac's age at the binding as between 15 and 30.

- - - - - - - - - - - - - - - - - -

This visual manifestation of God (theophany) must have greatly increased Abram's faith.

- - - - - - - - - - - - - - - - - -

# God Makes Himself Known

In an idol-worshiping culture, God made himself known.

## God Calls Abram

4.  (a) In Genesis 12:1, what happened to Abram? (b) What would God make of him (verse 2)? (c) How did Abram respond (verse 4)?

Unlike the idols, this God spoke. He promised to bless Abraham. Abraham hadn't done anything to earn his favor. In fact, until then, he and his family worshiped idols. Abram was 75 years old (Genesis 12:4). His wife Sarai was 65 (Genesis 17:17).

5.  ♥ Knowing their ages, how do you think the promise of a child affected this childless couple?

Abram and Sarai finally reached Canaan.

6.  In Genesis 12:7 below, circle what the Lord did. Underline Abram's response.

    Then the LORD appeared to Abram and said, "To your offspring I will give this land." So he built there an altar to the LORD, who had appeared to him.

This visual manifestation of God (theophany) must have greatly increased Abram's faith.

## God Protects Abram and His Loved Ones

Abram's nephew Lot moved to a city called Sodom in a fertile valley, even though it was already known as a wicked place (Genesis 13:12-13). The king of Sodom and four other kings went to war against another four kings—Sodom's five armies against four armies. Sodom's enemies defeated Sodom and captured the city's people, including Lot.

When Abram heard, he took 318 of his men and pursued the armies of the four kings. He defeated them and rescued all the prisoners.

Abram now saw tangible proof of God's promise to bless him in the land.

## God Makes a Covenant with Abram

7.  (a) What happened to Abram in Genesis 15:1? (b) What did Abram still lack (verses 2-3)? (c) What did God promise him (verse 5)?

8.  In Genesis 15:6 below, underline Abram's response. Circle what God counted his belief as. (The first *he* refers to Abram, while the second *he* refers to the Lord.)

    And he believed the LORD, and he counted it to him as righteousness.

That night, the Lord made a covenant with Abram. He said Abram's descendants would face affliction in a foreign land for 400 years, but he would bring them to Canaan to live as a nation. He told Abram to sacrifice some animals. Abram did so. He cut the animals in half and laid the pieces in two lines so that there was a passageway between them. The ancients *cut covenants* by walking between cut animal parts.[7] "When the sun had gone down and it was dark, behold, a smoking fire pot and a flaming torch passed between these pieces" (Genesis 15:17). This was how God let Abram "know for certain" the things he promised would happen (Genesis 15:13).

But a decade in Canaan passed, and there was still no child. Sarai asked Abram to give her a child through her maidservant (a common ancient practice). The servant (now a wife) bore a child whom Abram named Ishmael. He believed Ishmael was the child that God had promised. Thirteen more years passed.

9.  (a) What happened when Abram was 99 (Genesis 17:1)? (b) Why did God want Abram to walk before him and be blameless (verse 2)? (c) What did God change Abram's name to (verse 5)? (d) What did he change Sarai's name to (verse 15)?

*Abraham* means "father of many nations." *Sarah* means "princess."

10. (a) What had God made Abraham (Genesis 17:5)? (b) What would God do for him (verse 6)?

The covenant had a sign of acceptance: circumcision (Genesis 17:11). Today we show that we accept the terms of a contract by signing our names. God told Abraham to show his acceptance of the covenant by circumcising the men in his household and all future baby boys.

11. (a) What was God going to do for Sarah (Genesis 17:16)? (b) Why did Abraham laugh (verse 17)? (c) What did God affirm (verse 19)? (d) When would God's promise be fulfilled (verse 21)?

*Isaac* means "he laughs." Abraham showed he accepted the covenant by circumcising himself and all the men in his household.

Later, when Sarah heard the Lord repeat his promise, she laughed too. The Lord responded,

**The Little Details**
**Trent Hunter and Stephen Wellum on Covenant:**
*Covenant* is an older word that has fallen largely out of use today. It refers to a means by which we structure a relationship. Our contemporary word *contract* is the most familiar way we structure relationships today, and a covenant and a modern contract have some similarities. For example, both types of agreements involve parties and require obligations. If you buy a car, hire an employee, or rent a home, you need to enter into a contractual relationship with another person or party. But a contract and a covenant also have important differences. While a contract involves a relationship for the sake of obligations, a covenant involves obligations for the sake of a relationship. A covenant is *a chosen relationship between two parties ordered according to specific promises.*[8]

--------------------------

But a decade in Canaan passed, and there was still no child.

--------------------------

"Is anything too hard for the Lord? At the appointed time I will return to you, about this time next year, and Sarah shall have a son" (Genesis 18:14).

## God Produces a Miraculous Birth

12. ♥ (a) What happened one year later (Genesis 21:2)? (b) How did this miracle affect Abraham's faith that God keeps his promises and that nothing is too hard for him?

Abraham had seen angels and theophanies (physical manifestations of God). Angels protected his family. He knew God's faithfulness, justice, and power. The people all around him knew God was with him in everything he did (Genesis 21:22). God gave Abraham much more evidence of himself than he gives most people because Abraham played a central part in God's plan.

## Day 3

# A Father Gives His Son

At Isaac's miraculous birth, Abraham knew God could do anything and God kept his word. He watched Isaac grow into a young man. Then God tested Abraham's faith in his promise that Isaac would be his heir and the child of the covenant. God asked him to do something that appeared to make its fulfillment impossible.

## God Tests Abraham

13. (a) What does Genesis 22:1 say God did? (b) What did God call Abraham's son, Isaac (verse 2)? (c) Where was Abraham to go (verse 2)? (d) What did God ask Abraham to do with his beloved son, the only son of God's promise (Genesis 22:2)?

The Lord called Isaac "your son, your only son Isaac, whom you love." Yet Abraham had another son: Ishmael. Professor Andreas J. Köstenberger says *your only son* in Genesis 22:2,12,16 means "one-of-a-kind" son; that is, the son of promise.[11]

It was a test. God asked tenderly: The word *now* in "Take now your son" (NASB) is often translated "please" and has the sense of an entreaty. Professor Paul Copan says, "God's directive is unusual: 'Please take your son'…God is remarkably gentle as he gives a difficult order. This type of divine command (as a plea) is rare."[12]

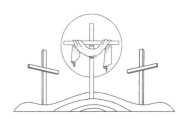

**14.** How did Abraham demonstrate his faith that obeying God wouldn't stop Isaac from being the child of promise (Genesis 22:5)?

Because of his culture, Abraham would not have thought that God's request to sacrifice Isaac was morally wrong. Still, he believed God's promises about Isaac and told his servants that he and Isaac would return together after the sacrifice (Genesis 22:5).

**15.** (a) Who carried the wood (Genesis 22:6)? (b) When Isaac asked where the lamb for the sacrifice was, what did Abraham reply (verse 8)?

Abraham built the altar of wood and bound his son Isaac. Abraham was well over 100; Isaac was between 15 and 30. Isaac could have stopped him but trusted his father.

**16.** (a) What did Abraham's willingness to obey God prove (Genesis 22:11-12)? (b) What did the angel of the Lord call Isaac at verse 12's end? (c) When God provided a ram to substitute as a sacrifice, what did Abraham call the place (22:14)?

The Lord provided the sacrifice that substituted for "your son, your only son."

## God Blesses Abraham
Abraham's faith in the God he knew and trusted brought blessing.

**17.** (a) Why would God bless Abraham (Genesis 22:16)? (b) How would God bless him (verse 17)? (c) What would happen through his offspring? (d) Why (verse 18)?

Most of these blessings expanded on God's earlier promises to Abraham. The last blessing was new: "In your offspring shall all the nations of the earth be blessed, because you have obeyed my voice" (Genesis 22:18). As in the promise to Eve, *offspring* is literally *seed*.

## God with Us Then
God revealed himself in miraculous ways to the prophet Abraham, including theophanies. He taught Abraham about righteousness and worship. He made a covenant with him and his descendants. He miraculously gave Abraham a child, showing his power.

## The Reveal Continued
Isaac grew, married, and had twin sons. God chose one of them—Jacob—to be the child of the covenant promise. He renamed Jacob *Israel*. Israel had 12 sons. The family moved to Egypt to escape a famine. There, Israel's 12 sons grew to be 12 tribes. Eventually, the Egyptians enslaved the Israelites.

## The Little Details
### Vern S. Poythress on the Angel of the Lord:
The Hebrew Old Testament uses the key word *mal'āk*...which is sometimes translated "angel." It is also sometimes translated "messenger," and that is what the word consistently means. The personage so designated functions to bring a message from someone. Thus, "the angel of the Lord" brings a message from the Lord. In itself, the Hebrew word for "messenger" does not give information about what *kind* of personage is being designated. It could be a created angel; it could be God himself; or it could be a prophet (Hag. 1:13) or a priest (Mal. 2:7)...Sometimes the context allows us to see that the being is himself divine. But in other cases he is human or angelic. Or we may not be sure, because in some cases there is not enough information.[13]

God revealed himself in miraculous ways to the prophet Abraham, including theophanies.

## The Little Details
### Jay Sklar on Atonement as Ransom:

In the Old Testament, a "ransom" has the following characteristics:

1. it is a legally or ethically legitimate payment;

2. it delivers a guilty party from a just punishment that is the right of the offended party to execute or to have executed;

3. it is a lesser punishment than was originally expected;

4. it is up to the offended party whether or not to accept the payment; and

5. its acceptance serves both to rescue the life of the guilty and to appease the offended party, thus restoring peace to the relationship.

This means that, in at least some instances, atonement is characterized by the payment of a ransom (sacrifice) on behalf of the guilty party (the sinner) to the offended party (the Lord).[14]

### Moses's Day

The Lord God sent Moses to free the Israelites from slavery in Egypt. When Moses asked his name, he replied, "I AM WHO I AM" (Exodus 3:14). God set up a system in which priests sacrificed animals to atone for people's sin so that they could approach him. They were substitutionary sacrifices like the ram that substituted for Isaac. God forbade sacrificing children to gods, a practice that had become common in Canaan (Leviticus 20:2). Moses taught that idol sacrifices were sacrifices to demons (Deuteronomy 32:17).

### David's Day

David told Solomon to build the temple at a spot where he had seen "the angel of the LORD standing between earth and heaven" (1 Chronicles 21:16). He built an altar there. The site was called Mount Moriah (2 Chronicles 3:1), thus linking the giving of temple sacrifices to the ram that substituted for Isaac on Moriah.

Written around this time, Psalm 49 revealed more of God's plan. It declared that no person could ransom another so that he or she could live forever (verses 7-9). "But God will ransom my soul from the power of Sheol, for he will receive me" (verse 15). One imperfect human couldn't ransom another, but somehow God will ransom his people.

### The Major Prophets' Day

By the time of the major prophets, the Israelites worshiped Canaanite gods. Violence, oppression, and injustice abounded. Israelites sacrificed their children to gods, filling a valley "with the blood of innocents" (Jeremiah 19:4). Instead of blessing the nations and leading them to God, Abraham's offspring became like the nations and sought the nations' gods.

The Lord revealed his plan's next stage: exile. He would avenge the children's deaths by sending a foreign army to punish the murderers. He would exile the survivors temporarily. After he brought them back, he would send a child who would reign righteously: "For to us a child is born, to us a son is given" (Isaiah 9:6).

As prophesied, foreign armies came and exiled the people in the major prophets' day.

### The Second Temple's Day

From exile, the people called to God. He brought them back from captivity. A psalmist recorded Israel's history of forgetting God's mighty deeds of salvation beginning with Moses's day and ending with the exile.

> **18.** In Psalm 106:37-41 below, underline the reason given for the exile. Circle to whom they sacrificed children.
>
> They sacrificed their sons and their daughters to the demons; they poured out innocent blood, the blood of their sons and daughters, whom they sacrificed to the idols of Canaan, and the land was polluted with blood…Then the anger of the LORD was kindled against his people, and…he gave them into the hand of the nations.

In human sacrifice, Satan and his demons had found another way to destroy human life.

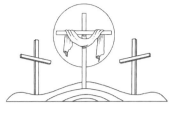

**19.** ♥ (a) What are other ways that sin destroys human life? (b) How does knowing that God intends to stop not just the sin that destroys life, but death itself, make you feel?

*Jesus's Day*
Abraham and Isaac didn't know it, but their actions foreshadowed how the offspring promised to Eve and now to them would one day crush the serpent and bless all peoples. That offspring was Jesus.

## Another Father Gives His Son

The key passages that link Abraham's test to the Father giving his Son are in the New Testament letters, but John's Gospel alludes to it with a catchphrase. Let's dig in.

### The Father's Only Son

Just as Isaac was a miracle child born in impossible circumstances to fulfill prophecy, so was Jesus. In Abraham's day, a 90-year-old barren woman well past menopause bore a child, Isaac. Two thousand years later, a young virgin bore a child, Jesus (Luke 1:26-38).

Jesus grew and became well known as a teacher and miracle worker. One night a religious leader named Nicodemus visited Jesus, convinced Jesus's miracles meant God sent him.

Nicodemus belonged to a popular Jewish sect called Pharisees, a mostly middle-class group who hoped God would send a king descended from David (the Messiah) when they were righteous enough. Not wanting to experience an exile again, they developed a set of oral rules meant to be a protective hedge around the law. They believed in an afterlife for righteous Jews who obeyed both the written Scripture and their oral traditions. They did not believe in an afterlife for the rest of the world.

**20.** (a) Who could have eternal life (John 3:15-16)? (b) Was eternal life limited to just righteous Jews? (c) Why did God send his Son to the world (verse 17)? (d) What would happen to those who believed in him (verse 18)?

Köstenberger says the phrase translated *his only Son* or *only begotten Son* (NASB) means one-of-a-kind son, the same as when God called Isaac *your only son* when he tested Abraham (Genesis 22:2,12,16). Thus, God giving his only Son would remind Jews of Abraham giving his only son in Genesis 22.[18] That the world (not just Pharisees) could have eternal life points to God's promise in the same chapter: "In your offspring shall all the nations of the earth be blessed, because you have obeyed my voice" (Genesis 22:18).

Abraham and Isaac didn't know it, but their actions foreshadowed how the offspring promised to Eve and now to them would one day crush the serpent and bless all peoples.

## The Little Details

### D.A. Carson on Loving the World:

Jews were familiar with the truth that God loved the children of Israel; here God's love is not restricted by race. Even so, God's love is to be admired not because the world is so big and includes so many people, but because the world is so bad: that is the customary connotation of *kosmos*... The world is so wicked that John elsewhere forbids Christians to love it or anything in it (1 Jn. 2:15-17). There is no contradiction between this prohibition and the fact that God does love it. Christians are not to love the world with the selfish love of participation; God loves the world with the self-less, costly love of redemption.[19]

Just as Isaac was a miracle child born in impossible circumstances to fulfill prophecy, so was Jesus.

## Abraham Saw Jesus's Day

Later, Jesus talked to some Jews who initially claimed to believe Jesus's teaching.

> **21.** (a) What did Jesus say true believers do (John 8:31)? (b) What would be the result (verse 32)? (c) About what kind of enslavement was Jesus talking (verse 34)?

Jesus's hearers were offended.

> **22.** (a) How did the Jews defend themselves (John 8:39)? (b) According to Jesus, if they were truly such, what would they do (verse 39)?

The true descendant of Abraham acted righteously, just as Abraham did.

Jesus said they weren't doing the works Abraham did, but instead, "You are doing the works your father did" (John 8:40-41). They replied, "We were not born of sexual immorality. We have one Father—even God" (verse 41). They were probably referring to Mary being pregnant before she married Joseph.

> **23.** (a) If God were their Father, what would they do (John 8:42)? (b) Since they wouldn't listen to the one the Father sent, who was their true father (verse 44)? (c) What was he like (verse 44)?

Jesus said, "Whoever is of God hears the words of God. The reason why you do not hear them is that you are not of God" (John 8:47). They retorted by calling him demon-possessed. Jesus said, "If anyone keeps my word, he will never see death" (John 8:51). They were incredulous because Abraham and all the prophets died. They asked if he thought he was greater than Abraham.

> **24.** In John 8:56 below, underline what Jesus said Abraham rejoiced over.
>
> Your father Abraham rejoiced that he would see my day. He saw it and was glad.

Abraham rejoiced over the day in which all God's promises to him would be fulfilled. By saying, "Abraham rejoiced that he would see my day," Jesus claimed that his own day would fulfill God's promises to Abraham. But his listeners didn't understand.

**25.** (a) Why did the Jews mock Jesus's words (John 8:57)? (b) Write out Jesus's reply (verse 58). (c) How did the Jews respond (verse 59)?

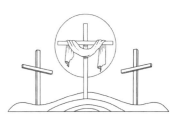

### The Little Details
*Akedah: The Binding*

The story of Abraham nearly sacrificing Isaac is called the Akedah, from *'aqedâ*, the Hebrew word for *binding*.[20] The title emphasizes that Isaac, who was stronger than his elderly father, submitted willfully to being bound, knowing by then that he was the sacrifice.

Jesus's reply riled them. First, Jesus claimed to have existed before Abraham was born. Second, he didn't say, "Before Abraham was, I was." He said, "Before Abraham was, *I am*," using God's name for himself (Exodus 3:14). To them, that was blasphemy.

## The Sacrifice

The Jews failed to kill Jesus that day but later succeeded.

Just as Abraham did not withhold his only son whom he loved, so the Father did not withhold his only Son whom he loved (Matthew 3:17; John 3:16). Just as Isaac carried the wood for the sacrifice on his back, so Jesus carried the wooden cross for his sacrifice on his back (John 19:17). Just as Isaac submitted to his father, so Jesus submitted to his Father (John 10:18). Just as the head of the ram that substituted for Isaac was caught in a thicket, so the head of Jesus who substituted for all the elect was caught in a crown of thorns (John 19:2).

Abraham not withholding his only son portended God not withholding his only Son. The Lord gave him a prophetic promise that "your offspring shall possess the gate of his enemies and in your offspring shall all the nations of the earth be blessed, because you have obeyed my voice" (Genesis 22:17-18). Abraham's actions foreshadowed the means by which his offspring would defeat humanity's enemy and bring blessing to all nations.

God stayed Abraham's hand and provided a ram to substitute for Isaac, sparing Isaac's life. Nothing stayed the Father's hand, for Jesus was the substitute the ram foreshadowed. Abraham prophesied, "God will provide for himself the lamb" (Genesis 22:8). In Jesus, God provided.

## The Sacrificed Son in Hebrews

Hebrews 11:8-19 commends Abraham's faith.

**26.** Read John 3:16 and Hebrews 11:17-19 (NASB) below. Box the four-word phrase that is the same in both. Underline in the first passage why God did this. Underline in the second passage what Abraham thought God could do. Circle how Abraham received Isaac back (the last word of the second passage).

For God so loved the world, that He gave His only begotten Son, that whoever believes in Him shall not perish, but have eternal life.

By faith Abraham, when he was tested, offered up Isaac, and he who had received the promises was offering up his only begotten son; it was he to whom it was said, "IN ISAAC YOUR DESCENDANTS SHALL BE CALLED." He considered that God is able to raise people even from the dead, from which he also received him back as a type.

Abraham received Isaac back as a *type* of resurrection. Professor Kenneth A. Mathews says:

In Hebrews [11:17-19] his [Isaac's] survival is termed a *parabola*, a "figure" (v. 19)

Jesus claimed to have existed before Abraham was born.

**The Little Details**
*The Early Church on the Binding of Isaac*

The early church fathers considered Abraham's words, "God will provide for himself the lamb" (Genesis 22:8), as a "theological foreshadow of Christ's sacrifice."[22] Mathews writes, "The church fathers...often read the Akedah episode typologically as the redemptive story of Christ's crucifixion, including the Greek, Latin, and Syrian branches of the church.[23] Augustine wrote of it this way in *The City of God*.[24]

of resurrection. The writer to the Hebrews recognized that Abraham believed the boy would return...which can only mean that Abraham trusted the Lord to raise him from the dead to fulfill his promise...This God did when the angel halted the knife, for the lad was as good as dead in the mind of his father—as well as in the reckoning of God.[21]

Abraham receiving Isaac back was a type of the Father receiving Jesus back when he raised him from the dead. The Father gave his Son so that Jesus could raise all those who believe in Jesus to eternal life: "For this is the will of my Father, that everyone who looks on the Son and believes in him should have eternal life, and I will raise him up on the last day" (John 6:40). Hallelujah.

27. ♥ What would you like to say to the Father and Son?

---

## Day 5

# Living by Faith

When as a teen I first heard that the Father gave his only Son, it didn't seem like a huge deal to me. God seemed untouchable and distant. But the story of Abraham's test gripped me and helped me sense the greatness of God's sacrifice and love.

### God with Us Still

*God with Us Today*
The New Testament authors drew lessons from Abraham's faith.

*Faith Looks to Eternity*
The author of Hebrews used Abraham, Sarah, and Isaac as models of faith.

28. (a) What is faith (Hebrews 11:1)? (b) Why is it important (verse 6)?

29. (a) What were Abraham, Sarah, and Isaac on the earth (Hebrews 11:13)? (b) What did they desire (verse 16)? (c) What has God prepared for them (verse 16)?

Abraham, Sarah, and Isaac didn't receive the land God promised to give their descendants

The Father gave his Son so that Jesus could raise all those who believe in Jesus to eternal life.

400 years later. God prepared for them instead a heavenly promised land. The earthly promised land was a mere type of the better country to come.

30. Read Hebrews 12:1-2. (a) What should we lay aside (verse 1)? (b) How should we run the race God sets before us? (c) To whom should we look (verse 2)? (d) Why did Jesus endure the cross?

Jesus endured the cross and scorned its shame because it was the way to joy: joy at perfecting those who love God, and joy at bringing us to the heavenly city with him.

### Faith Brings the Blessing of Abraham

The apostle Paul wrote of Abraham's faith in a letter to Gentile Christians in Galatia. Some Jewish Christians had told the Galatians that they had to be circumcised and follow all the law that Moses gave in order to be saved by Jesus's death. Paul pointed out that Abraham's faith was reckoned to him as righteousness long before he was circumcised (Genesis 15:6; 17:24).

31. In Galatians 3:7 below, circle who the true sons of Abraham are (three words).

    Know then that it is those of faith who are the sons of Abraham.

This is the same point we read that Jesus made.

32. In Galatians 3:8 (HCSB) below, underline what the Scripture saw in advance. Circle what was told to Abraham ahead of time (two words). Double-underline what Paul quoted (the words that follow "saying").

    Now the Scripture saw in advance that God would justify the Gentiles by faith and told the good news ahead of time to Abraham, saying, All the nations will be blessed through you.

The passage you double-underlined combines God's promises to Abraham.[25] Through them, God "preached the gospel beforehand to Abraham," as the ESV translates it.

### Faith Brings Assurance of God's Love

Paul gave us another important takeaway from the Father giving his Son.

33. In Romans 8:32 below, circle the verbs *spare*, *gave*, and *give*. Underline what God will do for us.

    He who did not spare his own Son but gave him up for us all, how will he not also with him graciously give us all things?

Professor Mark A. Seifrid writes, "'He who did not spare [*epheisato*] his own son' has the same verb used in Genesis 22:12,16 in the Greek Bible Paul used, 'You have not spared [*epheiso*] your beloved son.'"[27] D.M. Lloyd-Jones wrote this about Romans 8:32:

**The Little Details**

*Hunter and Wellum on a Substitute for Isaac:*

Whatever Abraham had in mind in saying, "God himself will provide the lamb," he spoke better than he knew. In truth, God did provide a substitute for Isaac, hinting that God himself must ultimately provide the proper substitute to pardon human sin.

Abraham's walk with his son to Mount Moriah foreshadows the journey of another Father and Son on another mountain many years later. God declares us just by grace *through faith,* yet the basis of our righteousness is found not in our righteous deeds but in the righteousness of God's own provided substitute for us, our Lord Jesus Christ. Isaac needed a substitute to die in his place, and God provided...The types and patterns of the Old Testament give way to fulfillment in the New, and no person can act as our substitute other than Jesus, God's own Son.[26]

------------------------

The earthly promised land was a mere type of the better country to come.

------------------------

## The Little Details
### *Sodom and Gomorrah*

After the Lord spoke to Sarah about her coming pregnancy, he told Abraham that he intended to visit Sodom and Gomorrah because he'd heard a great outcry against the people in the city, so he was going to examine them (Genesis 18:20-21). This was evidence to Abraham that God hears when people cry out about injustices, and he judges justly.

Abraham asked if the Lord would spare the city if he found ten righteous people in it, and the Lord said he would. This was evidence of God's justice and mercy.

But the cities did not have ten righteous people. Angels rescued Lot and his daughters before the Lord destroyed the cities. Abraham saw evidence of the Lord's power and of his ability and desire to rescue the godly.

The...term that confronts us is "spared." "He that spared not his own Son"..."Spared" is an old word which is used in connection with the offering up of Isaac by Abraham in Genesis 22:16...The offering of Isaac by Abraham is a type of what God Himself did on Calvary's hill...

It was not that God allowed cruel men to kill His Son; it was God Himself who smote His Son, as Abraham had been prepared to do with Isaac. It was God's action; it was "the determinate counsel and foreknowledge of God" that brought Christ's death to pass. It was the only way to forgive sin. Sin must be punished, as the entire Bible teaches. God is a God of righteousness and justice and holiness. He cannot wink at sin, He cannot pretend that He has not seen it, He cannot simply say, "I forgive you because I love you." The whole character of God demands justice and righteous retribution; and on the Cross that was meted out.[28]

**34.** ♥ Read Romans 8:31-39. What assurance stands out to you the most? Why?

### God with Us Forever
Revelation describes the city to which Abraham looked.

**35.** ♥ Read Revelation 21:1-8. What do you look forward to the most?

### God with Me Now
We read parts of Psalm 49 earlier in this chapter. Let's pray it to the Lord now.

Turn to Psalm 49 and read it. **Pray** the psalm to the Lord in worship.

**Praise** God for something you saw of his character this week. **Confess** anything that convicted you. **Ask** for help to do something God's Word calls you to do. **Thank** God for something you learned this week.

# The Heart and Art of Worship

Our imaginations are a gift from God, and we all have one. This creative collaborator works in unity with our thoughts and hearts visualizing mental images or ideas in our minds that are not actually real...or at least not unless or until you express them outwardly in some way.

If you're anything like me, your imagination was challenged multiple times throughout this week's lesson. I tried not to imagine what it must have been like for all those men to be circumcised. Ugh! I laughed with Abraham and Sarah as I could imagine their response to Sarah giving birth at 90 years old. My heart broke for Abraham as I walked up the mountain with him and watched him build the altar. And it was humbling to imagine him holding the knife ready to sacrifice his only son...humbling to witness faith so intensely confident.

But earlier, when God told Abraham to look up at the stars, I was right there with him. I saw the blackness of the night sky bursting forth with countless stars declaring the glory of the Lord; and all I could imagine was Abraham's awe and wonder at God's promises! Here he was without a child, but God said he was going to make a way where there seemed to be no way, and Abraham believed him! I could seriously "see" him dancing under the stars with exceedingly great joy! It was a night to remember!

When we engage with Scripture using our imaginations, it allows us to enter the story with more than our intellect. By imagining ourselves present in the story, we find ourselves connecting with the characters as real people, rather than fictional, and responding to them and to God with our hearts as well as our minds. Engaging with God's Word in this way oftentimes leads to discovering truths that we may otherwise have skimmed over...truths that may just touch our hearts, transform our lives, and draw us into more intimate and creative times of worship.

*Karla*

I will surely multiply your offspring as the stars of heaven...

and in your offspring shall all the nations of the earth be blessed.

Genesis 22:16-18

## Chapter 3

# Exodus 12
## Jesus the Sacrificed Lamb

The hope of freedom from sin and death

The Lord... will see the blood on the top and sides of the doorframe and will pass over that doorway,

and

he will not permit the destroyer to enter.

EXODUS 12:23 NIV

## Day 1

## Abraham's Children in Danger

One Sunday when I was around seven, my dad drove our blue station wagon to the park instead of to church. He said God didn't exist. He told me I could believe in God if I wanted to, but that would be stupid. At 14, I reasoned that a good God would want to tell people how to reach him. If the Bible was God's message, then an all-powerful God would be able to keep the message accurate. When I finally got a New Testament and read what the Gospels said about Jesus, I became convinced they were true.

When I told my parents that I had become a Christian, my dad told me he could easily destroy my faith with simple arguments, but he wouldn't because he'd destroyed someone else's faith and felt bad that the person left depressed. That propelled me to study the evidence for the resurrection and other topics related to the truth of Christianity.

Evidence. In our reading today, God will ask Abraham's descendants to become his people. The Hebrews needed to know they could trust God before they risked their lives leaving Egypt. They needed to know his saving power before they agreed to his covenant.

**The Reveal**

*Eve's Day*

After God judged Adam and Eve, he took care of their needs: "And the LORD God made for Adam and for his wife garments of skins" (Genesis 3:21). He covered their nakedness and protected them from the elements they would face outside the garden. But this protection came at a cost: the death of animals.[1]

*Moses's Day*

God renamed Abraham's grandson Jacob as Israel. Israel had 12 sons. A famine drove Israel's huge family to Egypt. There each of the 12 sons' families grew into a tribe. The Egyptians eventually enslaved them. To slow their rapid population growth, Pharaoh (the title of Egypt's ruler) commanded midwives to kill all Hebrew boys at birth.

One mom hid her baby boy for three months. Then she placed him in a basket among the river bank reeds. Pharaoh's daughter rescued and raised him as her own son, Moses.

When Moses grew up, he killed an Egyptian while trying to help the Hebrew slaves. He

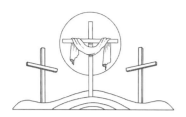

## The Little Details
### Exodus and Leviticus

The book of Exodus describes the Israelites' escape from Egyptian slavery, their journey to Mount Sinai, and the construction of a tabernacle where the people could meet with and worship God. It culminates with God's glorious presence entering the tabernacle.

The book of Leviticus describes the rules the priests needed to follow because of God's presence in the tabernacle. Professor Jay Sklar writes, "Leviticus describes a point in human history when the God who gives us meaning came and dwelt in the midst of some of our fellow human beings (the Israelites) and taught them what their purpose in life really was."[2]

Exodus and Leviticus together reveal much about the significance of the Passover lamb and how God intended to restore relationship with people.

---

The Israelites were thrilled that God intended to free them.

---

ended up fleeing for his life. When he was 80, the angel of the Lord appeared to him in a burning bush (Exodus 3). The Lord told him to lead his people to freedom.

Moses returned to Egypt and met with the Israelite leaders. He performed signs that God had given him the ability to do so that the Israelites would trust him. The Israelites were thrilled that God intended to free them (Exodus 4).

Moses went to Pharaoh and said, "Thus says the LORD, the God of Israel, 'Let my people go'" (Exodus 5:1). Pharaoh refused and punished the Hebrews by increasing their workload and beating them when they couldn't meet their quotas (Exodus 5).

That turned the people of Israel against Moses (Exodus 5:21).

The Lord sent Moses back to Pharaoh, this time with signs to convince Pharaoh that the powerful God of the Israelites was with Moses. Pharaoh again refused to let the people go. Moses returned and announced a plague. Pharaoh wouldn't budge. Nine times Moses announced the coming of a plague designed to show that the Lord was more powerful than Pharaoh and the Egyptian gods. Nine times Pharaoh refused to let the people go.

Pharaoh told Moses he would kill him if he ever saw his face again. So, the Lord announced one more plague—one that would convince Pharaoh to let the Hebrews go.

### God's Word to Us

 Take a moment to pray for insight as you read God's Word.

1. ♥ Read Exodus 1:8-22; 11:1-10; 12:21-42. What stands out to you? Why?

The Hebrews fled. When Pharaoh found out, he changed his mind and sent soldiers in pursuit. The soldiers trapped the people of Israel at the Red Sea. And then, the Lord miraculously parted the sea so that his people could escape. Pharaoh's armies pursued, but the waters crashed upon them (Exodus 14).

2. ♥ What are three ways God showed the Hebrews that he was trustworthy?

Today, God still gives evidence of his existence and of the resurrection.

3. (a) In Acts 17:31 (NIV) below, underline what will happen on the day God has set by the "man he has appointed" (Jesus). (b) Circle what God has given to everyone. (c) Double-underline how he did this.

   For he has set a day when he will judge the world with justice by the man he has appointed. He has given proof of this to everyone by raising him from the dead.

For more on the incredible evidence for the resurrection, go to www.DiscoveringTheBibleSeries.com.

# A Walk with Christ—Home

In Nancie Carmichael's book *The Unexpected Power of Home,* she shares that home is "a powerful metaphor for our lives. We have choices when it comes to making a home, and we can take the materials we have been given to make something beautiful and good. We have choices about our lives, to make them beautiful and good too."[3]

A sense of and the longing for home connects us with God and helps us to discover who we are and why we're here. This is illustrated in the life of Moses. Moses was born in captivity during a time of great chaos and inhumanity. Israel had grown significantly, and the large population made the new Pharaoh nervous.

> Come, we must deal shrewdly with them or they will become even more numerous and, if war breaks out, will join our enemies, fight against us and leave the country (Exodus 1:10 NIV).

Despite oppressive conditions and forced, grueling labor, the Hebrews continued to multiply. Eventually, Pharaoh became so worried, he commanded that every Hebrew male baby be cast into the Nile at birth. It was in this time of inhumane chaos and hostility that Moses was born. Where would Moses call home? And how do we find our home?

In *10 Best Decisions a Woman Can Make,* I use this snapshot of Moses's life to explore the skill needed to discern the will of God: the ability to look for spiritual markers. Once you've taken a look back, you can go forward in life. We are each created by God to live out our unique purpose that will be used to accomplish his plans. As you look back on your life, God will reveal your spiritual markers. These become road signs, pointing to your future.

One day while Moses was tending his sheep, God spoke to him through a burning bush. This interchange gives a glimpse into why God selected Moses as the leader to free his people. First God spoke:

> "And now the cry of the Israelites has reached me, and I have seen the way the Egyptians are oppressing them. So now, go. I am sending you to Pharaoh to bring my people the Israelites out of Egypt."

> But Moses said to God, "Who am I that I should go to Pharaoh and bring the Israelites out of Egypt?"

> And God said, "I will be with you...Now go; I will help you speak and teach you what to say" (Exodus 3:9-12; 4:12 NIV).

Moses's spiritual markers display he was uniquely prepared with the culture, language, and time with the people of Egypt:

- His mom saved his life by putting him in a basket and then into the water.
- His sister saved his life by following the basket.
- The princess saved his life by taking him into the palace and then chose his mom to care for him!
- God saved Moses's life by allowing him to flee to Goshen to guard sheep for a Midianite family.

It was there that the angel of the Lord appeared in the burning bush and spoke to Moses. He called him to tell Pharaoh to let God's people go. When you and I look back on our lives, we will see:

- Unique training that God can use for His purposes.
- Unique pain and experiences that God can use to prepare you for ministry and to walk through the doors he opens.
- Unique gifting, talents, and skills that God can use to further his mission.

When we scan the life of the Messiah and walk in his footsteps, we see pivotal markers where the carpenter's son points to our eternal home: heaven. "For we are his workmanship, created in Christ Jesus for good works, which God prepared beforehand, that we should walk in them" (Ephesians 2:10).

Pray, trace your life path, and then list your spiritual markers pointing to your *home*. "And your ears shall hear a word behind you, saying, 'This is the way, walk in it'" (Isaiah 30:21).

## Day 2

# The Passover Lamb Saves

Let's begin by picking up some of the details from our reading.

### The Call of Moses

> 4.  (a) Why did the Egyptians enslave the Israelites (Exodus 1:10)? (b) What were the Israelites' lives like (verses 13-14)? (c) What did Pharaoh command (verse 22)?

Pharaoh's daughter adopted the infant Moses. But when Moses grew up, he killed an Egyptian he saw beating a Hebrew. Pharaoh heard and wanted to kill Moses, so Moses fled to Midian, now an exile.

> 5.  (a) What happened to the Pharaoh who wanted to kill Moses (Exodus 2:23)? (b) What did the people of Israel do (verse 23)? (c) Who heard them (verse 24)?

When the Bible says God remembers something, it means he acted on it.

The angel of the Lord appeared in a flame of fire in a bush. The Lord called to Moses out of the bush and said, "I am the God of your father, the God of Abraham, the God of Isaac, and the God of Jacob...Come, I will send you to Pharaoh that you may bring my people, the children of Israel, out of Egypt" (Exodus 3:6,10).

> 6.  Exodus 4:22-23 below is what God told Moses to tell Pharaoh when he refused to set the people free. Underline what the Lord called Israel. Israel had been serving Pharaoh. Circle whom the Lord wanted Israel to serve instead.
>
>     Thus says the LORD, Israel is my firstborn son, and I say to you, "Let my son go that he may serve me." If you refuse to let him go, behold, I will kill your firstborn son.

"Israel is my firstborn son." That's an important phrase to which we'll return. For now, jump forward to just before the tenth plague.

---

**The Little Details**

*Theophanies in Moses's Day*

The Lord God gave physical manifestations of his presence in several ways in Moses's day. He appeared to Moses through fire in a burning bush (Exodus 3:2-6). The Lord led the people from Egypt to the promised land in a pillar of cloud by day and a pillar of fire by night (Exodus 13:21). On Mount Sinai, his presence manifested in a thunderstorm, cloud, fire, and trumpet blast (Exodus 19:16-20). At the dedication of the tabernacle, the glory of the Lord descended on it in a cloud (Exodus 40:34).

These displays assured the people of God's presence and guidance as they embarked on a journey they could not have made without his help.

## The Plague on the Firstborn

After nine plagues befell Egypt, Pharaoh told Moses he would kill him if he ever saw him again (Exodus 10:28). Moses announced the final plague: the death of every firstborn. He returned to the people of Israel to tell them what they must do to prevent the plague from falling on them.

7. (a) What kind of animal were the Israelites to slaughter (Exodus 12:21)? (b) What were they to do with the animal's blood (12:22)? (c) What would happen when the destroyer came to Egypt (12:23)? (d) What must not happen to the animal's bones (12:46)?

The Israelites in faith followed Moses's command and painted blood on the top and sides of their doors. They took care not to break any bones. They roasted the lambs and quickly ate them with unleavened bread and bitter herbs, fully clothed and ready to flee.

8. (a) What happened at midnight (Exodus 12:29-30)? (b) How did Pharaoh respond to the tenth plague (12:31-32)? (c) What indication is there in Pharaoh's words that he realized God was greater than he?

Judgment came, and the nation that had murdered Hebrew sons now lost their own.

## The Exodus

The Egyptians urged the Hebrews to leave quickly lest more of them die. The people of Israel left with all their belongings, herds, and flocks. They had no time to wait for yeast to make their dough rise, so they brought only unleavened dough.

The lamb had protected them from death. It had also redeemed them from slavery. They were free and on their way to the land God had promised to give Abraham's descendants.

As the people journeyed, God did something special to guide and assure them.

9. According to Exodus 13:21, who led the Israelites?

In the bright sun, the manifestation of the Lord's presence looked like a pillar of cloud, but at night, it looked like a pillar of fire. The pillar led them to the Red Sea.

Meanwhile, when Pharaoh heard his slaves were gone, he changed his mind and pursued them with chariots, horsemen, and troops. He hemmed them in at the Red Sea. The Israelites cried out in fear.

## The Little Details
### Paul M. Hoskins on Redemption:

God redeems his people from bondage without paying any redemption money...He says, "...I will bring you out from under the yoke of the Egyptians. I will free you from being slaves to them, and I will redeem you with an outstretched arm and with mighty acts of judgment" (NIV). Notice that there is no mention of payment of money...

Why all of the redemption and purchasing language if Pharaoh does not get paid? First, the language emphasizes God's goal in his dealings with Pharaoh...is nothing less than a transfer of ownership.

Second, God intends to redeem his people without money, because Pharaoh and the Egyptians unjustly enslaved God's people in the first place...God never sold them into bondage. Therefore, when God comes to redeem his people, he comes to break the yoke of slavery rather than to redeem them with money.[4]

## The Little Details

### Baylis on the Plagues Showing the Egyptian Gods' Powerlessness:

Many of the individual plagues directly demonstrate Yahweh's power over the gods. The Nile River was considered sacred, yet it was turned to blood. Associated with the river were the gods Khnum, Hapi, and Osiris (for whom the Nile served as his bloodstream). The goddess Heqt, the wife of Khnum, was represented as a frog...And where was the sky goddess Nut, from whose domain came the hail? Isis and Seth, responsible in part for agricultural crops, seem to have been overwhelmed. A number of gods are identified with the sun, including the sun god Re. Certainly these gods failed in allowing a heavy darkness to blanket Egypt for three days.[5]

- - - - - - - - - - - - - - - - - - -

God commanded the Israelites to celebrate this Passover yearly so that they would remember his power to deliver—and so that they would recognize the true Passover lamb when he came.

- - - - - - - - - - - - - - - - - - -

**10.** (a) What did Moses tell the Israelites to do (Exodus 14:13)? (b) What would the Lord do (verse 14)?

At the Lord's command, Moses stretched his hand out over the sea.

**11.** According to Exodus 14:21, what happened to the sea?

The Israelites passed through the sea on dry ground. When the Egyptians followed on their horses and chariots, the waters flowed back and destroyed them.

The Hebrews learned that the Lord was God, he had power over the sea, and he could keep his seemingly impossible promise to redeem them from slavery.

**12.** (a) In whom did the Israelites put their trust (Exodus 14:30-31)? (b) Would they have trusted as much if Pharaoh had let them go easily so that there was no need for a miraculous salvation? (c) Word of the miracle spread all around (Joshua 2:10-11); what did that tell the people of other nations?

**13.** ♥ Describe a difficulty you went through that helped others see God's glory.

God told the people to celebrate their escape from Egypt every spring.

**14.** Why should they celebrate Passover annually (Exodus 12:24-27)?

The Lord God told the people to commemorate their deliverance with an annual Passover feast that began a seven-day Feast of Unleavened Bread. Families reenacted events and ate a Passover meal of an unblemished roasted lamb, bitter herbs, and bread made without yeast (Exodus 12:5-8).[6] Parents told their children how on the day of judgment upon Egypt, the destroyer passed over all who trusted in lamb's blood so that God might deliver them from slavery to Egypt.

God commanded the Israelites to celebrate this Passover yearly so that they would remember his power to deliver—and so that they would recognize the true Passover lamb when he came. For there will be a day in which final judgment will pass over all who have trusted in that lamb's blood so that God might deliver them from slavery to sin and death.

## Day 3

# The Sacrificial Lambs Bring Near

The pillar of cloud led the people to Mount Sinai. The cloud stopped there for almost a year.[7] God explained why he brought the people out of Egypt.

## The Goal: A Kingdom of Priests

> **15.** (a) In Exodus 19:4, where did the Lord bring the people of Israel? (b) What did he ask them to do (verse 5)? (c) If they did, what would they be to him (verses 5-6)?

God wanted the people to be his treasured possession, so he made a covenant with them. A covenant is like a contract that governs relationships (such as marriage vows).

The Lord's part of the covenant was to provide the land in which they could live and to bless them in all ways. They would be a kingdom of priests, all serving God and showing other nations how to know God. They would be a holy nation, which means they would be set apart from other nations to serve the Lord.

The people's part of the covenant was to keep God's commands. At Sinai, the Lord gave the Ten Commandments (Exodus 20:3-17) as well as other commands. What would happen if they didn't keep his commands? He would remove his blessings and bring hardships on them as a warning. If they ignored his warnings and completely broke the covenant, he would exile them from the land.

Moses told the people all this, and they agreed to the covenant terms. Their "signature" to the covenant was Sabbath-keeping: "You shall keep my Sabbaths, for this is a sign between me and you" (Exodus 31:13). They would rest from Friday sundown to Saturday sundown. Pastor Trent Hunter and theology professor Stephen Wellum write, "Rest was the goal of the Law, a recovery of what was lost in creation because of sin, and something...that anticipated a far greater rest than was promised in the Law."[8]

## The Means: Preparing for God's Presence

God instructed Moses on what needed to be done so that people could draw near him.

### The Tabernacle for God's Presence

The Lord showed Moses how to build a tabernacle to enable people to approach him.

> **16.** In Exodus 25:9 below, circle the word describing what the tabernacle had to be like.
>
> Exactly as I show you concerning the pattern of the tabernacle, and of all its furniture, so you shall make it.

The earthly tabernacle was a pattern (or type) of heavenly things.

**The Little Details**

*Eugene H. Merrill on Kingdom of Priests:*

By this instrument [the covenant at Sinai] Yahweh confirmed his work of redeeming his vassal people from the overlordship of Egypt by making them his own servants, "a kingdom of priests and a holy nation" (Exod. 19:6). Their role thenceforth would be to mediate or intercede as priests between the holy God and the wayward nations of the world...

Both Exodus 20–23 and Deuteronomy follow the structure and contain the essential elements of classic suzerain-vassal treaties...

To clothe the profound theological truths of the Yahweh-Israel covenant relationship in the familiar garb of the form of international treaties was of inestimable value in communicating all that the covenant implied.[9]

----

God wanted the people to be his treasured possession, so he made a covenant with them.

----

## The Little Details
### Alexander on the Tabernacle:

A pair of curtains, embroidered with cherubim separated the Holy Place from the Most Holy Place. This latter room was the inner sanctum wherein was placed the ark of the covenant. This rectangular box served a double function, being both the footstool of a throne and a chest. Understood as a footstool, the ark of the covenant extends the heavenly throne to the earth; this is where the divine king's feet touch the earth. Consequently, the tabernacle links heaven and earth. As a chest, the ark of the covenant stores various items. The most important of these are the treaty or covenant documents that set out the obligations placed upon the Israelites by God.[10]

- - - - - - - - - - - - - - - - - -

A curtain embroidered with cherubim separated the Holy Place from the smaller Most Holy Place.

- - - - - - - - - - - - - - - - - -

**17.** (a) With what did the Lord fill Bezalel (Exodus 31:2-3)? (b) What could he do (verses 4-5)? (c) Why did God give the craftsmen these skills (verse 6)?

**18.** ♥ What skills has the Lord given you, and how do you use them to bless others?

The craftsmen made curtains to surround an outer courtyard containing the altar and a tabernacle (tent) with two rooms. The tabernacle's larger front room was called the Holy Place and contained a menorah for light. A curtain embroidered with cherubim separated the Holy Place from the smaller Most Holy Place. The Most Holy Place contained the ark of the covenant—a large chest holding the stone tablets engraved with the Ten Commandments. Its cherubim-adorned lid was called the mercy seat (NIV: atonement cover). Only the high priest could enter the Most Holy Place, and he only once a year.

Worshipers entered the courtyard and offered sacrifices at the altar. That would cleanse them so that they could worship at the tabernacle. The entrances to the courtyard, Holy Place, and Most Holy Place always faced east. The cherubim embroidered on the curtain would remind worshipers of other cherubim.

**19.** In Genesis 3:22-24 below, underline where God placed the cherubim and flaming sword. Circle what they guarded the way to (last three words). Box the reason God didn't want the man to eat (at the end of what God said).

Then the LORD God said, "Behold, the man has become like one of us in knowing good and evil. Now, lest he reach out his hand and take also of the tree of life and eat, and live forever—" therefore the LORD God...drove out the man, and at the east of the garden of Eden he placed the cherubim and a flaming sword that turned every way to guard the way to the tree of life.

Hunter and Wellum explain:

> The tabernacle points back to Eden as well—its construction in seven steps, ending with rest, echo the seven days of creation. The menorah reminiscent of the tree of life and the embroidered cherubim representing the cherubim remind us that the way back to Eden is guarded because of sin. Even as we approach from the east, we must be protected from God's holy presence—or we die.[11]

**20.** In Exodus 40:34 below, circle what covered the tent. Underline what filled the temple.

Then the cloud covered the tent of meeting, and the glory of the LORD filled the tabernacle.

God's presence was on earth. The ark of the covenant was his footstool.

### Sacrifices to Atone

God revealed that disobeying his commands brought guilt that separated people from him. He provided two ways to resolve this so that they could draw near without dying.

#### The Day of Atonement

Every fall, the people of Israel participated in the Day of Atonement. The high priest offered sacrifices for himself and then for all the people to cleanse them from sin: "For on this day shall atonement be made for you to cleanse you. You shall be clean before the LORD from all your sins" (Leviticus 16:30). On this day alone, the high priest carried some of the blood of the sacrifices into the Most Holy Place. There he sprinkled blood on the lid of the ark of the covenant. Next, he purified the objects in the Holy Place with blood. Then, he purified the altar in the courtyard with blood.

The Day of Atonement revealed that the people's sins separated them from God and defiled the tabernacle's holy objects. Only the shedding of blood could purify the tabernacle and the people again.

#### Other Offerings

When the people sinned or became defiled, they could offer purification, reparation, and burnt offerings (see sidebar). When they wanted to draw near to God in thanksgiving, they could offer dedication and peace offerings.

> **21.** (a) What sins does Leviticus 4:27-28 address? (b) What animals could be sacrificed (verses 28,32)? (c) What did the person do to the animal at the altar (verse 33)? (d) What did the priest do with the blood (verse 34)? (e) What happened to the person (verse 35)?

This ritual helped the worshiper know that sin was serious, but God was merciful.

## The Reminder: Preparing for the Future

When Moses knew he was about to die, he gave a pastoral farewell speech. He reminded everyone of the covenant blessings for obeying God and the covenant curses for disobeying him. He warned that one day they would break their covenant and God would exile them. But he gave them a message of hope.

> **22.** Read Deuteronomy 30:1-3. (a) If the future exiles remembered the covenant blessings and curses, what could they do (verses 1-2)? (b) How would God respond (verse 3)?

Even exile would not end their story.

### The Little Details
### *Old Testament Sacrifices*

Here's Dr. Allen P. Ross's summary of the temple sacrifices in the order they were offered.[12]

**Purification Offering** (also translated *sin offering*): animal sacrifice for purification from defilement and unintentional sin

**Reparation Offering** (*guilt offering*): money plus animal sacrifice for sins for which restitution could be and had been made (such as fraud)

**Burnt Offering**: animal sacrifice for atonement after either of the previous offerings

**Dedication Offering**: grains and crops for showing gratitude

**Peace Offering** (*fellowship offering*): animal sacrifice and bread for celebrating being at peace with God; a small part burned for the Lord, and the rest offered as a communal meal for the worshipers, priests, and the poor

The Day of Atonement revealed that the people's sins separated them from God and defiled the tabernacle's holy objects.

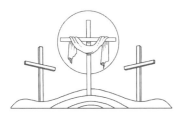

## The Little Details

### Craig L. Blomberg on Matthew's Use of Hosea:

It is better...to understand Matthew's actual use of Hos. 11:1 as a classic example of pure typology...That Israel had been delivered from Egypt, that Israel would again be exiled there but again restored, and that the child believed to be the Messiah also had to return to Israel from Egypt formed too striking a set of parallels for Matthew to attribute them to chance. God clearly was at work orchestrating the entire series of events...

"Out of Egypt" is the first of several parallels in Matthew's infancy narrative to events from the life of Moses, leading some to speak of a Christological portrait of Jesus as a "new Moses"...This motif is clearer elsewhere, however; here the parallel is more directly with Israel as a people. Clearly, though, a "new exodus" motif is present...Moreover, Jesus will prove faithful where the nation had been faithless; in numerous respects he recapitulates the history of Israel as a whole.[13]

# The Lamb of God Enters the World

In Moses's day, the Passover lamb redeemed the people from slavery. The sacrificial system tangibly showed that sin separated people from God, but God in his mercy provided the means for people to approach him.

## God with Us Then

At Sinai, skilled artisans created a lavish place of worship with three sections, each increasing in holiness. Worshipers entered the outer court first and offered sacrifices on the altar so that they could be cleansed of sin and defilement. Then they could approach the tabernacle and worship God. Priests could enter and view the curtain embroidered with cherubim that blocked the way to the Most Holy Place.

## The Reveal Continued

### David's Day

David wanted to build God a temple to replace the tabernacle. God gave him the plans so that his son Solomon could build it. The magnificent new temple had an outer courtyard for the altar, an inner Holy Place, and an innermost Most Holy Place.

After Solomon's death, the kingdom split in two: Israel in the north and Judah in the south. Most of the tribes belonged to the new Israel. Since the temple was in Judah, Israel's first king set up rival sanctuaries with golden calves and its own priesthood (1 Kings 12:28-31). Many of the legitimate priests in Israel fled to Judah (2 Chronicles 11:14-15). David's grandson ruled Judah.

### The Major Prophets' Day

Israel and Judah prospered in the mid-eighth century BC, but prosperity led to social injustice, oppression of the middle and lower classes, and idol worship. The prophets Hosea, Micah, and Isaiah all announced Israel's imminent exile for abandoning God's covenant (Hosea 7:13; Micah 1:6; Isaiah 5:13).

> 23. Read Hosea 11:1-6. (a) Verse 1 describes the exodus from Egypt. What two phrases describe Israel? (b) How does God's tenderness in verses 2-4 strike you? (c) Since they would not let God rule them, who would rule them instead (verses 5-6)?

Assyria conquered Israel and exiled its people in 722 BC. Micah and Isaiah decried wicked leaders in Judah and prophesied that Babylon—no threat at the time—would exile Judah (Micah 4:10; Isaiah 39:6). But the exile would be temporary. Light would shine over the land and draw the nations (Isaiah 60:1-3). God would send a suffering servant who would be "like a lamb that is led to the slaughter" and "an offering for guilt" (Isaiah 53:7,10).

Micah prophesied that Jerusalem would "become a heap of ruins" (Micah 3:12). The people would be exiled to Babylon, but the Lord would redeem them (4:10).

**24.** In Micah 5:2 below, underline who would come from Bethlehem. Double-underline from what time period he would come.

> But you, O Bethlehem Ephrathah, who are too little to be among the clans of Judah, from you shall come forth for me one who is to be ruler in Israel, whose coming forth is from of old, from ancient days.

As prophesied, in 586 BC, Babylon burned the temple, destroyed Jerusalem, and exiled the people. The people awaited the one who would come from Bethlehem.

### The Second Temple's Day

God opened the way for the people to return from exile. Some returned and rebuilt the temple, but it was nothing like Solomon's glorious temple. They had no king of their own but lived under foreign rule.

### Jesus's Day

In Jesus's day, Rome ruled the Jews. Jerusalem was in the Jewish province of Judea, but the Jews were scattered throughout the Roman Empire. Many eagerly awaited the fulfillment of the prophecies about a descendant of David who would be their king.

## Jesus Called Out of Egypt

After Jesus's birth, "wise men from the east came to Jerusalem, saying, 'Where is he who has been born king of the Jews? For we saw his star when it rose'"—an allusion to Isaiah's prophecy of a light arising over Zion and drawing other nations (Matthew 2:1-2; Isaiah 60:3). King Herod assembled the chief priests and scribes and asked where the Scriptures said the Christ would be born. They told him Bethlehem (Micah 5:2). When he couldn't find the child, he ordered the murder of all boys under two in Bethlehem.

But an angel of the Lord warned Mary's husband, Joseph, to flee, so he took Mary and Jesus to Egypt and lived there until Herod died.

**25.** According to Matthew 2:15, what was fulfilled by Jesus going to Egypt?

Matthew quoted Hosea 11:1, which was about God calling the people of Israel out of Egypt. Remember that God told Pharaoh, "Israel is my firstborn son" (Exodus 4:22). The people of Israel were a type of Jesus, God's Son. Many events that happened to Israel foreshadowed events that happened to Jesus. The Israelites went to Egypt to escape death from famine; Jesus went to Egypt to escape death from Herod's sword. While Israel was in Egypt, Pharaoh killed Israelite babies; while Jesus was in Egypt, King Herod killed Israelite babies. The Israelites came out of Egypt to become a people set apart for service to God; Jesus came out of Egypt to be a Son set apart for service to God. Israel faced temptation in the desert and failed; Jesus faced temptation in the desert and triumphed (see chapter 1 sidebars).

## Jesus the Lamb of God

Just before Jesus began his public ministry, a new prophet arrived—John the Baptist. When he saw Jesus, he said, "Behold, the Lamb of God, who takes away the sin of the world!" (John 1:29).

## The Little Details
### *"Rachel Weeping for Her Children"*

Jeremiah prophesied, "A voice is heard in Ramah, lamentation and bitter weeping. Rachel is weeping for her children; she refuses to be comforted for her children, because they are no more" (Jeremiah 31:15). The Lord comforted Rachel, saying there was hope for her exiled descendants' future, for they would return and he would make a new covenant (Jeremiah 31:17,31).

Rachel's tomb was near Ramah, which the Babylonians later used as a deportation site when they exiled the Israelites after killing children who couldn't make the trek.

Matthew 2:17-18 says that Herod killing the babies in tiny Bethlehem near Ramah fulfilled Jeremiah 31:15. Just as Rachel personified the mothers who lost children in the exile when their king was dethroned, so she personified the mothers who lost children when the new king arrived. They can take comfort that there is hope for their future, for a new covenant comes.

## Jesus the Passover Lamb

**26.** (a) To what is everyone who practices sin a slave (John 8:34)? (b) Who can free people from that slavery (verse 36)?

**27.** In John 5:24 below, circle what those who hear Jesus's words and believe the Father have. Underline what they don't come into. Double-underline where they pass from.

> Truly, truly, I say to you, whoever hears my word and believes him who sent me has eternal life. He does not come into judgment, but has passed from death to life.

Let's skip ahead to the end of Jesus's public ministry.

**28.** (a) What day was it and what happened on that day (Mark 14:12)? (b) What did Jesus want to do (verse 14)?

Jews reckoned days from sundown to sundown. The afternoon was when they killed the Passover lambs. Sundown started the feast, and Jesus had his final meeting with his disciples, the last supper. Jesus said he wouldn't drink wine with them again until "that day when I drink it new in the kingdom of God" (Mark 14:25). That night, the Jewish leaders arrested, tried, and condemned Jesus to be crucified.

**29.** Read John 19:31-36. (a) What didn't the soldiers do (verse 33)? (b) Why (verse 36)?

John quoted Exodus 12:46, which forbade breaking the bones of a Passover lamb. John saw the killing of lambs without breaking bones at Passover as portending the killing of Jesus without breaking bones at this Passover. The first Passover lambs rescued the Israelites from enslavement to Egypt and delivered them from the curse of death so that they could be God's people in the promised land. This Passover lamb rescues those who trust in him from enslavement to sin and delivers them from the curse of death so that they can have eternal life and be God's people in the new promised land, the kingdom of God.

**30.** ♥ How have the Passover lambs and the sacrificial system helped you understand Jesus's work on the cross for you?

## Day 5

# The Conquering Lamb Saves

John's Gospel proclaims that Jesus is the Lamb of God who takes away the sins of the world. Hebrews 9:1-14 explains that the entire sacrificial system with its offerings for sin was a type of something greater: Jesus's sacrifice of himself.

### The Sacrificed Lamb in Hebrews

31. (a) Which room did the priests enter regularly: the outer first section (the Holy Place) or the inner second section (the Most Holy Place), according to Hebrews 9:6? (b) Who was the only person who could enter the inner second section (the Most Holy Place), according to verse 7? (c) How often could he enter (verse 7)? (d) What did he need to offer before entering (verse 7)?

32. In Hebrews 9:8-9 (NIV) below, underline what the Holy Spirit was showing by these restrictions. Double-underline what the sacrifices were unable to do.

    The Holy Spirit was showing by this that the way into the Most Holy Place had not yet been disclosed as long as the first tabernacle was still functioning. This is an illustration for the present time, indicating that the gifts and sacrifices being offered were not able to clear the conscience of the worshiper.

The "present time" is the time since Christ's death. The word translated "illustration" is *parabolē* and is translated "parable" elsewhere. The tabernacle and offerings were pictures of—types of—something greater: Jesus's death on the cross.

33. In Hebrews 9:11-12 (NIV) below, circle what Christ came as. Underline the tabernacle through which he went. Box what he entered inside the tabernacle. Double-underline what he obtained.

    But when Christ came as high priest of the good things that are now already here, he went through the greater and more perfect tabernacle that is not made with human hands, that is to say, is not a part of this creation. He did not enter by means of the blood of goats and calves; but he entered the Most Holy Place once for all by his own blood, thus obtaining eternal redemption.

The tabernacle that Moses made was patterned after the heavenly true tabernacle (Hebrews 8:5). That's the tabernacle Jesus entered. He achieved eternal redemption, not just outward redemption to make someone ceremonially clean for a year.

### The Little Details
#### Kevin DeYoung on Sin:

Sin is another name for that hideous rebellion, that God-defiance, that wretched opposition to the Creator that crouches at the door of every fallen human heart. Sin is both a condition, inherited from Adam (Rom 5:12-21), and an action—manifesting itself in thought, word, and deed—that when full grown gives birth to death (Jas 1:15). In simplest terms, sin is lawlessness (1 John 3:4). It means we have broken God's commands and have fallen short of his glory (Rom 3:23). But sin goes deeper than merely missing the mark. Sin is idolatry (Col 3:5; 1 John 5:21). It is worshiping false gods, whether these deities are overt and physical or more subtle and internal...Sin is pollution (Jas 1:27). Sin is pervasive (Rom 3:9-20). And sin is *the* problem in the universe. The redemptive story of the Bible does not make sense without it.[14]

The tabernacle and offerings were pictures of—types of—something greater: Jesus's death on the cross.

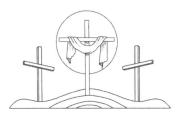

**The Little Details**
*Hunter and Wellum on the New Exodus:*

In Christ, God cures our problem of sin by Christ's life and redemptive death. Jesus speaks of his death as an *exodus* or "departure" (Luke 9:31) because his death is the event to which the exodus, as a type and pattern, ultimately pointed. In Jesus's cross and resurrection, redemption from sin has finally come in its complete sense. In Christ, an even greater exodus from slavery has occurred.[15]

34. Read Hebrews 9:13-14 (NIV) below. Box the two words at the end of the first sentence that describe the type of clean they received from animal sacrifices. Underline what Jesus's sacrifice cleanses us from (second sentence). Circle *Christ*, *Spirit*, and *God* (*God* appears twice). Double-underline the reason Jesus cleansed us (the last eight words).

> The blood of goats and bulls and the ashes of a heifer sprinkled on those who are ceremonially unclean sanctify them so that they are outwardly clean. How much more, then, will the blood of Christ, who through the eternal Spirit offered himself unblemished to God, cleanse our consciences from acts that lead to death, so that we may serve the living God!

Whereas the sacrificial system cleansed outwardly, Christ's blood cleanses completely.

### God with Us Still

*God with Us Today*
Paul and Peter describe how we should live since Jesus is the sacrificial lamb.

35. ♥ (a) Since Christ is our Passover Lamb, what should we remove from our lives (1 Corinthians 5:7-8)? (b) How have you seen these things hurt relationships? (c) What should we add to our lives? (d) How have you seen these things help relationships?

36. (a) What should our actions be like (1 Peter 1:14-16)? (b) How should we live out our time on this earth (verse 17)? (c) Why should we live this way (verses 18-19)? (d) From when was this lamb known/chosen (verse 20)?

*God with Us Forever*
Revelation 15 describes a heavenly scene involving those who have conquered the beast whose power is from the dragon (the devil). They celebrate the exodus Moses led into the promised land as a type of the new exodus into the new heaven and earth.

37. ♥ Read Revelation 15. What stands out to you the most?

Paul and Peter describe how we should live since Jesus is the sacrificial lamb.

*God with Me Now*

Psalm 114 celebrates God's mighty deliverance from Egypt, so it's a perfect way to close today. Think of a special time God delivered you from something, such as the day he delivered you from slavery to sin.

Turn to Psalm 114 and read it. **Pray** the psalm to the Lord in worship. Give thanks for your time of deliverance.

**Praise** God for something you saw of his character this week. **Confess** anything that convicted you. **Ask** for help to do something God's Word calls you to do. **Thank** God for something you learned this week.

# The Heart and Art of Worship

This week's study was so encouraging. At the first mention of paint, God had my attention, but the painting he was talking about had much greater purpose than my paintings of birds or flowers. The Lord told his people to paint the blood of the lamb on the sides and top of their doors, and it literally saved their lives. And then the parting of the Red Sea...no one saw that coming! Epic to say the least! But it just made me think about how amazingly creative God is when it comes to making himself and his will known to the inhabitants of this world...both believer and unbeliever!

God not only wanted to reveal his glory, but he wanted his glory to dwell with his people! And he had a vision for his house—down to the most minute details...and heaped with symbolism! Now you have to remember, he is God and could have spoken this tabernacle into existence, but he didn't. Instead, he wanted to work in and through his people...not only to dwell with them, but to give them a place to worship and the opportunity to reveal his glory to the nations through the works of their hands. He called his people to whom he had given creative abilities—people just like you and me—to use their skills to worship and bring him glory. And he still calls us today!

When I came to understand that my artistic ability was a gift from God, I prayed and asked if there was any way I could use my talent to bring glory to him and be a blessing to others. And he's answered that prayer more than I could have ever imagined. My hope is always that my art will touch your heart and draw you to worship Jesus. Today, God doesn't dwell in a building or a tabernacle but, because of Jesus, the Passover Lamb, he lives within us. Every time we share our art, our songs, our writings, our craft with the world, we're sharing him...his love and his glory!

The Lord...
will see the blood on the top and sides of the doorframe and will pass over that doorway,

and he will not permit the destroyer to enter.

EXODUS 12:23 NIV

## Chapter 4

# Psalm 22
## Jesus the Afflicted One

The hope of God hearing our cries

for he has NOT DESPISED or SCORNED the SUFFERING of the afflicted ONE

PSALM 22:24 NIV

## Day 1

## What's Right in God's Eyes

"God, I don't see what the big deal is if I don't follow this one verse as long as I don't sin." Yep, I actually prayed that. I probably should have tacked on "in any other way," but for some reason, I didn't see sidestepping this particular verse as an issue.

I had been invited to join a new ministry team and was excited about it. But soon I noticed the team's leader displaying jealousy toward someone. I thought, *I know this one. After all, my own mother struggled with jealousy. I'll simply gain her approval by making her look good, giving her credit for what I do, and showing her I'm not a threat.*

But Galatians 1:10 nagged me: "For am I now seeking the approval of man, or of God? Or am I trying to please man? If I were still trying to please man, I would not be a servant of Christ."

Things went well for a while. Then I received a phone call from the leader over her. He doubted she was in the right position and wanted to talk to her about moving to a different position. Would I be willing to take over if she agreed? I said "yes."

But she didn't agree, and the animosity she'd shown others now turned on me. I started to resign, but she told me, "You're the only one who can help in this area." *Lesson #1: It's easy to manipulate people pleasers.* Twice I heard her lie but did nothing. *Lesson #2: People pleasers compromise.* And then she lied about me. *Lesson #3: People pleasers lie to themselves.* She ousted me. *Lesson #4: Seeking approval from people who use approval to manipulate is stupid.* I learned the wisdom of Galatians 1:10 the hard way. *Lesson #5: The commands we least want to obey are the ones we most need to obey.*

**The Reveal**

In the passages we'll read this week, a young man who is trying to serve God and do what's right flees a jealous king.

*Eve's Day*

The Lord promised Eve that her offspring would crush the serpent's head, but the serpent would bruise her offspring's heel. The defeat would come, but only through suffering.

## The Little Details
### Hebrew Poetry

The psalms are poems meant to be sung and prayed. The psalm we'll read in this chapter is a lament, which is a prayer request psalm. It's a poem about things that have gone wrong. Psalm 22 is also a messianic psalm that foreshadows an important event in Jesus's life.

Psalm 22 comes from Book I of the Psalter (Psalms 1–41). Most of the psalms in Book I are about events that happened before David became king.

Laments such as Psalm 22 typically have five parts:

1. Address and introductory cry

2. Lament

3. Confession of trust

4. Petition

5. Praise or vow to praise

You can discover more about psalms and how to pray them in our book *Discovering Hope in the Psalms*.

---

For David, the path to the crown was through suffering.

---

### Abraham's Day

God promised Abraham that some of his descendants would be kings.

### Moses's Day

Through Moses, God provided commands for future kings to obey.

### David's Day

Under Moses and his successor, Joshua, the Israelites became a nation. Initially, God was their only king. When the generation that saw God's miracles died out, the people rebelled against God. He gave them over to enemies. They served enemies until they cried out to God, and he sent judges to rescue them. This cycle of rest, rebellion, repentance, rescue repeated over and over, with the people turning farther from God each time they rebelled. The book of Judges summarizes the situation: "In those days there was no king in Israel. Everyone did what was right in his own eyes" (Judges 21:25).

Eventually, the people demanded a king to lead them in battle, like other nations had. Their first king, Saul, settled on the throne around 1050 bc. But he promptly went his own way. A prophet told him his dynasty wouldn't last, for "the Lord has sought out a man after his own heart" (1 Samuel 13:14).

The prophet secretly anointed a shepherd boy named David as the future king. David became a mighty warrior for King Saul. But when Saul heard how the people loved David, jealousy drove him to try to kill David. When that failed, Saul falsely accused David of treason and dispatched soldiers to kill him. David fled into exile.

For David, the path to the crown was through suffering. It may have been during those dark times that he penned Psalm 22.

## God's Word to Us

 Take a moment to pray for insight as you read God's Word.

1. ♥ Read 1 Samuel 24 and Psalm 22. What stands out to you? Why?

2. ♥ Have you ever faced a time when it felt as if God had forsaken you? Explain.

3. ♥ Without giving names, describe a time you faced someone else's jealousy.

# A Walk with Christ—Christ Present

After my best friend's daughter unexpectedly died, Bill and I began rearranging our lives to be with my friend. This drive to be with a beloved friend in need is only a glimpse of the Father's nature, witnessed throughout the love story of the Bible, to be with us. The fulfillment of the Isaiah 7:14 prophecy of the coming of Immanuel (we'll study this in chapter 7) is found in Matthew when the angel speaks to Joseph:

> An angel of the Lord appeared to him in a dream and said, "Joseph son of David, do not be afraid to take Mary home as your wife, because what is conceived in her is from the Holy Spirit. She will give birth to a son, and you are to give him the name Jesus, because he will save his people from their sins."

All this took place to fulfill what the Lord had said through the prophet: "The virgin will conceive and give birth to a son, and they will call him Immanuel" (which means "God with us") (Matthew 1:20-23 NIV).

Underline each reference to God being with you:

"Have I not commanded you? Be strong and courageous. Do not be frightened, and do not be dismayed, for the Lord your God is with you wherever you go" (Joshua 1:9).

"Fear not, for I am with you; be not dismayed, for I am your God; I will strengthen you, I will help you, I will uphold you with my righteous right hand" (Isaiah 41:10).

"The Lord your God is in your midst, a mighty one who will save" (Zephaniah 3:17).

"Even though I walk through the valley of the shadow of death, I will fear no evil, for you are with me" (Psalm 23:4).

"And I will ask the Father, and he will give you another Helper, to be with you forever...he dwells with you and will be in you" (John 14:16-17).

"Where shall I go from your Spirit? Or where shall I flee from your presence? If I ascend to heaven, you are there! If I make my bed in Sheol, you are there! If I take the wings of the morning and dwell in the uttermost parts of the sea, even there your hand shall lead me, and your right hand shall hold me" (Psalm 139:7-10).

"For I am sure that neither death nor life, nor angels nor rulers, nor things present nor things to come, nor powers, nor height nor depth, nor anything else in all creation, will be able to separate us from the love of God in Christ Jesus our Lord" (Romans 8:38-39).

During my friend's season of grief, I tried to be present with her. And in her grief, she also found a way to be with others. In a First Place 4 Health online Bible study I lead, two women had lost children. My dear friend shared a comfort a Costa Rican pastor had expressed in sympathy, *Iré contigo*, which means "I go with you." In our times of sadness, joy, confusion, or celebration, Christ goes with us—Immanuel, God with us!

Visit www.DiscoveringTheBibleSeries.com for an acrostic to help you stay in STEP with Immanuel.

*Pam*

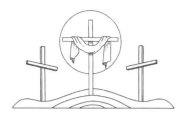

## The Little Details
### *Prophecy or Portent?*

The Gospels record that Jesus's crucifixion fulfilled Psalm 22. Details such as "they pierce my hands and my feet" and "cast lots for my garments" are clearly matched to events in Jesus's life.

The question arises, Did David receive Psalm 22 as purely a prophecy unrelated to his own life? Or did he write a psalm about an event in his own life that portended the crucifixion, with the Holy Spirit guiding him in language that fit both his situation and the crucifixion?

Most Old Testament scholars think that David wrote about an event in his own life, so we'll approach the psalm in that way. The event foreshadowed the crucifixion, and therefore we recognize the psalm as messianic.

Just as events in the lives of other prophets foreshadowed those in Jesus's life, so did events in David's life.

# David's Path to the Crown

Though God often spoke to David through prophets, at times the Holy Spirit spoke directly to David, who was a prophet himself (2 Samuel 23:2; Acts 2:30). Just as events in the lives of other prophets foreshadowed those in Jesus's life, so did events in David's life. Professor Paul M. Hoskins explains: "Part of God's plan for David's life was for David to suffer and for David to write about his suffering in such a way as to anticipate specific aspects of the suffering of Jesus, the Christ."[1]

## David's Situation

Saul was Israel's first king. But a prophet told him, "Because you have rejected the word of the LORD, he has also rejected you from being king...The LORD has torn the kingdom of Israel from you this day and has given it to a neighbor of yours" (1 Samuel 15:23,28).

Later, David impressed King Saul when he single-handedly defeated the giant Goliath. Saul was thrilled when he saw what a skilled warrior David was—until the women sang, "Saul has struck down his thousands, and David his ten thousands" (1 Samuel 18:7). Jealousy and rage overtook Saul. He feared that David was the prophesied replacement. When attempts to kill David failed, he falsely accused him of treason and pursued him.

4. (a) Briefly describe David hiding in the cave (yesterday's reading). (b) What did Saul admit in front of his men (1 Samuel 24:17)? (c) What did Saul know (verse 20)?

Now Saul's men knew he had lied. Saul continued to pursue David. The soldiers who obeyed him did so knowing it was unjust. David fled into exile (1 Samuel 27:1-2).

5. ♥ How does this encourage you that God can expose false accusations?

## David Cries Out to God

David lived exiled from the promised land until Saul's death in battle. He may have written Psalm 22 during the time Saul pursued him or during the battles he faced in exile.

6. In Psalm 22:1-2 below, circle what David called God three times. Underline his two questions. Box the times when David had cried out to God.

My God, my God, why have you forsaken me?
    Why are you so far from saving me, from the words of my groaning?
O my God, I cry by day, but you do not answer,
    and by night, but I find no rest.

David could neither sense God's presence nor see God's help. While God does not forsake those who belong to him, they sometimes feel forsaken (Hebrews 13:5). David sought answers as to why.

## David Confesses His Trust

David knew how to pray in ways that built hope and trust.

> **7.** In Psalm 22:3 below, circle the attribute of God in the first line (one word). Underline where God is enthroned.
>
> Yet you are holy,
>    enthroned on the praises of Israel.

God is holy and set apart. He is also enthroned on the praises of his people. Many of those praises were for answered prayers. That assured David that God answers prayer.

> **8.** (a) In whom had David's ancestors trusted (Psalm 22:4)? (b) In verse 4, what was the result of that trust? (c) What was the result of their crying out to God (verse 5)? (d) In verse 5, what was the result of their trust?

David recalled God's past saving acts and what happened when his ancestors trusted God. This built his hope that God would hear and deliver him too.

> **9.** (a) What did David call himself in Psalm 22:6? (b) How were others treating him (verses 6-7)? (c) How did they mock his faith (verse 8)?

David openly described his sorrows. Professor Allen P. Ross says, "With the metaphor 'worm' he is saying that (in their eyes) he is worthless because no one cares if he lives or dies. He is not regarded as a valuable human by his enemies; they consider him to be a worthless pest."[2] That fits well with David asking Saul why he pursued him when he was nothing but a dead dog or a flea (1 Samuel 24:14).

"Make mouths at me" in Psalm 22:7 can mean "make faces at me" (MSG) or "hurl insults" (NIV). Today, children commonly make faces at each other, but teens and adults tend to sneer or use crude hand gestures.

People wagged (shook) their heads at him, taunting him that his trust in God was unfounded. Their taunts reflected what David himself asked, "Why have you forsaken me?"

> **10.** (a) For how long had David trusted God (Psalm 22:9)? (b) What had the Lord been to him since birth (verse 10)?

## The Little Details
### Sklar on "Holy":

To be holy is to be set apart as distinct in some way. Normally, this takes place when a person or object is set apart as distinct by another person. In Exodus and Leviticus, the Lord himself frequently sets apart various people or objects as distinct. He does this with people either by entering into special relationship with them...or by having them go through various rituals that set them apart in a special way...He usually sets objects apart as distinct by means of various rituals as well...The holiness of these people or objects may be called "dependent holiness," for the simple reason that it is completely dependent on another. All of these people or objects were at one point not holy; they became holy only because another person had set them apart as distinct. The Lord's holiness, however, does not depend on anyone else...The Lord is set apart as distinct because of his very nature...Although there are many aspects to the Lord's holiness, the Pentateuch focuses on two in particular: his power and his moral purity.[3]

## The Little Details
### The Book of Psalms

Psalms is divided into five books, each containing collections of psalms.

**Book I** (Psalms 1–41) traces the rise of David's kingdom. The first two psalms introduce the entire book of Psalms. All but two of the rest are ascribed to David. Many concern his troubles before becoming king.

**Book II** (Psalms 42–72) is the establishment of the kingdom under David and his son Solomon.

**Book III** (Psalms 73–89) mourns the fall of the kingdom. It was probably compiled during the exile that followed the destruction of Jerusalem and the temple in 586 BC. It contains the most heart-breaking of the psalms and ends asking God why he rejected his people.

**Books IV & V** (Psalms 90–106 and 107–150) were compiled after the people returned from exile in 538 BC. They answer the questions of Book III and acknowledge God as king. The final five psalms are the doxology to the entire book of Psalms.

David again confessed his trust in God. He recalled his relationship with God, allowing truth to combat his enemies' taunts and accusations. David had seen God care for him since birth. There was no reason to think that his care had ceased.

### David Asks for Help

Once David had built up his hope in God by remembering God's attributes and past care, he made his request. He poured out to God what was wrong and told God what he wanted. This section is the prayer request part of the psalm.

> **11.** In Psalm 22:11 below, circle what David asked God to do. Underline the two reasons he gives.
>
> Be not far from me, for trouble is near, and there is none to help.

In verse 1, David asked why God had forsaken him because it felt as if God was not near. Yet David prayed anyway, trusting that God heard. In the next two verses, David compared his enemies to a large breed of dangerous bulls.

> **12.** (a) Summarize David's feelings in a word or two based on Psalm 22:14. (b) What happened to his strength (verse 15)? (c) What would happen if God did not rescue him soon (verse 15)?

David felt as if his bones were out of joint. His heart was weakening. His strength was gone. He was dehydrated and close to death.

> **13.** (a) Who surrounded David (Psalm 22:16)? (b) In verse 16, what do they do to him? (c) In verse 17, what do they do? (d) In verse 18, what do they do?

David continued using beast imagery. Wild dogs are scavengers, not pets (think jackals). They eat corpses and bite extremities. David called his enemies dogs as their swords nipped his hands and feet. He was so thin that his bones stuck out. Either his enemies took his garments and cast lots for them, or he wrote figuratively about how sure they were of his imminent death.

> **14.** (a) What did David call God in Psalm 22:19? (b) What did David request (verses 19-20)? (c) From what does he want to be saved (verse 21)?

And here the psalm abruptly changes.

## The Lord Rescues David

David wrote the first half of Psalm 22 about a dark time in his life when he feared enemies would kill him. He passionately called for God's help. And then, the second half of verse 21 makes an abrupt turn.

> **15.** In the second half of Psalm 22:21 below, circle the word describing God's action.
>
> You have rescued me from the horns of the wild oxen!

### David Praises God

God answered David's prayer, and the lament turned to praise.

> **16.** (a) In Psalm 22:22, what did David say he would do? (b) In verse 23, on whom did he call? (c) What three things did he tell them to do?

Ross says the Lord's "'name' refers to the nature of God, his attributes or perfections."[4]

Israel and Jacob were the same person. His descendants were the people of Israel, so David in these verses called on the nation to praise the Lord.

> **17.** (a) In verse 24, what had God neither despised nor abhorred? (b) Had God hidden his face from David, the afflicted one? (c) What happened when David cried to the Lord (end of verse 24)?

Job 12:5 describes how some people despise affliction as something that can happen only to those who have gone astray. But David knew that God is not like that. In verse 1, David asked why God had forsaken him; in verse 24, he knew that God had not hidden his face from him. In verse 2, David said God wasn't answering his cries; in verse 24, he knew God "heard, when he cried to him." In verse 6, David's enemies despised and scorned him; in verse 24, David knew that the Lord had done neither. In verse 19, David cried for the Lord to come quickly to his aid; in verse 24, God had done just that.

In troubles, it's normal not to sense God's presence. But that doesn't mean he's not there. That God hasn't answered a prayer favorably yet doesn't mean he won't.

> **18.** ♥ How does Psalm 22:24 comfort you in any current troubles?

### The Little Details
#### Why the Abrupt Change?

Psalm 22 suddenly changes from seeking help to praising God in the middle of verse 21. Why?

Perhaps David wrote the entire psalm after he received God's answer, and he wanted to express the suddenness of God's action.

Or perhaps David wrote the first half while in trouble and finished it after he received God's help. For instance, he might have written the first half when his men turned on him in Ziklag after their wives and children were kidnapped, and then finished it a short time later when Saul died in battle and David returned home to receive the crown (1 Samuel 30:6; 2 Samuel 2:4).

In troubles, it's normal not to sense God's presence. But that doesn't mean he's not there.

## The Little Details
### *God's Presence in Troubles*

In the book of Job, a righteous man endures numerous troubles. Job's friends claim that he must have hidden sin, for God always blesses the blameless, never allowing them to suffer.

In fact, the issue is that Satan has accused Job of being righteous only because God blesses him greatly. He demands to test Job's righteousness amid hardship.

Job can't sense God's presence and says, "Oh, for the days when I was in my prime, when God's intimate friendship blessed my house, when the Almighty was still with me" (Job 29:4-5 NIV).

But in the end, God reveals to Job that he has been watching Job carefully. He expresses anger with the friends for not speaking the truth about him, as Job did. For God to forgive them, they must present sacrifices with Job officiating and praying for them (Job 42:7-9). This restores relationships when the friends seek Job's forgiveness and Job grants it.

In David's time, when God answered a prayer, people gave public thanks while giving an animal and bread as a thanksgiving peace offering. The priest burned part on the altar, and the offeror shared the rest with family, friends, priests, and the poor.

19. In Psalm 22:25 below, circle where David's praise came from. Underline where he praised. Double-underline what he said he would perform.

> From you comes my praise in the great congregation;
>     my vows I will perform before those who fear him.

Most laments (prayer request psalms) end in a vow to praise the Lord publicly if he answers the request favorably. When David read or sang this psalm in the congregation, he fulfilled his vow.

20. (a) In Psalm 22:26, who would eat and be satisfied? (b) What would those who sought the Lord do when they heard David's prayer and praise? (c) How did David end this verse?

The afflicted (or poor) are those who came to the tabernacle in the hope that someone would sacrifice a peace offering that they could eat. While everyone in the congregation would praise the Lord when they heard David tell of his deliverance, the afflicted would praise him for two additional reasons: They were encouraged that God would deliver them from their own afflictions, and they were thankful for the food they received.

Their hearts should not melt like wax (Psalm 22:14) but should "live forever," a figurative way of telling others to be encouraged and keep praying.[5]

21. In Psalm 22:27 below, underline who will turn to the Lord and who will worship before him.

> All the ends of the earth shall remember
>     and turn to the LORD,
> and all the families of the nations
>     shall worship before you.

David anticipated that his story would be shared for generations, bringing others to God.

22. (a) To whom did kingship belong (Psalm 22:28)? (b) Who rules the nations?

This is what Saul missed. He thought the kingship belonged to him and that he should be able to make his own decisions without God's interference. He resented that God punished his disobedience by removing the crown from his family. He did his best to thwart God's plan to crown David.

**23.** (a) Who would eat and worship (Psalm 22:29)? (b) Who would bow down (verse 29)? (c) Future generations (posterity) would do what (verse 30)? (d) To whom would future generations proclaim the Lord's righteousness (verse 31)?

David anticipated that the afflicted, the prosperous, all nations, and future generations would all hear of the Lord and tell of his righteousness (verses 26-31). Just as hearing of the Lord's help in prior generations inspired David to trust God, so David hoped his story would inspire future generations to trust God (verses 4-5, 30-31).

When David became king, he formed choirs to worship the Lord and gave many of his psalms to the choirmasters, including this one (see the psalm's inscription). The choirs sang Psalm 22 for generations. Today, we still read this psalm that tells of the Lord's righteousness.

**24.** Compare verse 26 with verse 29 in Psalm 22. (a) What did David want the hearts of those who sought the Lord to do (verse 26)? (b) But who would bow before the Lord (verse 29)? (c) What could people not do for themselves (end of verse 29)?

David wrote, "May your hearts live forever!" (verse 26). Figuratively, this means "be encouraged." David realized all people die, and their bodies turn to dust. People cannot keep themselves alive, try as they may.

But there was a solution. It's hinted at in the last words of the psalm: "He has done it." The Lord intends to make hearts literally live forever. How he will do so we'll discover in how this psalm prefigures events in Jesus's life and death.

## The Path of Suffering

For Saul, the path to the crown was easy. The people of Israel demanded a king, and God selected one for them. He was a meek man, tall and handsome. He looked the part. There was no suffering on the way to the crown; it was handed to him. But it wasn't long before he considered the crown his right. He threw off God's rule. After all, kings in other nations had total rule. Why should he be different?

For David, the path to the crown was through suffering. He considered the crown to be God's right (Psalm 22:28). He embraced God's authority over himself.

Why did the path of ease produce a weak king who wanted his own way, while the path of suffering produced a strong king submitted to God? Perhaps the answer lies partly in the fact that Saul had never learned to trust God through hardship and suffering; whereas, David saw God rescue him time and again. Saul could believe the crown came through his own merits; whereas, David knew God gave it to him. Saul didn't have a history of relying on God in small things, while David had relied on God even as a young shepherd rescuing sheep from lions and bears (1 Samuel 17:37). The path through suffering is the path to exaltation.

Why did the path of ease produce a weak king who wanted his own way, while the path of suffering produced a strong king submitted to God?

## The Little Details
### *Suffering Psalms Fulfilled in Jesus*

Jesus said events in his life fulfilled passages in various psalms. That is, David suffered in a way that prefigured the way Jesus suffered.

**Psalm 31:5:** "Into your hand I commit my spirit." **Luke 23:46:** Jesus quoted this on the cross.

**Psalm 41:9:** "[He] who ate my bread, has lifted his heel against me." **John 13:18:** Jesus quoted this and said Judas eating bread with him at the last supper fulfilled it.

**Psalm 69:4:** "Who hate me without cause." **John 15:25:** Jesus said his enemies fulfilled this.

**Psalm 69:21a:** "They gave me poison for food" (the Greek translation of this verse is translated "gall" in English). [6] **Matthew 27:34:** Before the crucifixion, the soldiers offered Jesus wine mixed with gall.

**Psalm 69:21b:** "For my thirst they gave me sour wine to drink." **John 19:28-29:** On the cross, Jesus said, "I thirst" and was given sour wine.

# Jesus's Path to the Crown

Eventually, Saul died in battle, and the people crowned David king.

## God with Us Then

In David's day, God spoke through several prophets, including David.

## The Reveal Continued

### *The Major Prophets' Day*

Ungodly kings eventually led the people astray. Isaiah prophesied of a future suffering servant who would be "pierced for our transgressions" (Isaiah 53:5). Jeremiah 30:9 called a future king David, identifying David as a type of that future king.

### *The Second Temple's Day*

When the exile ended, a small number of people chose to return. Foreign kings ruled them. Zechariah prophesied, "When they look on me, on him whom they have pierced, they shall mourn for him, as one mourns for an only child" (Zechariah 12:10).

### *Jesus's Day*

When Jesus arrived and performed miracles such as healing the sick, raising the dead, and multiplying food, many wondered if he was the promised king. As with David, the crowds loved him, but rulers became jealous and sought to kill him. As David did, Jesus prayed for deliverance from enemies determined to kill him.

But there the similarities stop. While God rescued David and did not allow his enemies to kill him, the Father did allow his Son Jesus to die. Let's discover how Psalm 22 told the story of the cross.

## The Crucifixion

On a Friday, Roman soldiers scourged and crucified Jesus, the Holy One of God. They nailed his wrists and feet to a wooden cross and lifted him from the earth. He endured excruciating pain and the insults of bystanders and criminals. Around noon, darkness covered the land. About 3:00 p.m., Jesus cried out.

> **25.** In Psalm 22:1 below, underline what Jesus said in Matthew 27:46.
>
> My God, my God, why have you forsaken me?
> Why are you so far from saving me,
> from the words of my groaning?

In his prayer, Jesus quoted the first line of Psalm 22. Anyone who recognized the words could have turned to the psalm and read how David's divinely inspired figurative descriptions of his suffering prefigured Jesus's literal suffering in the crucifixion.

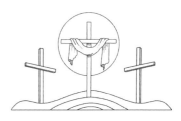

26. (a) How was Psalm 22:6 below fulfilled in Matthew 27:23 by the crowd? (b) How was it fulfilled in Matthew 27:27-31 by the soldiers?

> But I am a worm and not a man,
> scorned by mankind and despised by the people.

27. (a) How was Psalm 22:7 below fulfilled in Matthew 27:27-31 by the soldiers? (b) How was it fulfilled in Matthew 27:39 by the passersby?

> All who see me mock me;
> they make mouths at me; they wag their heads.

28. How was Psalm 22:8 below fulfilled in Matthew 27:43 by the religious leaders?

> He trusts in the LORD; let him deliver him;
> let him rescue him, for he delights in him!

Psalm 22:10 reads, "From my mother's womb you have been my God." This was literally true of Jesus, the Son of God.

29. Compare Psalm 22:14 with John 19:34 (both below). Circle what came out of the side in both verses. Underline what Psalm 22:14 says happened to joints.

> I am poured out like water,
> and all my bones are out of joint;
> my heart is like wax;
> it is melted within my breast (Psalm 22:14).

> But one of the soldiers pierced his side with a spear, and at once there came out blood and water (John 19:34).

According to *The Journal of the American Medical Association,* the sword likely pierced Jesus's lung and heart. What looked like water showed heart failure. The spikes were driven between the joints of his wrist and would have broken no bones.[8]

## The Little Details
### Allen P. Ross on Matthew's Use of Psalm 22:

[Psalm 22:8] is included in Matthew 27:43...In fact this use in Matthew is not a direct quote from the passage, but a general paraphrase: "He trusted in God, let him deliver him now, if he will have him, for he said, I am the Son of God." What was happening there is that Jesus's enemies were taunting him at the cross. They knew that he had claimed to be the Messiah, and they knew that Psalm 22 was in their tradition a Messianic psalm about the suffering Messiah. And so they simply used a line from the psalm to mock him on the cross—not realizing that at that very moment they were fulfilling the psalm. It is an amazing case of spiritual blindness.[7]

--------------------------

Psalm 22:10 reads, "From my mother's womb you have been my God." This was literally true of Jesus, the Son of God.

--------------------------

## The Little Details
### *JAMA on the Crucifixion*

According to *The Journal of the American Medical Association*, the sword thrust likely penetrated the right lung and right atrium of the heart (the Greek word translated "side" includes the ribs). The water was probably serous pleural and pericardial fluid due to hypovolemia (loss of blood from scourging) and impending acute heart failure.

Crucifixion involved driving iron spikes into the wrists and feet (ancients considered wrists to be part of the hand). When driven into the wrists through the joints between the radius and the carpals or between two rows of carpals and radius, there would be no fractures. The nails commonly went through the intermetatarsal space between the bones of the feet.[10]

----

In these words he proclaimed to humankind that he too suffered in darkness without sensing God's presence or hearing God's answer.

----

30. The Roman soldiers flogged Jesus before they crucified him, resulting in massive loss of blood and dehydration[9] (John 19:1). Underline how the first part of Psalm 22:15 was fulfilled in John 19:28 (both are below).

    My strength is dried up like a potsherd,
      and my tongue sticks to my jaws (Psalm 22:15).

    After this, Jesus, knowing that all was now finished, said (to fulfill the Scripture), "I thirst" (John 19:28).

31. Underline how the last part of Psalm 22:15 was fulfilled in John 19:42 (both below).

    You lay me in the dust of death (Psalm 22:15).

    Since the tomb was close at hand, they laid Jesus there (John 19:42).

32. How was Psalm 22:16 below fulfilled in John 19:23 and 20:24-28?

    For dogs encompass me;
      a company of evildoers encircles me;
    they have pierced my hands and feet.

"I can count all my bones—they stare and gloat over me" (Psalm 22:17) may refer to the removal of clothes before crucifixion, exposing ribs (John 19:23). Or it may refer to the fact that Jesus's leg bones were not broken (John 19:32-33).

33. How was Psalm 22:18 below fulfilled in John 19:23-24?

    They divide my garments among them,
      and for my clothing they cast lots.

Psalm 22:26's final blessing is "May your hearts live forever!" Jesus died so that those who trust in him could literally live forever. "He said, 'It is finished,' and he bowed his head and gave up his spirit" (John 19:30). As the last few words of Psalm 22 foretold, "He has done it" (22:31).

### "Why Have You Forsaken Me?"

Jesus's cry to his Father has a message to us. For in these words he proclaimed to humankind that he too suffered in darkness without sensing God's presence or hearing God's answer.[11] Even in this, he became like us.

34. ♥ Think of a hardship you suffered. How does it help you to know Jesus suffered like we do?

Shortly after uttering the first line of Psalm 22, Jesus echoed the psalm's last line by crying out, "It is finished."

Jesus died. The earth shook. Light returned to the land (Matthew 27:45-51).

Perhaps the spiritual forces of darkness thought they had won the victory.

## Day 5

# The Path to the Crown

On Friday, Jesus's followers placed his body in a tomb: "You lay me in the dust of death" (Psalm 22:15). But on Sunday, everything changed.

35. How was the second half of Psalm 22:21 below fulfilled in Matthew 28:5-6?

   You have rescued me from the horns of the wild oxen!

36. How was Psalm 22:22-23 below fulfilled in Matthew 28:10,19?

   I will tell of your name to my brothers;
       in the midst of the congregation I will praise you:
   You who fear the LORD, praise him!
       All you offspring of Jacob, glorify him,
       and stand in awe of him, all you offspring of Israel!

## The Afflicted One in Hebrews

The letter to the Hebrews expands on the next verses.

37. How was Psalm 22:24 below fulfilled in Hebrews 5:7?

   For he has not despised or abhorred
       the affliction of the afflicted,
   and he has not hidden his face from him,
       but has heard, when he cried to him.

### The Little Details
*Dates*

We're switching between BC and AD dates quite a bit, so here's a little explanation. The term BC is short for "before Christ." At the time the designation came into use, it was thought that Jesus was born in the first year AD. Now scholars think his birth was more likely around 5 or 6 BC. The BC designation follows the year.

The term AD is short for the Latin *anno Domini*, which translates "year of Lord" and is short for "in the year of our Lord." It is not short for "after death," which would skip the years between Jesus's birth and death. The AD precedes the year.

There is no year zero, so AD 1 immediately follows 1 BC.

Because of the religious connotation, some replace BC with BCE ("before common era") and AD with CE ("common era"). Both BCE and CE follow the year: 1 CE follows 1 BCE.

On Sunday, everything changed.

**38.** How was Psalm 22:26 below fulfilled in Hebrews 5:9?

May your hearts live forever!

## God with Us Still

*God with Us Today*
Psalm 22's last few verses apply to us today.

**39.** Underline how Psalm 22:27 is fulfilled in Jesus's words in Acts 1:8 (both below).

All the ends of the earth shall remember
    and turn to the Lord,
and all the families of the nations
    shall worship before you (Psalm 22:27).

You will be my witnesses in Jerusalem and in all Judea and Samaria, and to the end of the earth (Acts 1:8).

Psalm 22:28-29 was initially fulfilled when the wise men came to worship Jesus.

**40.** Underline how Psalm 22:28-29 will be fulfilled according to Philippians 2:9-10 (both below).

For kingship belongs to the Lord,
    and he rules over the nations.
All the prosperous of the earth eat and worship;
    before him shall bow all who go down to the dust,
        even the one who could not keep himself alive (Psalm 22:28-29).

God has highly exalted him…so that at the name of Jesus every knee should bow, in heaven and on earth and under the earth (Philippians 2:9-10).

**41.** ♥ (a) How has Psalm 22:30-31 been fulfilled since the time of the early church until now? (b) How are you fulfilling these verses?

Posterity shall serve him;
    it shall be told of the Lord to the coming generation;
they shall come and proclaim his righteousness to a people yet unborn,
    that he has done it.

This world is filled with suffering. Jesus didn't sidestep that to lead a comfy human life. Instead, he suffered as we do. His parents were poor, and the circumstances of his birth questionable to most.[12] He remained single. And he allowed humans to crucify him, one of the worst forms of execution humans ever devised, designed to torture victims over a few days as they slowly died, attacked by animals of prey and mocking crowds.

During our own dark times when we cannot sense God's presence or hear his voice, we can remember that when the Father's work is finished, light returns.

42. ♥ What encouragement can we take from Jesus's endurance through darkness?

### God with Us Forever
Revelation 1 describes the risen Jesus appearing to the apostle John.

43. ♥ Read Revelation 1:1-8. (a) What stands out to you the most in the descriptions of Jesus? (b) What stands out to you about what he's done for you?

### God with Me Now
David wrote Psalm 57 about hiding in a cave from Saul. As David sought imperfect refuge in a cave, he also sought perfect refuge in the Lord. He called on God to fulfill his purpose for him.

Turn to Psalm 57 and read it. Ponder God's purpose for you. **Pray** the psalm to the Lord in worship.

**Praise** God for something you saw of his character this week. **Confess** anything that convicted you. **Ask** for help to do something God's Word calls you to do. **Thank** God for something you learned this week.

During our own dark times when we cannot sense God's presence or hear his voice, we can remember that when the Father's work is finished, light returns.

# The Heart and Art of Worship

As I sketched this week's illustration, I was reminded of a craft show I was at years ago. I stopped to look at some greeting cards, and most of them were paintings of praying hands. As I stood there, I overheard the artist and her friend talking about how they chose to share their faith through the imagery of praying hands because it was more uplifting, and they couldn't understand why other Christians would want to paint crosses.

We all respond to art and visual imagery differently, partly because of how we relate to the message it conveys. These women found the image of the cross to be disturbing, but for us who know Christ and believe that without the cross we would still be dead in our sin, the cross is a symbol of love and hope.

Visual imagery has the potential to move our emotions. A painting of a butterfly can lift our spirit and inspire us to soar. A painting of a girl with her hands lifted high can draw us into an intimate time of worship. Whether I draw birds and flowers or a cross of nails and a crown of thorns, both can stir my heart to hope because both display an aspect of the character of God. In one we see an expression of a God who created the beauty of nature with us in mind. In the other we see a God of love who willingly endured the cross in order to give us the hope of eternal life with him.

How we creatively express and share our faith matters. I believe God is thrilled to see how women are expressing their love for Him through Bible journaling and coloring pages and sharing them on the internet. Every time we share, we are declaring the glory of the Lord and encouraging others. So as you color this week's illustration, let your heart be moved by the sacrifice Christ made for you. And then consider sharing it online with your friends and family to remind them of God's love for them too.

*Karla*

For he has not despised or scorned the suffering of the afflicted one

Psalm 22:24 NIV

## Chapter 5

## *2 Samuel 7*
# Jesus the King Forever

The hope of a righteous and just ruler

### Day 1

## The Anointed One

Soon after we bought our house, we planted fruit trees. The lemon, tangerine, and loquat trees all thrived in our sunny California yard. We found a peach tree developed especially for warm climates, and most years it bore a dozen or so sweet peaches.

But the plum and apricot trees never did well. Year after year we tried to nurse them into bearing fruit. My father-in-law was able to grow plums and apricots, but he lived farther from the coast where winters averaged ten degrees cooler. We finally gave up and dug them out.

Just as we expect our fruit trees to bear fruit, so God expects his people to bear fruit.

### The Reveal

*Eve's Day*
God made humans to rule the earth as vice-regents under him (Genesis 1:26). He placed them in a garden with many fruit trees. But when they believed the serpent over God, the serpent reigned instead (John 12:31). Outside of the garden, Adam toiled to bring forth food.

*Abraham's Day*
By Abraham's time, people filled the earth. They clustered together in kingdoms. Some were large, like Egypt. But in the promised land, most kings ruled over small city-states. Sometimes a powerful king ruled over weaker kings, making him a king of kings (the geeky name is *suzerain*). The Lord promised Abraham that some of his descendants would be kings (Genesis 17:6).

*Moses's Day*
God told the people that if they kept his covenant, he would bless the fruit of the ground and the fruit of their livestock so that they prospered. But if they broke his covenant, he would curse the ground and animals as a warning to return to him.

In Moses's time, the Lord God was king of the people of Israel (Deuteronomy 33:5). Moses recorded the Lord's commands about future kings in Deuteronomy 17:14-20. The king

## The Little Details
### 1 & 2 Samuel, 1 & 2 Kings, 1 & 2 Chronicles

First Samuel traces the history of the Israelites from the birth of the prophet Samuel to the end of Saul's reign. Second Samuel describes David's reign.

First and Second Kings begin with David's death and trace the history of the united and divided kingdoms. They end with a note of hope: the exiled king of Judah being released from prison.

First and Second Chronicles were written during the days of the second temple. They begin with genealogies before picking up the story of Saul's death and David's rise to power. They trace the history of David and the kings descended from him. They end with Cyrus's proclamation that the Jews may return to Jerusalem and rebuild the temple.

---

The former shepherd of sheep became shepherd over God's people.

---

must not multiply horses, wives, silver, or gold. He must write out the law, read it daily, and keep it, not lifting himself above others. In other words, God would be their King of kings.

### David's Day

Israel's first king, Saul, abandoned God. The prophet Samuel told him, "But now your kingdom shall not continue. The LORD has sought out a man after his own heart, and the LORD has commanded him to be prince over his people, because you have not kept what the LORD commanded you" (1 Samuel 13:14).

David became Saul's most successful and popular warrior. Jealousy filled Saul, and he tried to kill David, forcing him to flee into exile. Later, Saul died in battle along with three of his sons (1 Samuel 31:6). David returned home from exile.

The former shepherd of sheep became shepherd over God's people. First, the prophet Samuel anointed David king with oil, then the tribe of Judah anointed him, and finally all of Israel anointed him. The Hebrew word translated "anointed" and "anointed one" is *māshîaḥ*, from which we derive our English word *messiah*. David was anointed for service and therefore was an anointed one, or messiah.

David's heart remained grateful to God. He wanted to show his gratitude.

## God's Word to Us

1. ♥ Read 2 Samuel 7; 1 Chronicles 28:1-11; and 2 Chronicles 7:1-3,11-22. What stands out to you? Why?

Psalm 72 is a prayer for a righteous king. It was written either for or by Solomon.

2. (a) What did the psalmist ask God to give the king (Psalm 72:1)? (b) How would a righteous king judge (verse 2)? (c) What would the mountains then bear (verse 3)?

3. ♥ What stands out to you about what a righteous king accomplishes (Psalm 72:12-14)? Why is that important?

The psalmist describes grain and crops flourishing under a righteous king and concludes, "May people be blessed in him, all nations call him blessed!" (Psalm 72:16-17). Under a righteous king, God's promise to Abraham could be fulfilled.

# A Walk with Christ—Let Christ Reign

Oh, the beauty of God's anointing, favor, and hand of goodness covering our lives—we all want God's blessings!

The Father used several occasions to ensure the anointing of his son:

- Christ's anointing oils were provided when two of the three wise men gave oils at his birth: frankincense (the oil of royalty) and myrrh (the oil often used in burial).

- Christ was anointed at his baptism: "...after the baptism which John proclaimed. 'You know of Jesus of Nazareth, how God anointed Him with the Holy Spirit and with power, and how He went about doing good and healing all who were oppressed by the devil, for God was with Him'" (Acts 10:37-38 NASB).

- Mary, the sister of Lazarus, moved by gratitude, anointed Christ to prepare for his sacrificial death: "Mary then took a pound of very costly perfume of pure nard and anointed the feet of Jesus and wiped His feet with her hair; and the house was filled with the fragrance of the perfume" (John 12:3 NASB).

So how do we as believers today gain God's anointing on our lives? David's anointing reflects that God's favor over us begins with the heart. The Lord said to Samuel:

> You are to anoint for me the one I indicate...Do not consider his appearance...The LORD does not look at the things people look at. People look at the outward appearance, but the LORD looks at the heart...So Samuel took the horn of oil and anointed him in the presence of his brothers, and from that day on the Spirit of the LORD came powerfully upon David (1 Samuel 16:3,7,13 NIV).

So how do we gain this kind of heart for God? We ask God for it:

> Create in me a pure heart, O God, and renew a steadfast spirit within me (Psalm 51:10 NIV).

> Teach me your way, Lord, that I may rely on your faithfulness; give me an undivided heart, that I may fear your name (Psalm 86:11 NIV).

> Moreover, I will give you a new heart and put a new spirit within you; and I will remove the heart of stone from your flesh and give you a heart of flesh. I will put My Spirit within you and cause you to walk in My statutes (Ezekiel 36:26-27 NASB).

> In the Beatitudes, Jesus echoes this: "Blessed are the pure in heart, for they shall see God" (Matthew 5:8).

When our heart is centered on God, we naturally desire his anointing. During one hard year in ministry, an attendee at one of our conferences felt impressed by God to write down verses about God's favor and anointing. She said, "God is calling me to pray over you this year. I also believe God is wanting me to share these verses of hope of God's favor and anointing over you and your ministry so you two can use them as the prayer foundation for this, your year of God's anointing and favor over you." We needed miracles only God could provide, so we began to use these verses as prayer prompts for our lives. By the end of the year, we witnessed God's favor in our marriage; an important change for one of our sons; double speaking dates and book contracts; and the extension of our ministry to multiple nations.

"The anointing which you received from Him abides in you" (1 John 2:27 NASB). The legacy of anointing continues today as we receive the Holy Spirit.

📺 Read more about how anointing relates to your life and discover a list of verses to pray over your life at www .DiscoveringTheBibleSeries.com.

*Pam*

## The Little Details

### Psalm 2

David probably wrote Psalm 2 as a coronation psalm for his son Solomon, and all his descendants who reigned after him. Verse 7 calls the Davidic covenant "the decree." Verses 7-9 express God's words to David poetically.

Verse 2 says, "Rulers band together against the Lord and against his anointed" (NIV). The Hebrew word translated "anointed" is *māshîaḥ*, from which we get our English word *messiah*. Acts 13:33 identifies Psalm 2 as a messianic psalm that speaks of Jesus.

Psalm 2:7 says to the king, "The Lord said to me, 'You are my Son; today I have begotten you.'" Translations such as the ESV, NASB, and KJV capitalize *Son* so readers don't miss its connection to Jesus. Translations such as the NRSV, NIV, and NLT don't capitalize it so readers don't miss the connection to the earthly kings.

▬ Find more on Psalm 2 at www.DiscoveringTheBible Series.com. Learn more about Psalm 2 in our book *Discovering Hope in the Psalms.*

-------------------------

While the throne caused Saul's heart to turn *from* God, it caused David's to turn *to* God.

-------------------------

# God's Covenant with David

David built a magnificent palace in Jerusalem and brought over the ark of the covenant. In *From Eden to the New Jerusalem,* T. Desmond Alexander writes, "The thrones of the Israelite king and the divine king are now located side by side in the same city."[1]

### David's Heart Revealed

4.  (a) What seemed wrong to David (2 Samuel 7:2)? (b) What did the prophet Nathan tell him to do (verse 3)?

The fact that David thought it wrong that he should live in a cedar palace while a tent housed the ark of the Lord shows his reverence for and devotion to God. While the throne caused Saul's heart to turn *from* God, it caused David's to turn *to* God.

5.  (a) What happened that night (2 Samuel 7:4-5)? (b) What did the Lord do for David (verse 8)? (c) What was he going to make for David (verse 9)? (d) What was he going to appoint for his people (verse 10)?

God's pleasure at David's request is evident.

6.  (a) What did God declare he would build for David (2 Samuel 7:11)? (b) What would he raise up for David (verse 12)? (c) What would this person build (verse 13)? (d) For how long would God establish his throne (verse 13)?

David pleased the Lord. He wanted to build God a house in the form of a temple. In response, God promised to build David a house in the form of a dynasty—the house of David. David would not be the one to build God's house, however, because he had shed so much blood in wars. Instead, an offspring—seed—would build the house.

7.  (a) What relationship would David's offspring have with God (2 Samuel 7:14)? (b) What would God do if the offspring sinned (verse 14)? (c) What would God not do to the offspring (verse 15)? (d) What would God do for David (verse 16)?

God promised that one of David's sons would sit on David's throne after him, and that son would build God's temple. God would be a father to David's son, disciplining him. Great kings called the kings who served them *son*, and those kings called the great king *father*.[2] God gave the kings descended from David the title *sons of God*, indicating their status as kings under him.

Today, we call this promise the Davidic covenant. Like God's promises to Eve and Abraham, it contained a prophecy about an offspring, or seed.

## The Temple Builder

The Lord God told David to select one of his younger sons, Solomon, to follow him as king and build the temple. *Solomon* means "His Peace."[3] Even though it would cause turmoil with David's oldest living son, David obeyed. He instructed the prophet Nathan and the priest Zadok to anoint Solomon king so that he and Solomon could co-reign and the throne would pass securely. When a throne's successor was a son of the prior king, a priest anointed him king. When God chose a king who was not next in line for the throne, he sent a prophet to anoint him king. Both priest and prophet anointed Solomon, showing he was both David's and God's choice.

8. (a) In 1 Chronicles 28:9, what did David tell Solomon to do? (b) What does the Lord search and understand?

Serving God with a whole heart means complete devotion. Serving him with a willing mind means obeying willingly, not begrudgingly. Only people who understand God's goodness and love can do this (1 John 4:19).

9. ♥ Think of a current or upcoming situation that weighs on you. How can you serve God with a whole heart and willing mind in this situation?

To serve as king under the Lord, Solomon needed to be faithful to the covenant. If he forsook God, God would cast him off. The elderly David told Solomon that God had chosen him to build the temple, so he must be strong and do it.

David gave Solomon a detailed plan for the temple, its courts and treasuries, and golden cherubim (1 Chronicles 28:11-18). It was elaborate and ornate, with many garden motifs.

10. In 1 Chronicles 28:19 (NIV) below, circle from whom David received the plan.

    "All this," David said, "I have in writing as a result of the LORD's hand on me, and he enabled me to understand all the details of the plan."

11. In 1 Chronicles 28:21 (NIV) below, circle the word describing the skilled craftsmen who would help Solomon, according to David.

    Every willing person skilled in any craft will help you in all the work.

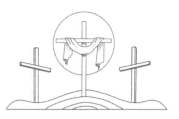

## The Little Details
### *Alexander on the City of God:*

The construction of the temple by Solomon transforms the status of Jerusalem as a city. It now becomes in a unique way the city of God. According to Psalms 78:68 and 132:13, the Lord chooses Jerusalem to be his dwelling place. Since God's creation project is to create a temple-city that will fill the whole earth, it is easy to see how Jerusalem is viewed as partially fulfilling God's plan. Consequently, Jerusalem/Zion becomes a model of God's creation blueprint and reflects in microcosm what God intends for the whole earth. [4]

## The Little Details
### Hebrews, Israelites, and Jews

Genesis calls Abraham's descendants *Hebrews,* after Abraham's ancestor Eber.

Abraham's grandson *Israel* had 12 sons who became 12 tribes collectively known as *Israelites.* The land in which they settled was called *Israel.*

After Israel split, the northern part kept the name *Israel* and the southern took the name *Judah.* Judah's people were *Jews,* though some translations use *people of Judah, Judeans,* and *Judahites* (see 2 Kings 16:6). The name *Israelite* during the divided kingdom could refer to all descendants of Israel or just those living in the north.

Israel ceased to be a nation in 722 BC. The term *Israelite* again referred to all descendants of Israel.

Judah ceased to be a nation in 586 BC. When the people returned from exile, they settled into what was now the province of Judah (later *Judea*). The names *Hebrew, Israelite,* and *Jew* were then interchangeable.

-----

The warning was a hint that Solomon might not be the offspring whose throne would last forever.

-----

After David died, Solomon built the temple. When he finished it, the people celebrated. The priests offered sacrifices. Choirs sang praises while musicians accompanied them with cymbals, harps, lyres, and trumpets. Finally, the Levites brought the ark into the new Most Holy Place.

A cloud filled the temple—it was the glory of the Lord (2 Chronicles 5:14). This showed Solomon and all Israel that God had accepted the temple as a replacement for the tabernacle.[5] Solomon stood to pray.

> 12. In 2 Chronicles 6:18 below, underline what Solomon realized about the inadequacy of the temple.
>
> But will God indeed dwell with man on the earth? Behold, heaven and the highest heaven cannot contain you, how much less this house that I have built!

When Solomon finished praying, "fire came down from heaven and consumed the burnt offering and the sacrifices, and the glory of the LORD filled the temple" (2 Chronicles 7:1). The people bowed and worshiped.

Later, the Lord appeared to Solomon.

> 13. (a) What did the Lord say he had chosen (2 Chronicles 7:12)? (b) If the people disobeyed God so that he brought the covenant curses on them as warnings, what could the people do (verses 13-14)? (c) What warning did God give Solomon (verses 17-20)?

The warning was a hint that Solomon might not be the offspring whose throne would last forever.

### God with Us Then

The thrones of the divine King of kings and the Israelite king resided together in Jerusalem on Mount Zion. The people came to consider all of Jerusalem to be God's dwelling place.[6]

## Day 3

# The Future Righteous King

Solomon started out with a heart after God, but it didn't last. He disobeyed the covenant commands that told kings not to multiply wives, military horses, and wealth. He took 700 wives and 300 concubines, built 40,000 stalls of horses for chariots, and amassed great wealth. Small steps of disobeying led to bigger steps. "When Solomon was old his wives turned away his heart after other gods" (1 Kings 11:4).

Because of Solomon's unfaithfulness, after his death, the Lord split the kingdom in two. Solomon's son retained the south. The north went to his son's rival.

## The Southern Kingdom of Judah

The southern part of the kingdom went to Solomon's son and took the name of Judah. Egypt attacked Judah and took the temple treasures, leaving it without the earthly glory that David and Solomon had poured into it so wholeheartedly (1 Kings 14:26).

## The Northern Kingdom of Israel

Jeroboam, the first ruler of the northern kingdom of Israel, feared that if his people continued to worship at the temple in Jerusalem, they'd abandon him for Judah's king. So, he set up two golden calves for the people to worship at instead of at the temple where God's presence resided (1 Kings 12:28). He built temples and set up his own priesthood. Many Levites and godly people fled south to Judah (2 Chronicles 11:14-16).

## The Reveal Continued

### The Major Prophets' Day

About 300 years after David, Isaiah prophesied that God would send Israel into exile. He encouraged Judah's King Ahaz to trust God, but to no avail. Ahaz rejected God as his King of kings and served Assyria's king instead. He installed an altar to Assyria's gods in Solomon's temple (2 Kings 16:10-17). Later, he shut the doors of the temple. He even burned his sons as offerings to idols (2 Chronicles 28:3,24).

> **14.** Read Isaiah 5:1-7. (a) When the Lord came to the vineyard, what was it missing (verse 4)? (b) What would he therefore do to it (verse 5)?

The Lord explained the meaning of the vineyard, the good grapes, and the wild grapes.

> **15.** In Isaiah 5:7 below, underline what the vineyard and planting symbolized. Circle the two types of fruit for which the Lord looked. Box what he found instead.
>
> For the vineyard of the LORD of hosts is the house of Israel, and the men of Judah are his pleasant planting; and he looked for justice, but behold, bloodshed; for righteousness, but behold, an outcry!

They lacked the two fruits that a righteous king should bear.

The Lord removed his hedge of protection from Israel, and an enemy overcame the nation and exiled the people in 722 BC. Isaiah prophesied to the king of Judah that in time God would exile Judah too, but a remnant would return (Isaiah 10:20).

Another century passed for Judah. Some kings were good, others wicked. The nation grew more corrupt. Judges accepted bribes. The rich oppressed the poor. The powerful oppressed widows and orphans. Parents—including another king—sacrificed children to Molech. False prophets said Israel fell because the people abandoned the temple, so Judah was safe as long as the people offered temple sacrifices (Jeremiah 7:1-15). After all, God promised that David's offspring's throne would last forever.

But Jeremiah prophesied that people sinning freely and coming to the temple to be delivered without repentance made the temple "a den of robbers" (Jeremiah 7:9-11). Just as robbers entered a cave until they felt it was safe to come out and rob again, so the people

## The Little Details
### Poisonous Fruit

Hosea prophesied in Israel around the same time as Isaiah.

Hosea 10:1-4 describes Israel as a luxuriant vine with fruit that Israel attributes to idols. As Israel's wealth increased, the people abandoned God and embraced idols even more. Therefore, God would exile the people and destroy their altars.

In exile, the people would realize, "We have no king, for we do not fear the LORD," but would express indifference, "And a king—what could he do for us?" (Hosea 10:3). Their experience showed that earthly kings "utter mere words; with empty oaths they make covenants; so judgment springs up like poisonous weeds in the furrows of the field" (verse 4).

Israel bore fruit "for himself," not for the Lord (Hosea 10:1 NASB). That fruit was poisonous.

## The Little Details
### Daniel's Prayer

In 539 BC, an elderly Daniel perceived that the 70-year exile that Jeremiah had prophesied should be nearly over. So, he sought God in prayer and fasting (Daniel 9:3). He confessed the people's sin. He asked the Lord God to turn his wrath from Jerusalem (verses 15-16). He prayed as both Moses and Solomon said to pray if the people were ever exiled (Deuteronomy 30:1-10; 1 Kings 8:46-48).

The angel Gabriel came to him and said the end of the 70-year exile began a process of 70 "'sevens'…to finish transgression, to put an end to sin, and to atone for wickedness, to bring in everlasting righteousness…From the time the word goes out to restore and rebuild Jerusalem until the Anointed One, the ruler comes, there will be seven 'sevens,' and sixty-two 'sevens'" (Daniel 9:24-25 NIV). The "sevens" are usually understood as seven years. Interpretations of Daniel 9 vary, but the gist is there would be quite some time before the future righteous king came.

----------------------

Ezekiel explained God's anger at leaders who ruled harshly and made themselves rich off the people entrusted to them.

----------------------

entered the temple with sacrifices so that they felt it was safe to come out and sin again. They wanted forgiveness without repentance.

16. ♥ (a) Why is repentance (turning from sin) important to God? (b) What's it like to receive an insincere apology?

God said he planned to destroy the temple to stop this misuse of it (Jeremiah 7:14).

The Lord had strong words for Judah's kings too. He said they were shepherds that scattered the flock instead of caring for them. The earthly kings had failed, but God promised a future righteous king, a son of David (Jeremiah 23:1-5).

The first stage of Judah's exile came in 605 BC and carried Daniel to Babylon.

The second stage came in 597 BC and took Ezekiel to Babylon. Five years later, God's Spirit transported Ezekiel from Babylon to the Jerusalem temple where he saw elders, women, and men using the temple to worship other gods (Ezekiel 8). Ezekiel watched the glory of the Lord leave the temple (Ezekiel 10–11).

The final stage came in 586 BC. Babylon demolished Jerusalem, burned the temple, and exiled the survivors.

Many thought God had broken his promise to David that his offspring's throne would last forever (Psalm 89:39). But in exile, Ezekiel explained God's anger at leaders who ruled harshly and made themselves rich off the people entrusted to them. He called them shepherds who ate the sheep they should have fed (Ezekiel 34:1-21).

17. In Ezekiel 34:23-24 below, circle the descriptions of the person God will place over the people. Underline what he will do.

> And I will set up over them one shepherd, my servant David, and he shall feed them: he shall feed them and be their shepherd. And I, the Lord, will be their God, and my servant David shall be prince among them. I am the Lord; I have spoken.

Hope budded for a future righteous king, a son of David whose throne would last forever.

### The Second Temple's Day

In 539 BC, Cyrus conquered Babylon and allowed all exiled peoples to return to their homelands. He returned many of the temple vessels (Ezra 1:7). Zerubbabel—a descendant of David, but governor, not king—oversaw construction of a new temple. He finished it on March 12, 516 BC.[7] The Most Holy Place was empty because the ark of the covenant was gone. When they celebrated its completion, the glory of the Lord didn't appear. Nonetheless, the prophet Haggai prophesied, "The latter glory of this house shall be greater than the former" (Haggai 2:9).

18. Read Zechariah 9:9. (a) Who was coming? (b) What would be his character? (c) What would he ride when he came?

In 458 BC, Ezra came to Jerusalem and taught from the Scriptures (Ezra 7:8-10). He showed the people that Moses had warned them that if they broke their covenant with God, God would exile them until their hearts returned to him.

Around this time, the Hallel psalms (Psalms 113–118) became part of the book of Psalms and part of the annual festivals, including the Passover celebration. In Psalm 118, a person leading a procession to the temple sang and those who followed responded. He calls the people Israel.

> **19.** (a) What gates did the leader want opened in Psalm 118:19? (b) What happened to the "stone the builders rejected" (verse 22)? (c) What did the people shout in the first half of verse 25? (d) What did they shout in the first half of verse 26?

The "gates of righteousness" (or "gates of the righteous" NIV) would be the gates to the temple. The leader brought people to the temple to give thanks that God disciplined, but did not destroy, Israel (verse 18). "Cornerstone" could also be translated "head of the corner" and was "probably referring to the capstone."[8]

### Jesus's Day

By Jesus's day, a Roman emperor was king of kings. One of the lesser kings, King Herod, ruled Judea. He began rebuilding the Jerusalem temple in 19 BC,[9] a grand project that would take until AD 64 to complete.[10] He built it of white marble and covered it with gold.

Meanwhile, around 5 BC, a couple named Joseph and Mary took their 40-day-old baby to the temple to present him to the Lord.

## Day 4

# The King Has Come

The angel Gabriel appeared to a young virgin named Mary at a time when many Jews hoped for a son of David to come and free them from Rome's rule.

### The Throne of David

> **20.** (a) What did Gabriel tell Mary would happen (Luke 1:31)? (b) What would the child be called (verse 32)? (c) What would he be given (verse 32)? (d) What would he do forever (verse 33)?

People had thought God's promise to David of a throne that lasted forever meant his earthly dynasty would last forever. But Gabriel said this child would reign forever.

---

**The Little Details**

*Allen P. Ross on the Cornerstone in Psalm 118:*

The language is figurative, probably inspired by the rebuilding of the temple where some of the existing stones were discarded and others used.

…The stone was a type of what was happening to the nation and its leader; the stone symbolizes Israel, represented by the Judean prince; and the builders symbolize the empire builders, the great powers of the world. As these nations swept through the land to establish their empires, they considered the little country of Judah to be of no value to them—they rejected it and would have destroyed it. But now that which was rejected by them as worthless has been chosen by God. It not only was restored to the land, but was also made the center of God's theocratic program—and Babylon no longer existed![11]

---

But Gabriel said this child would reign forever.

---

## The Little Details

### G.K. Beale & Benjamin L. Gladd on Jesus Being Greater than the Temple:

Jesus is greater than the temple now because "God's presence is more manifest in him than in the temple (cf. Matt. 12:6: 'But I say to you that something greater than the temple is here.'). On him, not on the temple, rests the 'Shekinah' glory" in an even greater way than previously in the temple (echoing perhaps the prophecy in Hag. 2:9: "the latter glory of this house will be greater than the former"). Therefore, not only is Jesus identified with the temple because he is assuming the role of the sacrificial system, but he is also now, instead of the temple, the unique place on earth where God's revelatory presence is located. God is manifesting his glorious presence in Jesus in a greater way than it was ever manifested in a physical temple structure.[12]

The glory of the Lord had finally come to the temple.

Mary asked how she could be a mother since she was a virgin. Gabriel explained that the Holy Spirit would overshadow her and this child would be "the Son of God" (Luke 1:34-35). For prior kings, the title *son of god* signified God was king over them. Gabriel's words showed that their title foreshadowed this king's literal relationship to God.

Mary visited her relative Elizabeth, who was pregnant with the child who would be John the Baptist. Elizabeth prophesied, "Blessed are you among women, and blessed is the fruit of your womb! And why is this granted to me that the mother of my Lord should come to me? For behold, when the sound of your greeting came to my ears, the baby in my womb leaped for joy" (Luke 1:42-44). This must have greatly encouraged the pregnant, unmarried Mary.

Mary was engaged to Joseph when her pregnancy was discovered, and he intended to break off the marriage quietly. "But...an angel of the Lord appeared to him in a dream, saying, 'Joseph, son of David, do not fear to take Mary as your wife, for that which is conceived in her is from the Holy Spirit'" (Matthew 1:20).

21. ♥ (a) What must it have been like for Mary and Joseph, knowing many people would not believe their tale of a virgin birth? (b) Think of an embarrassing circumstance in your life. How does it comfort you that the Son of God chose to relate to people in humble circumstances?

Mary gave birth in Bethlehem. Not far away, an angel of the Lord appeared to shepherds and said, "For unto you is born this day in the city of David a Savior, who is Christ the Lord" (Luke 2:11). *Christ* means "Anointed One." It's from the Greek equivalent of *Messiah*. Bethlehem was tiny and insignificant except for being known as David's birthplace. "Born...in the city of David" points to David's birth being a type of this child's birth.

Many angels then appeared, praising God. The shepherds found Mary and her baby and told what the angel said.

A few weeks later, Joseph and Mary took Jesus to the temple. There, the prophets Simeon and Anna prophesied that the baby was the long-awaited Christ (Luke 2:25-38).

John's Gospel tells us that Jesus was the Word of God who "became flesh and dwelt among us, and we have seen his glory, glory as of the only Son from the Father, full of grace and truth" (John 1:14). The word translated "dwelt" is literally "tabernacled." The glory of the Lord had finally come to the temple.

## The King Revealed

Elizabeth's son grew and became known as John the Baptist. John told the religious leaders to bear fruit befitting repentance, for the axe would cut down fruitless trees to be burned. He said Jesus was the one coming after him who would gather the wheat but burn the chaff (Matthew 3:7-12). When he baptized Jesus, he saw the Holy Spirit descend on him and heard a voice from heaven say, "This is my beloved Son, with whom I am well pleased" (Matthew 3:17).

Jesus began preaching the good news: "The time is fulfilled, and the kingdom of God is at hand; repent and believe in the gospel" (Mark 1:15). He showed power over demons and healed the sick. After he fed 4000 people with seven loaves of bread and a few small fish, Jesus asked his disciples who they thought he was.

> **22.** (a) Who did Peter say Jesus was (Mark 8:29)? (b) How did Jesus respond (verse 30)?

The people weren't sure yet who Jesus was, but Peter realized he was the Christ—the Anointed One, the Messiah, the longed-for King. Jesus told them not to tell the crowds yet because the crowds expected the Messiah to overthrow Rome and restore the kingdom of Israel on earth. He explained he had to suffer, die, and rise. But they didn't understand.

As he neared Jerusalem, a blind beggar heard Jesus was passing by.

> **23.** What did Bartimaeus call Jesus (Mark 10:46-48)?

It was no longer just the disciples who knew Jesus was the Messiah, the Son of David.

Jesus sent two disciples ahead to retrieve a colt on which no one had ever sat. They threw their cloaks on it as for a king, and Jesus sat on it (Mark 11:1-7), fulfilling Zechariah 9:9: "Behold, your king is coming to you; righteous and having salvation is he, humble and mounted on a donkey, on a colt, the foal of a donkey."

> **24.** Read Mark 11:8-10. (a) What did the people do as Jesus rode the colt into Jerusalem (verse 8)? (b) What did the people shout?

At Jesus's triumphal entry, the crowds treated him like royalty by spreading cloaks and branches before him,[13] signaling they believed he was the Messiah. *Hosanna* means "LORD, save us." The crowd's shouts came mainly from Psalm 118:25-26. Their shout, "Blessed is the coming kingdom of our father David," showed their expectation that Jesus was coming as king to bring back David's kingdom.

But absent from the excited crowds were the Jewish leaders.

## The King Looks for Fruit

The next day, Jesus saw a fig tree and looked for fruit but found none. He said, "May no one ever eat fruit from you again" (Mark 11:14). Then he went into the temple and drove out those who were buying and selling there. He taught the people, "Is it not written, 'My house shall be called a house of prayer for all the nations'? But you have made it a den of robbers" (Mark 11:17, quoting Isaiah 56:7 before referring to Jeremiah 7:11). The chief priests and scribes heard him, feared him, and sought to destroy him. He escaped.

The following day Jesus and his disciples returned to Jerusalem. As they passed the fig tree, they saw it had withered. He entered the temple and the religious leaders asked him by what authority had he cleansed the temple. He said he would tell them only if they told him whether John's baptism was from heaven or from man.

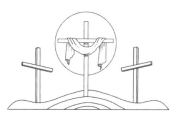

**The Little Details**
*Allen P. Ross on Jesus as the Stone in Psalm 118:22-24:*
According to the usage of the passage in the New Testament, Israel represented by its prince was a type of Christ. Jesus is presented in the Gospels as the true Israel, the promised seed...And so in Matthew Jesus claims to be the "stone" of the psalm, the true king and representative head of the nation (Matt. 21:42-44). And the "builders" then are the political and religious leaders, the chief priests and Pharisees (see Matt. 21:45), the kings, and the Romans, most of whom...rejected him and tried to destroy him. In spite of their efforts, this stone became the center of God's new program, a new kingdom that would produce fruit...This came about through the resurrection...Renewed Israel may have been the head of the corner at the return from the exile; but Jesus is the stone of the eternal covenant (Eph. 2:20).[14]

## The Little Details

### Carson on the Temple as Jesus's Body:

The words "his body" [in John 2:21] can refer only to the physical body of Jesus...For Jesus to make this identification, after cleansing the temple in Jerusalem, means that he himself saw the connection between the temple and his own body to be fundamentally typological. We are inclined to think of "prophecy" as verbal prediction that is "fulfilled" when the event predicted by the prophecy has come to pass. But...New Testament writers...understood that some things "predicted" in the Old Testament were not set out as verbal predictions, but as pictures, events, people, institutions...The temple in Jerusalem is being viewed in such a typological way...The temple itself pointed toward a better and final meeting-point between God and human beings...Jesus cleansed the temple; under this typological reading of the Old Testament, he also replaced it, fulfilling its purpose.[15]

- - - - - - - - - - - - - - - -

Now the Son of God stood in the temple looking for fruit.

- - - - - - - - - - - - - - - -

They were stuck. If they said from heaven, then Jesus would ask why they didn't believe his words about Jesus. But if they said from man, the crowds would turn on them, for they all believed John was a prophet. They refused to answer (Mark 11:29-33). Jesus told them a parable.

**25.** Read Mark 12:1-9. What is the gist of the parable?

This was a warning, a chance to see where they were headed and to repent.

Centuries before, the Lord had come looking for fruit in Israel and Judah but found none and so cut down the nation through exile (Isaiah 5:1-7). John the Baptist warned that the Lord was sending the Son of God to look for fruit and cut down fruitless trees (Matthew 3:10). Jesus acted out a parable before his disciples when he looked for fruit on the fig tree and, finding none, withered it with a word. Now the Son of God stood in the temple looking for fruit.

**26.** What additional warning did Jesus give them (Mark 12:10-11)?

Jesus quoted Psalm 118:22-23, claiming he was the cornerstone the builders rejected.

When Jesus left the temple, his disciples extolled its beauty. Jesus said, "There will not be left here one stone upon another that will not be thrown down" (Mark 13:2). Just as Jeremiah foretold the destruction of Solomon's temple after declaring it a den of robbers (Jeremiah 7:11,14), so now Jesus foretold the destruction of Herod's temple after declaring it the same.

## Day 5

# The Temple Builder

At the last supper, Jesus told his disciples that he was the true vine and they were branches (John 15:1-17). If they remained in him, they would bear fruit and glorify God.

Later, the religious leaders arrested Jesus. At his trial, the high priest asked, "Are you the Christ, the Son of the Blessed?" Jesus said, "I am" (Mark 14:61-62). They condemned him to die and delivered him to Rome, asking Pontius Pilate to put him to death.

**27.** (a) What did Pilate ask Jesus (John 18:33)? (b) What did Jesus say about his kingdom (verse 36)?

Pilate told the Jews, "I find no guilt in him" (John 18:38). But they insisted he die. Pilate wrote his crime on a placard (John 19:19). A Roman soldier carried it before Jesus on the way to his execution. There they nailed it on the cross. It read,

Jesus of Nazareth,
the King of the Jews

## The King Forever in Hebrews

Hebrews 1:8-9 quotes Psalm 45:6-7 as God speaking of his Son:

> But of the Son he says,
> "Your throne, O God, is forever and ever,
>     the scepter of uprightness is the scepter of your kingdom.
> You have loved righteousness and hated wickedness;
> therefore God, your God, has anointed you
>     with the oil of gladness beyond your companions."

The author of Hebrews called Jesus *Christ* throughout the letter, telling readers that Jesus is the anointed king promised to David. The author admonished them not to let persecution lead them astray.

> **28.** Read Hebrews 12:3-11. (a) When we struggle, what should we do (Hebrews 12:3)? (b) Why should we endure hardship (verse 7)? (c) Why does God discipline us (verse 10)? (d) What does discipline yield (verse 11)?

Fruit. The Lord our God wants us to bear fruit: "The fruit of the Spirit is love, joy, peace, patience, kindness, goodness, faithfulness, gentleness, self-control" (Galatians 5:22-23).

> **29.** ♥ Describe a way that hardship grew one of the fruit of the Spirit in your life.

## God with Us Still

Not all believed Jesus was the Christ. Herod's temple was finished in AD 64. In AD 66, Jews in Judea revolted in the hope of establishing a kingdom on earth under a different messiah. Rome's reaction was swift. In AD 70, Rome destroyed Jerusalem, razed Herod's temple, and crucified countless Jews. Those the soldiers didn't execute they exiled.

The earthly temple was no more. But there remained hope of another temple. For kings built temples, and Jesus was no exception.

### God with Us Today

Ephesians 1:20-21 says that God seated Jesus "at his right hand in the heavenly places, far above all rule and authority and power and dominion, and above every name that is named, not only in this age but also in the one to come."

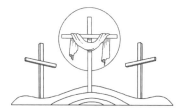

## The Little Details
### Psalm 118

This chapter's God with Me Now section includes reading Psalm 118. It's a thanksgiving psalm for groups going to the temple after being delivered from the Lord's chastening (verse 18).[16] Verses with *I* or *me* are the group's leader singing. Verses with *we* or *us* are everyone joining in.

During the days of the second temple, verse 18's severe discipline likely reminded worshipers of the nation's exile. They cried to the Lord for help. The Lord saved them from exile, and they could go to the rebuilt temple with thanksgiving.

Bible versions translate verse 27 in different ways. Dr. Ross says the Hebrew translates literally to "bind the festal sacrifice with cords."[17]

In the Gospels, verse 25's "Lord, save us" (NIV) is usually translated *Hosanna*, which is a transliteration of the Hebrew for "Lord, save us." The crowds shouted verses 25-27 during Jesus's triumphal entry into Jerusalem.

**30.** In Ephesians 1:22-23 below, circle *church*. Circle what the church is (two words).

And he put all things under his feet and gave [Jesus] as head over all things to the church, which is his body.

God's people are the body of Jesus. Paul wrote to the Gentiles in Ephesus that through Jesus, both Gentiles and Jews "have access in one Spirit to the Father" (Ephesians 2:18).

**31.** In Ephesians 2:19-22 below, underline the foundation of the household of God. Circle who the cornerstone is. Double-underline what the structure is growing into. Box for whom the temple is a dwelling place.

You are...members of the household of God, built on the foundation of the apostles and prophets, Christ Jesus himself being the cornerstone, in whom the whole structure, being joined together, grows into a holy temple in the Lord. In him you also are being built together into a dwelling place for God by the Spirit.

God's people are the temple of the Holy Spirit.

**32.** (a) How then should we live (Ephesians 4:1)? (b) What fruit should we bear (verses 2-3)? (c) Why should we live in unity with other believers (verse 4)?

### God with Us Forever

Revelation 11:15-19 describes a heavenly view of the kingdom of this world becoming the kingdom of God and the time of judgment having arrived. Revelation 19 depicts Jesus as King of kings.

**33.** ♥ Read Revelation 11:15-19 and 19:11-16. What encourages you the most?

### God with Me Now

We read this week about how Jesus fulfilled Psalm 118:22,25-27. This psalm is also special because it was the last one sung at the Passover meal, and therefore at Jesus's last supper. Professor Allen P. Ross writes this about Psalm 118:24 and Jesus's final meal:

Psalms 113–116 were sung before the meal, and Psalms 117 and 118 closed the evening. This psalm, then, was the hymn that Jesus and the disciples sang in the upper room after the last supper (Matt. 26:30). After the evening concluded with the line "Bind the sacrifice with cords to the horns of the altar," Jesus and his disciples went out into the Garden of Gethsemane to watch and pray—and await the fulfillment of their hymn.[18]

Let's conclude with the same two psalms. (The sidebar on the previous page explains some of the verses.)

Turn to Psalms 117–118 and read them. **Pray** the psalms to the Lord in worship.

**Praise** God for something you saw of his character this week. **Confess** anything that convicted you. **Ask** for help to do something God's Word calls you to do. **Thank** God for something you learned this week.

## The Heart and Art of Worship

I loved learning this week about how God gave David the plans for the temple. It wasn't David's design. It was God's design, down to the most minute details. David was simply the vessel God used to bring his plans from heaven to earth. It made me think about how God longs to use us, as vessels created for his glory, to reveal his design for kingdom living here on earth. It might be by him inspiring the royal colors you choose for this week's illustration or the poem of praise you write with thanksgiving, but it could also be him inspiring you to help a stranger in need or make that phone call to say you're sorry. Whenever we respond to God's inspiration…his nudgings…his still, small voice…we are revealing his character and his glory here on earth in a very tangible way.

Another thing that spoke loudly to me was when David told Solomon that every willing craftsman would be with him as he built the temple. Did you catch it? That one word? *Willing*. It jumped off the page. The one word that set some craftsmen apart from others. *Willing*. I want to believe that because of all that God had done for them as a people that they all had a willing heart to use their skills, talents, and abilities for his glory. But if so, why did he insert that one word? *Willing*. Maybe because they were no different than us…than me. Because despite all God has done for me, I can still choose to ignore his inspiration and his calling. I can choose to believe the lies that I'm not good enough or skilled enough to serve God with my talents. We choose. And I hope today we choose to give our best to the One who is seated on the throne and trust him to use us, like he did David, to bring his plans from heaven to earth…for his glory!

*Karla*

Your Throne shall be established Forever

2 Samuel 7:16

## Chapter 6

# Psalm 110
## Jesus the High Priest Forever

The hope of approaching God

---

**Day 1**

## The King-Priest Melchizedek

As I write, the twenty-first highest grossing movie of all time (adjusted for inflation) is *Raiders of the Lost Ark*.[1] The movie is set in 1936. Indiana Jones wears a wide-brimmed fedora and carries a bullwhip. He wants to recover the lost ark of the covenant before the Nazis do because they all believe that carrying the ark into battle makes an army invincible. In the movie's climax (spoiler alert), the Nazis open the ark and spirits attack them, melting their faces and killing them all. Indiana Jones survives by keeping his eyes closed until the spirits reseal the ark.

Yes, the ark of the covenant was lost when Babylon invaded Jerusalem. No, the ark didn't make armies invincible (the Israelites would have ruled the world!). But the ark was holy, and God instructed the Levites and priests to always treat it as such. Two irreverent priests who carried the ark into battle died (1 Samuel 4:1-11). So did 70 Levites who looked inside the ark and another who touched it (1 Samuel 6:19; 2 Samuel 6:7).

**The Reveal**

*Eve's Day*
God placed cherubim before the east entrance to the garden to guard the way to the tree of life, signifying that the way to eternal life was blocked (Genesis 3:22-24).

*Abraham's Day*
When God granted Abraham an astounding victory over the armies of four kings, Abraham showed his gratitude by tithing to Melchizedek, the priest-king of Salem.

*Moses's Day*
God's presence appeared in a cloud above the ark of the covenant in the Most Holy Place (Leviticus 16:2). A curtain embroidered with cherubim barred the way to the Most Holy Place, reminding worshipers of the cherubim who barred the way to the tree of life. God assigned the Levites the responsibility to know and carry out the laws about the tabernacle's holy things.

The high priest performed his most important duty annually on the Day of Atonement.

## The Little Details
### Royal Psalms

Royal psalms are about the monarchy. Some of the royal psalms are messianic psalms; that is, they tell us something about the coming of the future righteous king, Jesus. The New Testament identifies both Psalms 2 and 110 as messianic. These are the royal psalms and their themes:

Psalm 2—King's coronation

Psalm 18—King's battle victory

Psalm 20—Prayer for king for battle victory

Psalm 21—Praise for king for battle victory

Psalm 45—King's wedding

Psalm 72—Prayer for king's dominion

Psalm 89—Davidic covenant

Psalm 101—King's charter

Psalm 110—Priestly kingdom

Psalm 144—Peace by king's victory

---

The high priest performed his most important duty annually on the Day of Atonement.

---

He offered animal sacrifices for his own sin and the sin of the people. He sprinkled blood from sacrifices on the front of the ark's cover to atone for people's sin (Leviticus 16:14).

### David's Day

In David's time, Salem was called Jerusalem. David's throne was in Jerusalem on Mount Zion, just as Melchizedek's throne had been. When David's son Solomon built a temple for the Lord, he made a new curtain embroidered with cherubim to block the way to the new Most Holy Place (2 Chronicles 3:10-14).

### God's Word to Us

In our last chapter, we saw that Jesus is the king who will rule forever based on God's promise to David. David wrote Psalm 110 about a vision God showed him of a warrior king who will rule from Zion (Jerusalem) while serving as priest forever.[2]

> Take a moment to pray for insight as you read God's Word.

1. ♥ Read Genesis 14:17-24 and Psalm 110. What stands out to you? Why?

Abram rescued the people and plunder taken from Sodom.

2. (a) Who came to greet Abram (Genesis 14:18)? (b) What two offices did he hold?

Most Canaanite kings worshiped gods they believed resided in their cities. But Melchizedek worshiped God Most High, the Creator of heaven and earth.

3. (a) What did Melchizedek do for Abram (Genesis 14:19)? (b) What did he call God (verse 19)? (c) To whom did he credit Abram's victory (verse 20)? (d) What did Abram give him (verse 20)?

Abram tithed from what he recovered to show appreciation for God's help.

4. ♥ How can giving to ministries show appreciation for the gifts God gives us?

# A Walk with Christ—#Sabbath

The biblical account of Sabbath is in relation to the time from Friday sundown to Saturday sundown. Many Christians today keep the principle of what is taught about the Sabbath on Sunday to disconnect from what distracts us so we can worship God. One day I investigated the modern-day Sabbath by surveying the social media #hashtags revealing how people spend their Sundays. I discerned two diverse paths.

## The Selfish Path

The majority of these posts use tags like #SundayFunday and share innocent activities like eating or creating foodie meals, watching sports or movies, shopping, or walking the dog. However, as I continued my exploration, I ended up on a digital alley revealing a "selfie" trend that compels people to place themselves on the throne and live out hedonistic activities exploiting themselves, their bodies, and others in an attempt to gain followers or even mock worship. The social media site I was on brags about keeping posts clean, yet the raunchiness I was exposed to made me want to scrub my eyes with chlorine!

I was saddened by and called to pray over this brokenness. The Holy Spirit reminded me that Christ looked at the crowds and "felt sorry for them. They were confused and helpless, like sheep without a shepherd" (Matthew 9:36 CEV). The Spirit took me to the heart of Jesus who went to the cross for *all* of us.

To stand strong in a culture of always-shifting morality, we can choose God-honoring ways to enjoy the Lord's Day that will refuel, reignite, refresh, and renew us:

> Remember the Sabbath day by keeping it holy. Six days you shall labor and do all your work, but the seventh day is a sabbath to the LORD your God. On it you shall not do any work...For in six days the LORD made the heavens and the earth...but he rested on the seventh day. Therefore, the LORD blessed the Sabbath day and made it holy (Exodus 20:8-11 NIV).

Jesus said that the Sabbath was made for man (Mark 2:27). God considers weekly rest important for us.

## The Sabbath Path

The intended principle of the Sabbath is rest, but year after year, Jewish traditions and laws added more rules. Jesus, in Matthew 12:8 (NIV), says he is "Lord of the Sabbath." In simple terms, Jesus fulfilled the law (including the Sabbath), so when we focus on our relationship with Christ, we are enjoying Sabbath rest. On my social media Sabbath quest, I read plenty of memes reflecting a Sabbath of wholesome freedom: Scripture verses and lyrics to praise songs and hymns juxtaposed on images of family, fellowship, food, and creation. I saw a host of inspiring quotes from faithful and favorite pastors, speakers, writers, and teachers. I witnessed images of healthy forms of rest: spending time with family and in the Word; creating art and enjoying wholesome interests; using God-given talents as well as nurturing self-care that bolsters rest and renewal of body, soul, and spirit. God's #SundaySabbathPlan is refreshing and restful.

Is God asking you to make any changes in the way you spend your Sabbath?

At www.DiscoveringTheBibleSeries.com you'll find the *Sabbath Planning* devotional sheet I created. It's filled with ideas and verses to honor the heart of your High Priest and his path for your Sabbath.

*Pam*

# The Future King-Priest

Psalm 110 begins with, "The LORD says to my lord" (NIV). Dr. Ross writes that the literal translation is "An oracle of Yahweh to my lord."[3] An oracle is a form of prophecy. He says the Hebrew word that the NIV translates "says" is "a prophetic term that means 'utterance, declaration, revelation'…The term emphasizes that this is a divine oracle, an announcement of the will and plan of God; and it ensures the certainty of its being fulfilled."[4]

David probably received the oracle after he moved his throne to Jerusalem, thereby taking the throne previously held by the king-priest Melchizedek. We'll discover first how people in David's day likely interpreted Psalm 110.

### Exaltation: A Great King Comes[5]

Let's begin by identifying the persons in the first verse.

> **5.** In Psalm 110:1-2 (NIV) below, circle the speaker. Box where the speaker tells the other person to sit. Underline what the speaker tells the lord to do.
>
> The LORD says to my lord:
>
> "Sit at my right hand
>  until I make your enemies
>  a footstool for your feet."
>
> The LORD will extend your mighty scepter from Zion, saying,
>  "Rule in the midst of your enemies!"

English translations usually translate the first name as LORD and format it with small capital letters to let us know it's the name of God, Yahweh. Yahweh was the speaker. He spoke to someone David called "my lord." This translates a different Hebrew word that can refer to a person or God. Since the New Testament identifies this person as Jesus, many English translations capitalize it. But people in David's day didn't have that insight. This lesson will call the speaker "Yahweh" and the one to whom he spoke "lord" so that we can view it as David's contemporaries did.

Yahweh told David's lord to rule with his "mighty scepter." That made him a future king. Since David's offspring would rule forever, he must descend from David. But David called him "my lord," making him greater than David. Ross explains:

> David clearly sees this future coming king, who is the one to whom God is speaking, as his sovereign master. His use of the word "my lord" does not indicate that the king was divine, only that he is lord and master. If it is referring to David's descendant, it means he will be greater than David.[7]

This raises a question: *How could one of King David's sons be greater than King David?*

---

## The Little Details

### Prophetic Psalms

Most of the prophetic psalms that point to Jesus have a meaning in David's or his sons' lives. For example, Psalm 2 is a coronation psalm that David probably wrote for Solomon's coronation. The New Testament tells us it's a prophecy about the Christ, so Solomon's coronation was a type of Jesus's coronation.

Psalm 110 is different. Not only is there no known event in David's life that it could apply to, its topics don't seem possible to ascribe to David. David was never considered a priest, and under the Law of Moses, kings were forbidden to take on the priestly duties assigned to the Levites. Dr. Ross writes that this psalm may be the only psalm in the Psalter that is purely prophetic: "All the [other royal psalms] have a primary reference to an event in the life of a king that becomes typological of the greatest of the David kings, the Messiah."[6]

- - - - - - - - - - - - - - - - - - - - - - -

David probably received the oracle after he moved his throne to Jerusalem, thereby taking the throne previously held by the king-priest Melchizedek.

- - - - - - - - - - - - - - - - - - - - - - -

**6.** (a) What did Yahweh tell David's lord to do (verse 1)? (b) For how long?

*Footstool* is a figure of speech meaning "complete rule." In those days, rulers put their foot on the neck of those they conquered. David was used to God delivering him from enemies, so this part of the verse isn't unusual. The rest is.

God is normally invisible to humans, his throne is in heaven, and for a person to sit at God's right hand implies great exaltation. The next question is, *How could David's descendant sit at Yahweh's right hand?*

**7.** In Psalm 110:2 (NIV) below, circle from where Yahweh will extend the king's scepter. Underline what Yahweh commands the king to do.

> The LORD will extend your mighty scepter from Zion, saying,
> "Rule in the midst of your enemies!"

The scepter symbolized rule. "Mighty scepter" means the king will be powerful. The king will rule from Zion, the hill on which Jerusalem sat, just as Melchizedek and David did. The king holds the scepter, and Yahweh extends it. Yahweh will extend the king's domain and commands the king, "Rule!" Ross notes, "He will not only subjugate his enemies but will rule among them."[8]

## Consecration: The King Is a Priest

**8.** In Psalm 110:3 below, underline what the people the king rules over will do (first line of the verse). Circle what they wear.

> Your people will offer themselves freely
>   on the day of your power,
>   in holy garments;
> from the womb of the morning,
>   the dew of your youth will be yours.

The words translated "offer...freely" are elsewhere translated "freewill offerings." So, the king's people offer themselves as freewill offerings in the king's service. Freewill offerings came from love and worship, as opposed to the sacrifices that seek atonement for sin.

"Holy garments" probably reminded people of the ornate garments the high priest wore. They were consecrated and holy, set apart for priestly use (Exodus 28:4). The "womb of the morning" is dawn, when dew appears. "The willing servants of the king will be with the king suddenly, and in abundance," like dew.[10] Ross summarizes:

> Thus, when the king appears to put down his enemies and establish his earthly reign, he will be accompanied by a myriad of willing servants who will be adorned in holy array, meaning that they have been set apart to his service and are characterized by holiness.[11]

Still, that the king's servants wear holy garments raises a question: *Why are the king's servants wearing holy garments like priests wear?*

Freewill offerings came from love and worship, as opposed to the sacrifices that seek atonement for sin.

**The Little Details**
*Your Sketch of a Cherub*
(See question 12)

**9.** (a) What does God say about this king in Psalm 110:4? (b) Will he change his mind?

According to Moses, priests came from the tribe of Levi and descended from Aaron. David came from the tribe of Judah. This, then, speaks of a different priesthood and produces another question: *Why is there a need for another priesthood?*

## Vindication: The King-Priest Is a Conqueror

Now the psalm turns to the day of judgment. In verse 5, the word translated "Lord" isn't the same as either of the words in verse 1, but we'll take it to refer to Yahweh.

**10.** Read Psalm 110:5-6. (a) What will the Lord God do for the king (verse 5)? (b) What is the day when that happens called (verse 5)? (c) What will he do among the nations (verse 6)? (d) Where will this happen (verse 6)?

In verses 5-6, the Lord executes judgment against kings and nations over the earth. *Shatter kings* is literally "crush the head," with *head* being the same word used in Genesis 3:15: "He shall bruise your head." Ross writes that *head* is "a singular form" and could refer to crushing every head, or to crushing the heads (leaders) of the enemies, or to crushing the main head (leader).[12] People in David's day could see in this a reference to God's promise to Eve of a serpent crusher. Not only will the serpent fall, but all enemies of the king will fall.

Therefore, a day of judgment comes which involves a great battle in which God executes all the king's enemies. *What is this day of judgment?*

**11.** In Psalm 110:7, what two things will the king do?

Brooks in Israel were often dry, so a flowing brook is a sign of God's blessing. "The picture of the conquering king drinking from such a brook is a sign that in his kingdom the streams will flow in great abundance."[13] "The way" is what God puts before him to do. "Lift up his head" means the king will be exalted, as in Psalm 3:3: "But you, O LORD, are a shield about me, my glory, and the lifter of my head."

## God with Us Then

Through Moses, God gave the Israelites a priesthood and sacrificial system that taught them that they needed holiness and righteousness to approach him. When they sinned or became ceremonially unclean, they could take an animal to the tabernacle's court and lay their hand on its head, symbolizing the transfer of sins (Leviticus 1:4).[14] They killed the animal. A priest threw its blood on the altar and burned the carcass. The forgiven Israelites could then worship. But the way to the Most Holy Place was blocked by a cherubim-embroidered curtain.

> 12.  ♥ Ezekiel describes cherubim as having four faces (cherub or ox, human, lion, eagle), four wings, feet like calves, and something like human hands under the wings. Their bodies and wings were covered with eyes, and they appeared to burn like coals of fire (Ezekiel 1:4-14; 10:8,12-15). Sketch a cherub in the margin.

## *Day 3*

# "The Lord Said to My Lord"

A priest's duties included instructing people in holiness, interceding with God on behalf of people, and offering sacrifices for people. We'll see today how Jesus did all of these.

## The Reveal Continued

### *The Major Prophets' Day*

Isaiah watched an ungodly priest place an altar to an idol in the Lord's temple, abandoning God's ways for favor with a corrupt king (2 Kings 16:10-16). He prophesied the coming of a future righteous king who would be called Prince of Peace (Isaiah 9:6-7).

Around the same time, Hosea prophesied against priests, saying, "My people are destroyed for lack of knowledge; because you have rejected knowledge...and...have forgotten the law of your God" (Hosea 4:6). Micah prophesied that ungodly priests and false prophets misled people into believing they could be secure in sin (Micah 3:11).

A century later, Ezekiel said the priests had "done violence" to God's laws by teaching that there wasn't a "difference between the unclean and the clean" (Ezekiel 22:26). Jeremiah prophesied that the priests didn't know the Lord (Jeremiah 2:8).

### *The Second Temple's Day*

The prophet Zechariah prophesied of a Branch who would build the temple of the Lord and would be a priest ruling on a throne (Zechariah 6:11-13). Decades later, the prophet Malachi rebuked the second-temple priests for stumbling people by ignoring God's ways and showing partiality in their teaching (Malachi 3:1-9). Then the priest Ezra came to Jerusalem and taught Scripture accurately, spurring a revival.

During the time between the Old and New Testaments, Judaism divided into sects. Jewish scholars called scribes taught Scripture according to which sect they belonged.[15] The hereditary office of high priest became a political appointment.

### *Jesus's Day*

At Jesus's coming, the Jewish religious leadership consisted of members from two Jewish sects: Sadducees and Pharisees. Both considered Jesus a threat to their power.

## The Little Details
### Jewish Sects and Messianic Beliefs

**Pharisees** were mostly middle-class businessmen and a few priests who had a system of oral laws meant to be a hedge around the Mosaic law. For example, they interpreted how far one could walk without breaking the Sabbath. They believed God equally inspired the Old Testament and their oral law, called the *tradition of the elders*. They hoped their righteousness would cause God to send the Messiah.[16]

**Sadducees** were wealthy, aristocratic priests who may have accepted the Old Testament as we have it today, but believed the later writings were subordinate to the five books of Moses. They were not looking for an anointed king (messiah).[17]

**Zealots** were activists who believed God would send a king (messiah) when the people took up arms against Rome.[18]

-----------------------

Many Pharisees refused to believe Jesus could be from God because he wouldn't submit to their traditions.

-----------------------

## Jesus Instructs in Holiness

One of the priests' duties was to instruct people on holiness. When Jesus began his ministry, he taught at synagogues: "And they were astonished at his teaching, for he taught them as one who had authority, and not as the scribes" (Mark 1:22).

His most famous holiness instruction was the Sermon on the Mount. He taught that holiness needed to be in the heart, not just in actions. For example, he said that the command, "You shall not commit adultery," included lust, which was adultery in the heart (Matthew 5:27-28).

### Jesus Instructs the Pharisees

The Pharisees taught that holiness came from obeying a long list of dos and don'ts that they'd added to the law as a protective hedge. They called this list the *tradition of the elders*. They prohibited many actions on the Sabbath. When they saw Jesus healing the sick and casting out demons on the Sabbath, they demanded he do so only on other days of the week.

> **13.** Read Mark 3:1-6. (a) Why were the Pharisees watching Jesus in the synagogue (verse 2)? (b) What did Jesus ask the people (verse 4)? (c) What did the Pharisees choose to do on the Sabbath: good or harm, save life or kill (verse 6)?

Jesus pointed out ways the Pharisees put their "tradition of men" above God's commands (Mark 7:8). He tried to get them to look in their hearts, telling them they were like whitewashed tombs, outwardly clean but inside full of decay (Matthew 23:27). Many Pharisees refused to believe Jesus could be from God because he wouldn't submit to their traditions.

### Jesus Instructs the Sadducees

Jesus taught that holiness involved storing up treasures in heaven rather than on earth (Matthew 6:19). The wealthy Sadducees tried to prove Jesus mistaken.

> **14.** Read Mark 12:18-27. According to Jesus, why were the Sadducees wrong (verse 24)?

### Jesus Instructs the Scribes

The scribes were teachers of the law.

> **15.** Read Mark 12:28-34. (a) What did Jesus say the most important command was (verses 29-30)? (b) What was the second most important command (verse 31)? (c) How did the scribe react (verses 32-33)? (d) How did Jesus respond (verse 34)?

The scribe noted that obeying these two commands was more important than burnt offerings, which were for seeking forgiveness.

**16.** ♥ What is a way you can act on each of the two commands in a current situation?

Jesus continued to teach.

**17.** Read Mark 12:35-37. (a) What did Jesus ask about Psalm 110:1? (Note: New Testament translations capitalize "my Lord" because the New Testament identifies him as Jesus, as we'll see.) (b) Who guided David in writing this psalm (verse 36)?

Many scribes had a problem with holiness too. In Mark 12:38-40, Jesus said:

> Beware of the scribes, who like to walk around in long robes and like greetings in the marketplaces and have the best seats in the synagogues and the places of honor at feasts, who devour widows' houses and for a pretense make long prayers. They will receive the greater condemnation.

## Jesus Intercedes

John 17 is called the *high priestly prayer* because in it, Jesus interceded for believers. He asks for his disciples to be kept from the evil one, and he asks the Father to sanctify them in the truth. He prays that future believers may all be one. He desires that they'll be with him and see his glory.

## Jesus Sacrifices

In the crucifixion, Jesus offered himself as a sacrifice to atone for people's sins and purify them from all uncleanness. This was the greatest high priestly act of all. He did this so that people could dwell with God.

Let's look at something that happened during the crucifixion.

**18.** In Mark 15:33,37-39 below, circle what was over the land for three hours. Double-underline what Jesus did. Box what tore in the temple. Underline the centurion's conclusion.

> When the sixth hour had come, there was darkness over the whole land until the ninth hour…Jesus uttered a loud cry and breathed his last. And the curtain of the temple was torn in two, from top to bottom. And when the centurion, who stood facing him, saw that in this way he breathed his last, he said, "Truly this man was the Son of God!"

The darkness covering the land was a sign to all of God's judgment and of the significance of what was happening. The centurion grasped what so many of the Jewish leaders refused to see. This man was the Son of God. That is why he was both David's son and David's Lord.

At Jesus's death, the cherubim-embroidered curtain separating humans from God tore. The way to God was opened, and the way was Jesus, the Son of God, David's Lord, and the high priest of a new order forever.

---

### The Little Details
#### *Alexander on Atonement:*

These sacrifices made God and human beings "at one"…

To appreciate the necessity of atonement, we must grasp clearly that God is not indifferent to our immoral thoughts and behavior. On the contrary, his holy nature is deeply offended by such things. As a perfect God, he cannot ignore anything evil. The smallest lie is offensive to the One who is truth. The tiniest feeling of animosity towards another person is repulsive to the One who is love. Due to his holy and perfect nature God cannot turn a blind eye to perverse human behavior as if it does not matter.

We also need to appreciate that due to our own perversity, we do not realize fully how objectionable our imperfections are to God. If we contemplate our shortcomings and failures at all, we merely dismiss them as something natural; this is part of our human nature—we are like this.[19]

---

The way to God was opened, and the way was Jesus, the Son of God, David's Lord, and the high priest of a new order forever.

---

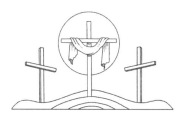

## The Little Details
### Psalm 110 in the New Testament

The New Testament references Psalm 110 more than any other psalm.

Matthew 22:44

Acts 2:34-35

1 Corinthians 15:25

Ephesians 1:20

Colossians 3:1

Hebrews 1:13

Hebrews 5:6

Hebrews 7:17

Hebrews 7:21

1 Peter 3:22

*Day 4*

# The New Priestly Order

The author of Hebrews explained to Jewish Christians that Aaron's priesthood foreshadowed the superior priesthood that Jesus brought. Aaron's priesthood laid the foundation so that when Jesus came, people could recognize how Jesus fulfilled his priesthood and understand what the offering of himself meant.

## The High Priest Forever in Hebrews

Let's discover what Hebrews tells us about Jesus as high priest.

> **19.** In Hebrews 6:19-20 below, underline where our hope enters. Circle who went there first. Double-underline what he has become.
>
> We have this as a sure and steadfast anchor of the soul, a hope that enters into the inner place behind the curtain, where Jesus has gone as a forerunner on our behalf, having become a high priest forever after the order of Melchizedek.

The "inner place behind the curtain" is the Most Holy Place we've been talking about. The curtain is the cherubim-embroidered curtain that blocked the way to it—the curtain that tore. Jesus entered so that our hope could enter too.

Hebrews 7:2 reads that Melchizedek's name means "king of righteousness." His title, king of Salem, means "king of peace." This made him a type of the Prince of Peace who would sit on David's throne and uphold the kingdom in righteousness (Isaiah 9:6-7).

Hebrews 7:3 notes that Genesis gives genealogies for most people, but not for Melchizedek. His lack of beginning and end in Genesis is a type of the literal lack of beginning and end of the Son of God. Types are always fulfilled in something greater.

Hebrews 7:4 states that Melchizedek was greater than Abraham because Abraham tithed to him; therefore, Melchizedek was greater than Levi, the father of Aaron's priesthood.

> **20.** Could perfection come through the Levitical priesthood (Hebrews 7:11)?
>
> ☐ Yes    ☐ No

The argument is that God would not have announced a priest after the order of Melchizedek if such a priest weren't needed. Therefore, perfection couldn't have come through the Levitical priesthood.

> **21.** Read Hebrews 7:12-14. (a) What did a change in priesthood require (verse 12)? (b) From what tribe did Jesus our Lord come (verse 14)? (c) What did the law of Moses say about priests from Judah (verse 14)?

Jesus brought a change in law—a new covenant. The new covenant had a new priesthood.

The new covenant had a new priesthood.

22. In Hebrews 7:16-17 below, circle the power that Jesus has that enables him to be a priest forever, unlike the priests descended from Levi. Underline the quotation from Psalm 110 that the author says is a witness about Jesus.

> [Jesus] has become a priest, not on the basis of a legal requirement concerning bodily descent, but by the power of an indestructible life. For it is witnessed of him, "You are a priest forever, after the order of Melchizedek."

Hebrews addresses the change in priesthood.

23. In Hebrews 7:18-19 below, underline why a former commandment about high priests was set aside. Double-underline why it was that way (the phrase within parentheses). Circle what was introduced instead.

> For on the one hand, a former commandment is set aside because of its weakness and uselessness (for the law made nothing perfect); but on the other hand, a better hope is introduced, through which we draw near to God.

Jesus brought a better hope than what the first covenant offered.

24. Read Hebrews 7:20-24. (a) For how long will Jesus hold the priesthood (verse 21)? (b) What does that make him a guarantor of (verse 22)? (c) Why is Jesus's priesthood permanent, unlike the Levites' (verses 23-24)?

Remember how some Levitical priests were godly and served well, but others were self-serving and didn't teach God's ways? That can't happen with this priest!

25. In Hebrews 7:25 below, circle what Jesus can do because his priesthood is permanent. Underline for whom he does it. Double-underline what he always lives to do.

> Consequently, he is able to save to the uttermost those who draw near to God through him, since he always lives to make intercession for them.

26. ♥ Do you take comfort in the fact that Jesus intercedes for you? Why or why not?

We have one permanent, righteous priest forever. Hallelujah!

27. Read Hebrews 7:26-28. (a) How does verse 26 describe Jesus? (b) Could that description fit any priest descended from Levi? (c) Did Jesus need to offer sacrifices for his own sins, like the Levitical priests (verse 27)? (d) The law appointed what kind of men to be high priests (verse 28)? (e) In contrast, who did God by oath appoint as priest forever, and what kind of man is he?

**The Little Details**
*Allen P. Ross on the New Priesthood:*

In Israel there could be only one order of High Priest (or priests), and in biblical times that was the order of Aaron, in the line of Levi. The Davidic kings came from the line of Judah, and any function they had in the sacrificial ritual would have been under the authority of the priesthood. The only way that a descendant of David could become the official priest was for the order of Aaron to come to an end, which happened at the death of Christ according to the New Testament teaching. The saints now have a new High Priest and King. And God declared with a solemn oath that this king would be a priest forever, a royal priest—making his loyal subjects a kingdom of priests.[20]

- - - - - - - - - - - - - - - - - - - - - -

We have one permanent, righteous priest forever. Hallelujah!

- - - - - - - - - - - - - - - - - - - - - -

## The Little Details

### Baylis on the Torah of Moses:

The Torah of Moses was *instruction in knowing God.* Its center is relationship, not ritual. Its ritual is educational, not magical or manipulative. Its purpose was to picture relational truth and enrich memory, not promote a form of buying off God. God was not interested in bribes (Deut. 10:17). Pagans brought offerings to their deities to encourage divine generosity. Yahweh received thanksgiving offerings from his children for whatever had already been received.[21]

What a high priest we have!

> **28.** Read Hebrews 8:1-5. (a) Where is Jesus seated (verse 1)? (b) Where does he minister (verse 2)? (c) The Levitical priests on earth served in a temple that was what (verse 5)?

Moses built an earthly tabernacle (tent) that was "a copy and shadow of the heavenly things"; that is, it was a *type* of heavenly things. The Levitical priests served at the tent which was a copy; Jesus served at "the true tent that the Lord set up, not man." Allen P. Ross summarizes:

> The book of Hebrews explains how Melchizedek was a type of Christ because he did not owe his priesthood to his physical lineage, because he was both a king and a priest in Jerusalem, and because he remains a priest forever in human memory. The Aaronic priesthood did come to an end when Jesus the Messiah completely satisfied the demands of the Law and made the perfect sacrifice, fulfilling all the temple ritual once and for all. No longer was there a need for sacrifices, or the temple, or the Levitical sacrificing priests. Jesus became the high priest, consecrated by his own blood, and confirmed forever when he went into the heavenly sanctuary. Because his sacrifice was made once and for all, and because it remains the basis for salvation and sanctification forever, his priesthood will never end.[22]

In AD 70, Rome burned the Jerusalem temple. Sacrifices ended. The Levitical priesthood was over. There has been no temple or temple sacrifice since.

Because the Sacrifice that they foreshadowed came and lives.

## Day 5

# Holy Garments

Now that we understand the New Testament's teaching about Psalm 110, let's revisit the questions raised in Day 2. Then we'll discover an amazing gift from our high priest.

### Psalm 110's Questions Answered

*How could one of King David's sons be greater than King David himself?* Jesus descended from David through his mother, but he was the Son of God (Hebrews 7:3).

*How could David's descendant sit at Yahweh's right hand?* God raised him from the dead and he rules from the heavenly Zion of which the earthly Zion was a type. He came from heaven and to there he returned (Hebrews 1:3).

*Why is there a need for another priesthood?* The Levitical priesthood was imperfect and left the way to God barred because it was merely a type of the perfect priesthood to come (Hebrews 7:11). Jesus's death tore the curtain that symbolized that the way to God was

The Sacrifice which they foreshadowed came and lives.

barred. With the way now open, the Levitical priesthood and the entire sacrificial system was obsolete.

***Why are the king's servants wearing holy garments, something priests wore when performing their duties at the tabernacle?*** Jesus's servants are a royal priesthood (1 Peter 2:9). Jesus's blood shed on the cross made his servants holy so that they could be clothed "'with fine linen, bright and pure'—for the fine linen is the righteous deeds of the saints" (Revelation 19:8).

***What is this day of judgment?*** "It is appointed for man to die once, and after that comes judgment" (Hebrews 9:27).

## God with Us Still

### God with Us Today

The author of Hebrews told us how we should live since Jesus is our permanent high priest.

29. Read Hebrews 10:19-22. (a) What confidence do we have (verse 19)? (b) What was the curtain that opened up a type of (verse 20)? (c) What do we have (verse 21)?

Jesus's flesh in the crucifixion opened the way through the temple curtain, giving us access to God.[23] We can now enter the holy places.

30. In Hebrews 10:22 below, circle the action we should take because we have confidence to enter the holy places. Underline the type of heart we should have. Double-underline the type of faith with which we should draw near. Bracket the ways our high priest has cleansed us (hint: left bracket before "with our" and right bracket after "water").

    Let us draw near with a true heart in full assurance of faith, with our hearts sprinkled clean from an evil conscience and our bodies washed with pure water.

A true heart is a sincere heart, a heart that approaches God honestly because we have full assurance of faith, for our high priest has cleansed us.

31. Read Hebrews 10:23-25. (a) To what and how should we hold fast (verse 23)? (b) Why (verse 23)? (c) What should we consider (verse 24)? (d) What should we not neglect (verse 25)? (e) What should we do with each other (verse 25)?

We can't stir one another up and encourage each other unless we're meeting together. When we meet with our Christian brothers and sisters, we can ask ourselves, How can I encourage them and stir them up to love others and pursue good works? Hebrews isn't

### The Little Details
### *Alexander on Adam and Eve as Priests:*

If Genesis portrays the Garden of Eden as a sanctuary or temple-garden, a number of things follow: (1) Since the garden is a place where divinity and humanity enjoy each other's presence, it is appropriate that it should be a prototype for later Israelite sanctuaries. This explains why many of the decorative features of the tabernacle and temple are arboreal in nature. (2) Because they met God face to face in a holy place, we may assume that Adam and Eve had a holy or priestly status. Only priests were permitted to serve within a sanctuary or temple. (3) Although it is not stated, the opening chapters of Genesis imply that the boundaries of the garden will be extended to fill the whole earth as human beings are fruitful and increase in number.[24]

---

The Levitical priesthood was imperfect and left the way to God barred because it was merely a type of the perfect priesthood to come.

---

## The Little Details
### Sklar on Atonement as Cleansing:

Sin...pollutes. The Israelites are described as being "cleansed" from their sin on the Day of Atonement (Lev. 16:30). Furthermore, it appears that sin was viewed as that which defiled the sanctuary in particular, almost as though it were an impure dust that settled on the tent of meeting and its contents, or a defiling dishonour that clung to the home of the sinner's covenant Lord...This in turn suggests that *kipper* [sacrificial atonement] in these contexts can refer to an element of cleansing as well as ransom...

But not all cleansing rites are the same. In particular, while minor impurities can be cleansed by means of various rites other than sacrifice, the cleansing of a major impurity always involves sacrificial atonement...Why is this so?...Those who suffer from a major impurity defile the sanctuary and its contents, even if they have not had direct contact with them.[25]

talking about pursuing good works to earn salvation—we have full assurance of faith. Rather, because we've been cleansed, we love others, pursue good works, and encourage others to do the same.

**32.** ♥ (a) How can you stir someone up to love and good works this week? (b) How can you encourage someone this week?

The Day is drawing near. Let us use our time wisely.

### God with Us Forever
Revelation 19 describes the marriage supper of the Lamb. His Bride is the saints. It has been granted to her to dress for the wedding in a special way.

**33.** ♥ Read Revelation 19:6-10. What encourages you the most?

### God with Me Now
Psalm 115 is one of the Hallel psalms that Jesus likely sang with his disciples. It celebrates trust in God rather than in the things of the earth, including idols. We can make idols out of money, positions, and possessions.

🗨 Consider prayerfully if you're putting money, positions, or possessions ahead of the Lord. Turn to Psalm 115 and read it. **Pray** the psalm to the Lord in worship.

🗨 **Praise** God for something you saw of his character this week. **Confess** anything that convicted you. **Ask** for help to do something God's Word calls you to do. **Thank** God for something you learned this week.

# The Heart and Art of Worship

Have you ever planned a road trip? You start with a vision of where you want to go and what you want to accomplish. Maybe you want to visit several national parks and enjoy the beauty of God's handiwork. Or maybe you're more fun-loving and want to stop at amusement parks. Whatever your plan or purpose, you always start at home and end at home. You already know the beginning and the end, so now it's all about the journey in between!

This week's study really made me think of the journey we're all on and how building the temple and everything in it, including the curtain, was all God's plan to reveal himself to us along the way. You see...God knew while we were still in the garden that we'd be going on a road trip, so he went before us and set up road signs, monuments, and highway markers all along our journey, in order to point us in the right direction and lead us back home again in due time. Even the menorah...this week's illustration. It was a road sign pointing us to Jesus our High Priest and the light of the world.

But we could only get so far on our own. Our sin was an insurmountable roadblock. We couldn't go over it, under it, or around it. Until Christ died on the cross. That's when the curtain was torn in half and the highway was opened for us to enter the presence of God and complete our journey home.

I'm so thankful for the visual imagery God uses to point us to Jesus. As you color this week's illustration, think about how God wants to use your light to shine for him. How can your words speak life to those who are lost? What can you do to point people to the love and kindness of Christ? How can he use your creative abilities to be God-signs of blessing to others along their journey and prepare their hearts...and yours...to worship Him as he welcomes us back home?

*Karla*

## Chapter 7

# Isaiah 9
## Jesus the Mighty God

The hope of Immanuel, God with us

His name shall be called WONDERFUL counselor, Mighty God, everlasting FATHER, prince of PEACE.

ISAIAH 9:6

**Day 1**

## God with Us

In high school, about 65 students attended a fellowship at my then-boyfriend Clay's house on Friday nights. We excitedly committed our entire lives to following Jesus and professed undying faith in a loving God.

As we grew older, though, the unexpected difficulties of life caused some to fall away. One friend in her thirties told her fiancé she couldn't marry him unless he became a Christian. When he left her, she left God, saying she had done her part, but God hadn't done his by making her ex a Christian. She feared never marrying. My sorrow over her increases my joy when I encounter those who traverse hardship with their hand in God's.

In this chapter, we'll encounter people whose fears drive them to either trust or abandon God. One king's choice launches the next big reveal of God's plan.

### The Reveal

So far, the Lord has repeatedly shown his people that he is with them by rescuing those who call on him. He has also shown faithfulness to his covenants.

### *Moses's Day*

The Lord miraculously rescued the Israelites from slavery and made a covenant with them. The covenant included blessings if they "faithfully obey the voice of the LORD your God, being careful to do all his commandments" (Deuteronomy 28:1-2). The blessings included defeating enemies (Deuteronomy 28:7). But the covenant included curses if they broke it, such as falling to enemies (Deuteronomy 28:25). The curses were warnings to repent and turn back to the Lord. If they refused to heed the warnings, then God would remove them from the land and scatter them in exile (Deuteronomy 28:63-64). Yet, he would remain willing to forgive.

### *David's Day*

God saved David from the wicked and powerful, keeping his promises even when it seemed impossible. He also revealed himself as one who was willing to forgive even as he disciplines (Psalm 51).

## The Little Details
### Key People and Places

#### People

**Ahaz**: king of Judah who became a vassal of Assyria in place of God

**Isaiah**: prophet

**Pekah**: king of Israel; Isaiah called him "son of Remaliah" to emphasize that he usurped the throne

**Rezin**: king of Syria/Aram

#### Places

**Aram**: See *Syria*.

**Assyria**: an aggressive, rapidly expanding empire north of Israel and Syria/Aram

**Babylon**: in Isaiah's day, a kingdom east of Assyria

**Damascus**: capital of Syria/Aram

**Ephraim**: the main tribe of the north and what Isaiah often called the northern kingdom of Israel

**Jerusalem**: capital of Judah

**Samaria**: capital of Israel

**Syria**: kingdom north of Israel and south of Assyria, also called **Aram**

*The Major Prophets' Day*

Two hundred years after David's death, both Judah and Israel had come through a time of great prosperity. But that prosperity led to more sin. The rich greedily oppressed the poor. The powerful stole. Judges accepted bribes. Violence spread.

In the southern kingdom of Judah, young Ahaz sat on David's throne. In the north, Pekah—the son of the military captain, Remaliah—assassinated Israel's king and usurped the throne. He conspired with Rezin, the king of Syria (NIV Aram), to conquer Judah and replace Ahaz with a puppet king. Meanwhile, the superpower Assyria was a growing threat to all three.

### God's Word to Us

Use the sidebar to help you keep track of people and places throughout this chapter. In Isaiah, *Israel* can refer to the present northern kingdom or the past unified kingdom. Just as we use Washington and Moscow to refer to the United States and Russia, so Isaiah uses the names of capital cities (Jerusalem, Samaria, Damascus) to refer to kingdoms. The names *Syria* (ESV) and *Aram* (NIV) are interchangeable; different translations prefer one or the other for the small kingdom threatened by the huge Assyria.

As you read, contrast the two sources of help: God's gentle help through children and Assyria's armed help through military dominance.

> Take a moment to pray for insight as you read God's Word.

1. ♥ Read Isaiah 7:1-17; 8:1-22; 9:1-7. What stands out to you? Why?

   *Optional:* Read 2 Kings 16 and 2 Chronicles 28 to understand Ahaz's actions and character better.

If you've never read these verses in context before, you may be a little surprised. Hang in there. These signs had fulfillments in Isaiah's day that foreshadowed future events.

2. ♥ Without giving names, describe someone who abandoned God because life didn't go how he or she wanted.

# A Walk with Christ—Hope for Humanity

Is this familiar? You enter your home exhausted and with your arms overloaded with work. You drop the burden with a cry of exasperation. You keep the light off because you can't bear to see the house in disarray. You're hungry, but the idea of cooking is overwhelming. You crave a hot bath because you ache all over; yet, you're tempted to skip food and bathing so you can collapse into bed.

You are soul sick. It's an illness brought on by too many demands, too much coffee and adrenaline boosters, and not enough prayer and stillness. You hate to admit it, but you're sick of life. Everyone needs a piece of you: family, friends, neighbors—people you love; but at this moment, you can't summon the strength to help yourself. You lean against the wall and slowly slide down, collapsing in a heap. Your head slumps toward your knees, and you wrap your arms around yourself because you could really use a hug. You can't keep going this way. Something has to change.

Dear friend, there is hope. Change is the good news of the Christmas story. Each Advent, I speak on "The Christmas Light." The heartbeat of the message is "In him was life, and the life was the light of men" (John 1:4). Jesus is our light as we journey through life, and he is our ultimate hope based on Isaiah 9:6: "For to us a child is born, to us a son is given, and the government will be on his shoulders. And he will be called Wonderful Counselor, Mighty God, Everlasting Father, Prince of Peace" (NIV). In Handel's *Messiah* concerts, this verse is when the audience stands during the Halleluiah chorus. Does your heart stand in honor of the Messiah of hope? When life seems impossible, heaven sends help:

> And the angel came to her [Mary] and said, "Rejoice, favored woman! The Lord is with you...Do not be afraid, Mary, for you have found favor with God...You will conceive and give birth to a son, and you will call His name Jesus. He will be great and will be called the Son of the Most High, and the Lord God will give Him the throne of His father David. He will reign over the house of Jacob forever, and His kingdom will have no end."

Mary asked the angel, "How can this be, since I have not been intimate with a man?"

The angel replied to her: "The Holy Spirit will come upon you, and the power of the Most High will overshadow you.

Therefore, the holy One to be born will be called the Son of God...*For nothing will be impossible with God*" (Luke 1:28-37 HCSB, emphasis added).

What do you want the Christ to accomplish in your life? Choose a name of the Messiah you want to rest your hope on. Just as in the times of Isaiah, people carry desperately heavy burdens. We all need a Savior.

> **Wonderful Counselor:** *an astonishing adviser*
> **Mighty God:** *the Almighty; a strong, heroic Warrior Champion*
> **Everlasting Father:** *the first and forever Father of all*
> **Prince of Peace:** *Ruler, Captain, Chief, Commander of perfect peace and prosperity*

🖥 At www.DiscoveringTheBibleSeries.com, find my devotional on how "the zeal of the LORD" (Isaiah 9:7) breaks the yoke of burden, and our family's *Christmas Dinner and Dialogue* devotional based on Isaiah 9:6.

*Pam*

## The Little Details

### Uzziah, Ahaz, and Hezekiah

King Uzziah led a mostly righteous life until he decided to offer incense in the temple, which only a priest could lawfully do. The Lord struck him with leprosy. In Isaiah 6, he has died, and his disfigured corpse showed the weakness and frailty of human kings in contrast to the holy and eternal divine King.

Uzziah's grandson, King Ahaz, looted the temple to buy Assyria's favor. He closed the temple doors, nationalized idol worship, and sacrificed his sons to the god Molech.

Ahaz's son, King Hezekiah, reopened and cleansed the temple. He demolished idols. Nonetheless, he earned Isaiah's rebuke when he showed off temple treasures to the Babylonians.

The nation was still in need of a righteous king.

God explained that Isaiah would speak many words from him, calling the people to be true servants of the Lord.

# A Sign Is Given

Isaiah arranged his book by theme, not date. Here's a simple outline we'll use:

    I. The Problem: Israel Is Unrighteous (Isaiah 1–5)

    II. God's First Solution: A Future Righteous King (Isaiah 6–39)

    III. God's Second Solution: A Future Righteous Servant (Isaiah 40–55)

    IV. God's Third Solution: A Future Righteous People (Isaiah 56–66)[1]

## The Problem: Israel Is Unrighteous

Chapters 1–5 introduce the problem: the Israelites (Israel and Judah) were unrighteous and estranged from God (Isaiah 1:2-4). Their sacrifices weren't accompanied by repentance but were attempts to manipulate God (Isaiah 1:13). Such offerings neither cleansed them nor pleased God. The Lord wanted people to "cease to do evil, learn to do good; seek justice, correct oppression; bring justice to the fatherless, plead the widow's cause" (Isaiah 1:16-17).

In Isaiah 1:18-20, the Lord gave the people a choice:

> Come now, let us reason together, says the LORD: though your sins are like scarlet, they shall be as white as snow; though they are red like crimson, they shall become like wool. If you are willing and obedient, you shall eat the good of the land; but if you refuse and rebel, you shall be eaten by the sword.

## God's First Solution: A Future Righteous King

Chapters 6–39 present the first way God would solve Israel's unrighteousness. He would bring a future righteous king whose ways would sharply contrast with current kings' ways.

### The Divine King Appears to Isaiah

This section jumps back in time to the death of one of Judah's kings, the leprous Uzziah.

> 3. What did Isaiah see in the temple (Isaiah 6:1-4)?

The divine King's holiness and glory made Isaiah keenly aware that he and his people had "unclean lips" (6:5). Their sacrifices were ineffectual. He confessed his uncleanness and his fear that he would die in God's holy presence. But a heavenly being touched his mouth with a burning coal and took away his guilt. Clearly, the rest of the people needed to confess and turn from their sin so that the Lord would take away their guilt too.

The Lord asked, "Whom shall I send?" Isaiah responded, "Here I am! Send me" (Isaiah 6:8). God explained that Isaiah would speak many words from him, calling the people to be true servants of the Lord. But the words would fall on ears that didn't want to hear. Instead of causing repentance, they would harden the hearts of the rebellious, setting them in their ways.

Isaiah saw that prediction fulfilled when a few years later God sent him to Uzziah's grandson Ahaz, the new king of Judah.

## The Lord Offers King Ahaz a Sign

Shortly after young Ahaz became sole king of Judah, two neighboring kings took advantage of his inexperience and attacked, intending to depose him. They were Pekah, the king of Israel, and Rezin, the king of Syria/Aram.

> 4. (a) How did Ahaz react when he heard about the attack (Isaiah 7:2)? (b) Whom did the Lord send to help him (verse 3)? (c) What did the Lord tell Ahaz to do (verse 4)?

Isaiah uses poetic language, so let's discover what some of it means. Isaiah often called the kingdom of Israel *Ephraim*, the name of its largest tribe, to emphasize that the split between Israel and Judah was a tribal dispute. He called Pekah *the son of Remaliah* to underscore that Pekah was an inconsequential usurper of a throne, while Ahaz received David's throne legitimately. Isaiah's son's name means "a remnant shall return." "Two smoldering stumps of firebrands" means Ephraim and Syria/Aram were like the smoldering embers that glow after a fire is out, so Ahaz shouldn't fear them.

> 5. In these verses, Damascus is the capital city of Syria/Aram, and Samaria is the capital city of Israel (here called Ephraim). (a) What did the Lord say about Pekah's plan to overthrow Ahaz (Isaiah 7:7)? (b) What would happen within 65 years (end of verse 8)? (c) What did the Lord warn Ahaz (end of verse 9)?

Next, the Lord offered exceptional assurance to the terrified king.

> 6. (a) What did the Lord tell Ahaz to do so he would know for certain his enemies would not replace him (Isaiah 7:11)? (b) To whose God did Isaiah refer?

Isaiah reminded Ahaz that the Lord was Ahaz's God—or should have been under the covenant by which they lived in the Lord's land.

Ahaz replied, "I will not ask, and I will not put the LORD to the test" (Isaiah 7:12). Ahaz hid his refusal in pious-sounding words. He didn't want a sign because he had already decided how he would deal with his enemies. Professor John N. Oswalt explains: "Evidence cannot create faith; it can only confirm it. Where there is not faith, evidence is merely unwelcome, something which needs to be explained away."[3]

### The Little Details
### *John N. Oswalt on Signs:*

[In Isaiah 7:11] Ahaz is now challenged to give God a chance to prove his trustworthiness. Although our faith is not to be in the signs, nevertheless God has, throughout all the ages, given his people evidence by which their faith might be strengthened. To this extent "the leap of faith" concept, as popularly held, is incorrect, presuming as it does that God cannot, or will not, intersect the world of space/time/matter and that thus there is no evidence for faith external to our own psyches. Rather, according to the Scriptures, God has always given such evidence, sometimes in greater or lesser abundance, but he never asks us to believe without rational foundation. True, the will to believe must come first, but when that will is exercised, there is evidence freely offered (John 7:17).[2]

- - - - - - - - - - - - - - - - - - - - - - -

The Lord offered exceptional assurance to the terrified king.

- - - - - - - - - - - - - - - - - - - - - - -

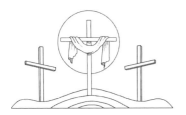

## The Little Details

### Oswalt on "Virgin":

[The word translated *virgin* in Isaiah 7:14 is the] Hebrew *'almâ*, which means "young woman of marriageable age." In Israelite society a young woman of marriageable age would have been a virgin (as the Septuagint, the pre-Christian Greek translation of the OT, makes plain)...But the Hebrew word is not the technical term meaning "virgin." Isaiah uses this more ambiguous term because of the double reference of this sign. In its immediate reference the virginity of the mother is not the most significant point. Rather, God is saying that before a child conceived at that time would reach age 12 or 13 (v. 16), the two nations of which Ahaz was so terrified would cease to exist. But in the long term, this sign, higher than heaven and deeper than hell...referred to the coming of Jesus Christ, the true Immanuel (Matt. 1:23), and the virginity of his mother was vitally important. This is why Isaiah did not use a simple word meaning "woman" or "young woman."[4]

7. (a) What did Isaiah call Ahaz in Isaiah 7:13? (b) What did Isaiah say Ahaz was doing to God (verse 13)? (c) To whose God did Isaiah now refer?

Isaiah called Ahaz a name that reminded him who he was: a king in the line of David, who served the King of kings, God. The shift from "your God" to "my God" showed that Ahaz's refusal to ask for a sign meant he did not consider the Lord God to be his God.

8. (a) What would God give Ahaz (Isaiah 7:14)? (b) Who would conceive? (c) What would the child's name be?

*Immanuel* means "God is with us."

9. (a) What would the child eat (Isaiah 7:15)? (b) By the time the child knew how to choose good (age 12 or 13), what would happen (verse 16)?

The woman in the *immediate* context of this sign was a young, unmarried woman. This woman would marry, conceive, and bear a son. The child would eat curds and honey, rich food normally reserved for the wealthy. By the time the child was old enough to know right from wrong, the two kingdoms attacking Ahaz would be deserted. (Again, if you've never read these verses in context before, you may be surprised. It'll all make sense in the coming pages.)

10. What king would attack Judah because of Ahaz's choice (Isaiah 7:17)?

Assyria would attack not just the two nations Ahaz feared, but also Judah. The reason the child would eat curds and honey is that the devastation would leave too few people to consume the milk produced. The remnant would turn the unused milk into curds and everyone—not just the rich—would eat curds and honey (Isaiah 7:22). Judah's vineyards would become "briers and thorns" (Isaiah 7:23). Because Ahaz refused God's help, he would suffer the consequences of relying on an ungodly and cruel superpower intent on annexing as many kingdoms as possible.

11. ♥ Look back at how Isaiah encouraged Ahaz in Isaiah 7:4,9. How can you apply his words to something facing you now?

Ahaz gave the temple treasures and his own treasures to Assyria's king, saying "I am your servant and your son" (2 Kings 16:7-8). This phrase means that Ahaz offered himself as a vassal to the king of Assyria. A *vassal* king was a lesser king who served a king of kings, called a *suzerain*. Ahaz was supposed to be the vassal of God. Vassals called themselves "sons" of their suzerain. This meant he would have to pay tribute, offer his army for Assyria's use, and worship Assyria's gods.

## A Future Righteous King

The Lord responded to Ahaz's rejection of him with a message of judgment and hope, for *God is with us* is judgment for God's enemies, but hope for his people.

### The Judgment: Devastation

> 12. In Isaiah 8:3 below, circle what Isaiah did with the prophetess. Underline the result.
>
> And I went to the prophetess, and she conceived and bore a son.

The Hebrew translated "went to" "is a euphemism used several times in the OT for the first intercourse between a man and his wife."[5] Many scholars believe Isaiah's first wife died, and his prediction about a virgin being with child in chapter 7 was fulfilled in the immediate context by this maiden. The child was not the crown prince Hezekiah because he was born before Ahaz became king.[6] Before this newborn reached three, Assyria would plunder Ahaz's two enemies: "Before the boy knows how to cry 'My father' or 'My mother,' the wealth of Damascus [Syria/Aram] and the spoil of Samaria [Israel] will be carried away before the king of Assyria" (Isaiah 8:4).

Within three years, both the kings that had threatened Ahaz were dead.

> 13. (a) What had the people of Judah rejected (Isaiah 8:6)? (b) Instead, they rejoiced over the two kings' deaths. What River would flow over Judah (verse 7)? (c) Whose land would it fill (verse 8)? (d) Why would Assyria not conquer Judah (verse 10)?

Assyria would attack like floodwaters, but would not destroy Judah, Immanuel's land, because "God is with us" still (Isaiah 8:10). Oswalt explains the significance:

> That Judah is called Immanuel's land makes it abundantly clear that [Isaiah's newborn] Maher-shalal-hash-baz, or someone else who may have constituted the initial fulfillment of the sign, was not the ultimate fulfillment. Ultimately, Immanuel is the owner of the land, the one against whom Assyria's threats are ultimately lodged, the one upon whom deliverance finally depends. That cannot be Isaiah's son, nor even some unknown son of Ahaz. It can only be the Messiah, in whom all hope resides. It is as if Isaiah, plunging deeper and

### The Little Details
#### Oswalt on Isaiah's Child:

The similarity of 8:1-4 to 7:10-17 [in Isaiah] is too close to be coincidental. The relation of the sign to the birth and naming of a child is the same, even to the use of the same language ("she shall conceive and bear a son," 7:14; "she conceived and bore a son," 8:3). Moreover, the significance of the signs is the same: before the child reaches a certain age, Samaria and Damascus will cease to be a threat to Judah. These similarities have prompted some writers to conclude that it is these events to which 7:10-17 (at least initially) refers. This seems highly likely in that it satisfies the demand of those verses for some specific fulfillment of that prophecy during Ahaz's time...This is not to say that [Isaiah's son] in any way exhausts or completes the Immanuel motif. In fact, it is evident that he does not, for Assyria will destroy not only Damascus and Samaria, she will sweep on into Judah. Obviously, then, the unfolding of the actuality of God's presence waits some larger personage than the son of the prophet.[7]

## The Little Details
### Oswalt on Emphasizing a Child:

First, it emphasized that...the divine ruler will not merely be God, but although partaking of the divine attributes, will have the most human of all arrivals upon the earth, namely, birth. The expected perfect king will be human and divine. But the language also makes another point. This point underlines the central paradox in Isaiah's conception of Yahweh's deliverance of his people. How will God deliver from arrogance, war, oppression, and coercion? By being more arrogant, more warlike, more oppressive, and more coercive? Surely, the book of Isaiah indicates frequently that God was powerful enough to destroy his enemies in an instant, yet again and again, when the prophet comes to the heart of the means of deliverance, a childlike face peers out at us. God is strong enough to overcome his enemies by becoming vulnerable, transparent, and humble—the only hope, in fact, for turning enmity into friendship.[9]

---

But darkness was not the end of Judah's hope.

---

deeper into the dark implications of his sign, is suddenly brought up short by the deepest implication: God *is* with us, and best of all, will be with us, not merely in the impersonal developments of history, but somehow as a person.[8]

> **14.** In Isaiah 8:17-18 below, underline the two actions Isaiah will take. Circle the two words that describe Isaiah and his children.
>
> I will wait for the Lord, who is hiding his face from the house of Jacob, and I will hope in him. Behold, I and the children whom the Lord has given me are signs and portents in Israel from the Lord of hosts.

They were signs of how to trust God as well as portents of what was to come.

Isaiah exhorts, "Consult God's instruction and the testimony of warning. If anyone does not speak according to this word, they have no light of dawn" (Isaiah 8:20 NIV). Indeed, those who ignore God's instruction and warning will behold "distress and darkness, the gloom of anguish. And they will be thrust into thick darkness" (Isaiah 8:22).

> **15.** ♥ (a) How are you following Isaiah's exhortation to consult God's instruction? (b) What's something that helps you do so?

## The Hope: The Promise of a Future Righteous King

But darkness was not the end of Judah's hope.

> **16.** In Isaiah 9:1-2 below, underline the two time periods. Circle the names of the three lands. Box what they will see and what will shine on them.
>
> In the former time he brought into contempt...Zebulun and...Naphtali, but in the latter time he has made glorious...Galilee...The people who walked in darkness have seen a great light; those who dwelt in a land of deep darkness, on them has light shone.

Assyria attacked the northern lands of Israel first (including the three you circled) and plunged them into the darkness of exile. But in the future, they would see "a great light" and rejoice (Isaiah 9:2-3). The oppressor's strength would be broken (verses 4-5).

> **17.** Read Isaiah 9:6. (a) Who will be born? (b) What will be on his shoulder? (c) What will he be called?

***Wonderful Counselor.*** People will wonder at his great wisdom and counsel.

***Mighty God.*** At the least it refers to God's might being with him, but every other instance of this name refers to God himself, including this nearby passage: "A remnant will return, the remnant of Jacob, to the mighty God" (Isaiah 10:21).

**Everlasting Father.** Sometimes kings referred to themselves as a "father" to their subjects, but never as such forever.

**Prince of Peace.** He will bring lasting peace.

> 18. Read Isaiah 9:7. (a) What will increase without end? (b) On whose throne will he sit? (c) With what two characteristics will he rule? (d) For how long will he rule? (e) What will accomplish all this?

The child will sit on David's throne, so he will be an anointed king (messiah). But the child theme begun in chapter 7 here transcends an earthly king.

## The Immediate Fulfillments

In 732 BC, Assyria destroyed Syria/Aram and killed its king. Israel's King Pekah was assassinated. Assyria plundered and exiled parts of Israel and became its new king's suzerain. All this was about three years after Isaiah's son was born and fulfilled Isaiah 8:3-4.

Israel later rebelled against Assyria; Assyria demolished Israel in 722 BC, about a decade after Isaiah told Ahaz, "Before the boy knows how to refuse the evil and choose the good, the land whose two kings you dread will be deserted" (Isaiah 7:16).

Yet Ahaz saw all this as due to his turning to Assyria and Assyria's gods. Ahaz met Assyria's king in Damascus, formerly the capital of Syria/Aram. There he saw an altar he admired. He told Uriah the priest to build him such an altar and put it in the temple. Ahaz shoved aside the Lord's altar to make room for the idol's altar. This idol had not saved Damascus from Assyria, but Ahaz embraced it anyway. Not only that, he planned to use the Lord's altar for divination—a practice God forbade.

Uriah the priest did not stop him. He allowed Ahaz to dismantle holy implements and oversee worship. Second Chronicles 28:1-4 lists Ahaz's actions:

> Ahaz...made metal images for the Baals, and he made offerings in the Valley of the Son of Hinnom and burned his sons as an offering...And he sacrificed and made offerings on the high places and on the hills and under every green tree.

Was trusting a human king over the divine King worth it?

> 19. (a) What did the king of Assyria do to Ahaz (2 Chronicles 28:20-21)? (b) Where did Ahaz turn next (verses 22-23)? (c) What did Ahaz do to the temple (verse 24)? (d) With what did he replace worship of God (verse 25)?

Ahaz rejected God and shut the temple doors. He died in 716/15 in his thirties, leaving his

### The Little Details
**Baylis on Prophecy:**

While prophets would give short-term predictions, called "signs," to verify their calling as God's messengers...their messages often contain a longer view down the tunnel of history. Note the following features: (1) *Connection.* Rarely is a prediction given that is detached from present events. The predictive element is there to spotlight God's ultimate plan and so to influence present conduct by awareness of ultimate concerns. (2) *Telescoping.* A long-term prediction is often fulfilled in several stages in the future, even though the prophecy seems to read as a single event. To the prophetic eye, the future is telescoped into one picture. This has been graphically illustrated by several mountain peaks off in the distance. In prophetic oracles those higher and more distant peaks seem a continuation of the first peak. In fact, they are. They deal with the same theme coming to pass in the future. As part of the same mountain range time gaps simply are not revealed.[10]

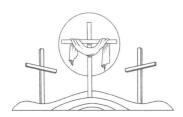

*The Use of Isaiah 9:1-2 in Matthew 4:15-16*

Professor Craig L. Blomberg notes that Isaiah 9:1-2 was originally fulfilled when exiles passed through Zebulun and Naphtali on their return to their hometowns. The light in that context was freedom from exile, whereas it was spiritual light in the context of the Messiah.

He writes, "Matthew recognized a short-term fulfillment during OT times but also saw a longer-term fulfillment in the coming of Jesus the Messiah. What began as physical liberation from the exile culminates in spiritual liberation in the messianic age."[11]

Isaiah warned of exile but gave hope in the promise of a child called Immanuel.

son Hezekiah to deal with the problems he left behind. The people refused to bury him in the tombs of the kings of Israel.

### The Lord Offers King Hezekiah a Sign

Hezekiah opened the doors of the temple and readied it for worship again. He tried to throw off Assyria's yoke, but Assyria struck back hard, overthrowing many cities on its way to Jerusalem and fulfilling Isaiah 8:8's prediction that Assyria would "sweep on into Judah, it will overflow and pass on, reaching even to the neck." Hezekiah prayed for deliverance. God sent Isaiah with a sign: In the third year, the land and Judah's remnant would again bear fruit (Isaiah 37:30-32). The Lord himself would defend the city (37:35).

That night, the angel of the Lord struck down 185,000 Assyrian soldiers (Isaiah 37:36).

Hezekiah trusted God and saw a miracle.

## The Word Was God

We left off with the story of the Lord miraculously delivering Hezekiah. Isaiah 38 tells of God miraculously healing Hezekiah of a fatal disease. They're high notes of hope fulfilled.

But Isaiah 39 reveals that Hezekiah's trust was imperfect. Envoys from Babylon arrived to hear about his healing. "God left him to himself, in order to test him and to know all that was in his heart" (2 Chronicles 32:31). Hezekiah treated the Babylonians as allies against Assyria and showed off his treasures. There's no record of him telling them about God.

Isaiah told Hezekiah that a future Babylonian king would take away all the treasures Hezekiah had showed them (Isaiah 39:5-7). Babylon would exile Judah just as Assyria exiled Israel. That announcement closes the second section of the book of Isaiah.

### God with Us Then

Isaiah warned of exile but gave hope in the promise of a child called Immanuel.

### The Reveal Continued

Two evil kings followed Hezekiah. Judah survived a little more than a century after Israel's fall. In 586 BC, Babylon stripped the palace and temple treasuries, and it exiled the inhabitants, just as Isaiah prophesied.

*The Second Temple's Day*

Isaiah's first son's name meant "a remnant shall return." Just as a remnant survived Assyria's attack, so a remnant survived Babylon's attack. In 538 BC, a remnant returned to Jerusalem to wait for the messianic child whom Isaiah promised.

*Jesus's Day*

Five hundred years passed, and the people still waited for the Prince of Peace who would sit on David's throne in an everlasting rule, as Isaiah 9:1-7 promised.

## The Virgin and Child

Matthew's description of Jesus's birth includes a point important to his Jewish audience.

> **20.** Read Matthew 1:18-25. (a) How did the angel say Mary had conceived (verse 20)? (b) From what will the child save people (verse 21)? (c) What did Matthew say her conception as a virgin fulfilled (verse 23)?

**The Little Details**
*Fulfillments of Isaiah 9:3-5*

Isaiah 9:3-4 says that the coming of the light will bring great joy and enlarge the nation, breaking the burdensome yoke of their oppressor as when God through Gideon broke Midian's yoke with a tiny army. Isaiah 9:5 says battle gear will burn.

*Great joy:* In Luke 2:10, the angel tells the shepherds he brings "good news of great joy" when he announces Jesus's birth.

*Enlarge the nation:* Jesus brought many into the kingdom of God (Revelation 5:9-10).

*Break the oppressor's yoke:* Jesus will destroy the devil, who had the power of death and thereby enslaved people (Hebrews 2:14-15).

*Burn battle gear:* Fire from heaven will defeat Satan (Revelation 20:9-10).

Matthew says Mary's conception as a virgin fulfilled Isaiah 7:14: "Behold, the virgin shall conceive and bear a son, and shall call his name Immanuel." He explains the name's meaning from Isaiah 8:10: "God is with us." *Jesus* means "the LORD saves."[12] Matthew means that the woman and infant who were signs of Judah's salvation in Isaiah's day foreshadowed Mary and infant Jesus, who were signs of a greater salvation (Luke 2:11-12). The prophecy was predictive to Ahaz, but its fulfillment was typological prophecy. Craig L. Blomberg in the *Commentary on the New Testament Use of the Old Testament* explains:

> Matthew recognized that Isaiah's son fulfilled the dimension of the prophecy that required a child to be born in the immediate future. But the larger, eschatological context, especially of Isa. 9:1-7, depicted a son, never clearly distinguished from Isaiah's, who would be a divine, messianic king. That dimension was fulfilled in Jesus...who was unequivocally born to a young woman of marriageable age, but to a woman who also was a virgin at the time of the conception. Whether or not Matthew was aware of any previous interpretation of Isa. 7:14 as referring to a sexually chaste woman, the "coincidence" of Jesus being born of a virgin was too striking not to be divinely intended.[13]

Typological prophecies are always fulfilled by something greater. The woman in Isaiah's day was a virgin at the time of the prophecy; Mary was a virgin at the time of conception. The temporary salvation of Judah's people from enemies foreshadowed the final salvation of God's people from sin (Matthew 1:21). The child in Isaiah's day was a sign that God was with his people; the child Jesus was literally God with his people (John 1:14).

## The Land of Zebulun and Naphtali

Turn now to just prior to the start of Jesus's public ministry.

> **21.** Read Matthew 4:12-17. (a) To where did Jesus withdraw? (b) He moved from Nazareth in Galilee to Capernaum. What areas were near Capernaum (verse 13)?

Matthew says Jesus living first in Galilee and then by Zebulun and Naphtali fulfilled Isaiah 9:1-2. In Day 2's lesson, we read that Assyria plunged these three lands into the gloom, anguish, and deep darkness of exile. But Isaiah promised that "in the latter time" the people there would see "a great light" that would shine on them. By living there and beginning his public ministry there, Jesus honored the territories that Assyria had dishonored. Jesus as the light of the world shone on them (John 1:4-9).

The child in Isaiah's day was a sign that God was with his people; the child Jesus was literally God with his people.

## The Little Details

*Oswalt on "Mighty God":*

Such extravagant titling was not normal for Israelite kings. It is an expression of a belief that the one who would be born to rule over Israel in justice and righteousness would be possessed of divine attributes. All of this points to a remarkable congruence with the Immanuel prophecy. Somehow a virgin-born child would demonstrate that God is with us (7:14). Now he says "to us a child is born" (Isaiah including himself with his people in their deliverance as he did in their sin [6:1]) and this child has those traits which manifest the presence of God in our midst. Surely this child (also described in 11:1-5) is presented to us as the ultimate fulfillment of the Immanuel sign.[15]

## To Us a Son Is Given

We move now to the heart of the oracle, Isaiah 9:6-7 (see sidebar on page 119 for verses 3-5).

*For to us a child is born.* In Luke 2:11, the angel told the shepherds, "For unto you is born this day in the city of David a Savior."

*To us a son is given.* John 3:16 reads, "God...gave his only Son" to bring us eternal life.

*And the government shall be upon his shoulder.* We've already seen that Jesus is King forever, which puts the government on his shoulders.

*And his name shall be called Wonderful Counselor.* People were astonished by Jesus's authority and wisdom (Matthew 9:8; Mark 6:2). Even his detractors said he taught truthfully, not caring about people's opinions and not swayed by appearances (Matthew 22:16). He is "wisdom from God" (1 Corinthians 1:30).

*Mighty God.* Every other time the Old Testament uses this title, it is a title for God (for instance, Isaiah 10:21).[14] The New Testament tells us how it applies to Jesus.

> **22.** (a) Who was the Word (John 1:1)? (b) Where was the Word in the beginning (verse 2)? (c) What did the Word become (verse 14)? (d) Of what is his glory (verse 14)?

Hebrews 2:14 says that since the children Jesus was bringing into God's family "share in flesh and blood, he himself likewise partook of the same things." He was made like us.

*Everlasting Father.* This could be another divine title, or *Father* might be used as a substitute for *King* (as David called King Saul "my father" in 1 Samuel 24:11). Hebrews 2:13 applies Isaiah 8:17-18 (NIV) to Jesus: "I will put my trust in him. Here am I, and the children the LORD has given me." Just as the trust that Isaiah and his children showed were signs to wayward people around them, so the trust that Jesus and his children showed were signs to the wayward people around them. Isaiah and his children were portents of Jesus and the children of God.

As to everlasting, Jesus "was in the beginning with God" (John 1:2).

> **23.** In Revelation 1:18 below, circle how long Jesus said he would be alive.
>
> I died, and behold I am alive forevermore, and I have the keys of Death.

*Prince of Peace.* Jesus makes peace with God possible: "Since we have been justified by faith, we have peace with God through our Lord Jesus Christ" (Romans 5:1).

> **24.** In Colossians 1:19-20 below, underline what dwelt in Jesus. Box what he reconciled to himself. Circle what the blood of his cross made.
>
> For in him all the fullness of God was pleased to dwell, and through him to reconcile to himself all things, whether on earth or in heaven, making peace by the blood of his cross.

**25.** (a) According to Romans 5:10, what is our status before we are saved by Jesus's death? (b) What reconciles us to God? (c) What is our natural response (verse 11)?

**26.** ♥ Write a one-sentence prayer rejoicing in your reconciliation with God.

*He will reign on David's throne…establishing and upholding it with justice and righteousness…forever.* He is Messiah, the righteous King who will reign forever.

## Day 5

### The Stone of Offense

We skipped a passage in Isaiah 8 that Jesus fulfilled. Let's look at that now.

**27.** (a) What did the Lord warn Isaiah not to do (Isaiah 8:11)? (b) How should Isaiah be different (verse 12)? (c) Whom should he honor and hold in awe (verse 13)?

In Isaiah's day, conspiracies and assassinations abounded, bringing uncertainty and dread. But Isaiah did not need to fear the future. Instead, he could honor and fear the LORD of hosts who had more power than any conspirators.

**28.** (a) List what the Lord would become to the two kingdoms (Isaiah 8:14). (b) In your list, circle the one positive item. (c) What would many do with the "stone" (verse 15)?

The Lord is a sanctuary to those who trust him, but a stone of offense that causes stumbling to those who don't. Jesus is this stone (Luke 2:34; 1 Peter 2:8; Romans 9:33).

He is Messiah, the righteous King who will reign forever.

The Lord is a sanctuary to those who trust him, but a stone of offense that causes stumbling to those who don't.

## The Little Details
### *The Use of Isaiah 8:17-18 in Hebrews 2:13*

Isaiah 8:17-18 reads, "I will hope in him. Behold, I and the children whom the LORD has given me are signs and portents."

Hebrews 2:13 says Jesus fulfilled this, just as he fulfilled the surrounding messianic verses. Just as Isaiah put his trust in the Lord, so Jesus put his trust in the Father. Just as Isaiah had children whom the Lord gave him, so Jesus had children whom the Lord gave him—all those he brought into God's family to be adopted as children of God.

Professor George H. Guthrie writes, "At John 6:37; 10:27-29; 17:6 Jesus says that his followers are given to him by the Father, and this seems to parallel Isa. 8:18 quite closely."[16]

29. ♥ My friend feared never marrying. Ahaz feared losing his position and life. When you face fear, how can you trust the Lord like Isaiah without stumbling like Ahaz?

## The Mighty God in Hebrews

Let's look at the first chapter of Hebrews.

30. In Hebrews 1:1-2 below, circle whom God has spoken through in the last days. Underline what God appointed his Son. Double-underline what God did through the Son.

> Long ago…God spoke to our fathers by the prophets, but in these last days he has spoken to us by his Son, whom he appointed the heir of all things, through whom also he created the world.

God created the world through his Son. The Son existed before creation.

31. In Hebrews 1:3 below, underline what the Son is. Circle what he upholds.

> He is the radiance of the glory of God and the exact imprint of his nature, and he upholds the universe by the word of his power.

32. In Hebrews 1:3-4 below, underline where the Son sat. Circle what he is to angels.

> After making purification for sins, he sat down at the right hand of the Majesty on high, having become as much superior to angels as the name he has inherited is more excellent than theirs.

33. (a) What does Hebrews 1:8 call the Son? (b) How long will his throne last? (c) Why did God anoint him (verse 9)?

## God with Us Still

*God with Us Today*
The apostle Paul explains how Jesus as God took on human form.

34. In Philippians 2:5-8 (NIV) below, circle who Jesus was in nature. Underline what he did not use to his own advantage. Box the likeness in which he was made when born to Mary. Double-underline the appearance in which he was found.

> In your relationships with one another, have the same mindset as Christ Jesus: Who, being in very nature God, did not consider equality with God something

to be used to his own advantage; rather, he made himself nothing by taking the very nature of a servant, being made in human likeness. And being found in appearance as a man, he humbled himself by becoming obedient to death—even death on a cross!

Jesus's actions should affect our own lives.

35. ♥ (a) In Philippians 2:5-8 above, what mindset should we have in our relationships? (b) How did Jesus make himself nothing? (c) How can you humble yourself in a relationship like Jesus did?

By taking the form of a human, Jesus was temporarily in a form lower than that of angels (Hebrews 2:9). But he is now crowned with glory and honor, which he amply deserves.

### God with Us Forever

In Isaiah 48:12, the Lord said, "I am he; I am the *first*, and I am the *last*." In Revelation 21:6, the Lord said, "I am the *Alpha* and the *Omega*, the *beginning* and the *end*."

In Revelation 22:13, Jesus said, "I am the *Alpha* and the *Omega*, the *first* and the *last*, the *beginning* and the *end*." Jesus gave himself the same titles that the Lord God gave himself. That is why Jesus is called Immanuel, "God is with us."

36. ♥ Read Revelation 1:9-20. What stands out to you the most?

### God with Me Now

Luke records a song Mary wrote about being pregnant with Messiah Jesus. The song is known as the Magnificat. It's a beautiful song of praise.

Turn to Luke 1:46-55 and read it. **Pray** the Magnificat to the Lord in worship.

**Praise** God for something you saw of his character this week. **Confess** anything that convicted you. **Ask** for help to do something God's Word calls you to do. **Thank** God for something you learned this week.

---

## The Little Details
### Poythress on "Last Days":

Hebrews [1:1-3] labels the time of Christ's coming "these last days," because in them, "by his Son," God has brought to fulfillment the plans articulated and foreshadowed throughout the Old Testament. "For *all* the promises of God find their *Yes* in him" (2 Cor. 1:20).

So, in a broad sense, the entirety of the record in the Gospels constitutes a theophany. More than the other Gospels, John explicitly uses language linked to theophanic themes: "And the Word became flesh and *dwelt* among us, and we have seen his *glory*, *glory* as of the only Son from the Father, full of grace and truth" (John 1:14). The Greek word for *dwell* in this verse...is not the most common one, but one linked to the Old Testament tabernacle. The word for *glory* has links with the glory of God that appears in the cloud, the cloud that settles on the tabernacle (Ex. 40:34-38)...

When Jesus comes, God appears. Jesus is the final form of God's presence among human beings.[17]

# The Heart and Art of Worship

We closed this week's study reading Mary's song, the Magnificat, and I don't know about you, but when I read her words and hear her heart, an overwhelming sense of awe and wonder wells up within me. With every fiber of her being, she proclaims, "My soul magnifies the Lord, and my spirit rejoices in God my Savior." I so want this to be my song. I want my soul...my heart, my life, my words, my works...every fiber of my being to magnify and glorify the Lord.

I've drawn since I was a little girl, but being rather shy, I was more of a mouse-in-the-corner kind of artist who never signed her name and wanted no glory. It made me happy when someone admired my work, but I was even happier when they didn't know it was me who drew it. When I first realized that my ability to draw was a gift from God, I remember praying and asking the Lord if he would allow me to use my art in some way to be a blessing to others and, most importantly, to bring glory to him. This prayer changed my perspective. My art was no longer about me at all, but instead, it became all about him.

God gives us our creative gifts, talents, and abilities as a means to express our faith and to be his hands, his heart, and his voice to the world. When we spend creative time with God in his Word through Bible art and journaling, our hearts are transformed, and our lives glorify the Lord even more. When we create an inspirational post on social media, our words magnify the character of God and give people hope and encouragement. When we create a meal for a person in need, we're sharing the love of God in a tangible way, and people are blessed. However we creatively express our faith—through our life, our words, and our works—God is glorified, and we can sing along with Mary: "My soul magnifies the Lord, and my spirit rejoices in God my Savior."

*Karla*

## Chapter 8

# Isaiah 52–53
## Jesus the Suffering Servant

The hope of being made righteous

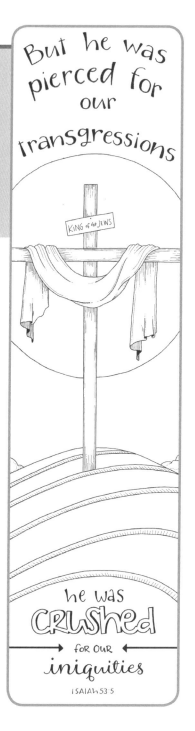

But he was pierced for our transgressions

KING of the JEWS

he was CRUSHED → FOR OUR ← iniquities

ISAIAH 53:5

## Day 1

## Two Servants

One summer when I was about 13, my girlfriend Linda and I lay on towels at the beach, listening to the rhythmic roar of the green waves and the loud call of seagulls. I asked her how to get to heaven. She told me if the good outweighed the bad, you went to heaven, but if the bad outweighed the good, you went to hell. My dismay must have shown on my face because she raised up on one arm and laughed. "Don't worry!" she said. "You'll go to heaven." I turned my head away and thought, *She doesn't know how bad I really am.*

That fall, we ran into one of Linda's friends in front of the glass entrance of a store. Rich told us that Jesus died to save us from our sins so that we could go to heaven. He said we needed to pray to make Jesus Lord of our lives. I said, "You've got to be kidding. Moses and David were great leaders, and everybody liked them. One of them might save people. But Jesus? He was just some shepherd who liked children, but he didn't get along with people, so adults killed him. How could he save anyone?"

Some months later, I got hold of a paperback New Testament with *Good News for Modern Man* on the cover. I started reading it that day. I discovered Rich was right. Jesus the Son of God died so that our sins could be forgiven and we could dwell with God eternally.

But it wasn't until I later read the Old Testament that the reasons started making sense. The prophecies we'll read today drove into my heart the magnitude of Jesus's sacrifice. And they amazed me with the proof that God planned it all before even creating us.

**The Reveal**

From the beginning, the Lord revealed that rescuing humans involved suffering.

*Eve's Day*
Eve's offspring—her seed—would crush the serpent's head, but at a cost: The serpent would strike the serpent crusher's heel.

*Abraham's Day*
Abraham's near-sacrifice of Isaac foreshadowed how Abraham's offspring—his seed—would be a blessing to all nations. The ram that took Isaac's place revealed that one life could substitute for another.

## The Little Details
### *Isaiah*

The book of Isaiah is the first book of the Major Prophets. Isaiah delivered his messages between 740 BC and 681 BC. He arranged the material later (which accounts for the material not being in chronological order).

Baylis writes, "Isaiah has long been considered the prince of prophets. In fact, his access to kings suggests a noble birth."[1]

There are a few prose sections, but most of the book is written in the style of Hebrew poetry. Isaiah uses poetic devices such as parallelism, figures of speech, and vivid imagery.

How will he strengthen and uphold them? The answer is found in four passages called servant songs.

### *Moses's Day*

The night the Hebrews escaped from Egypt, the Passover lamb took the place of Hebrew firstborn sons. Later, animal sacrifices atoned for people's sin so that the Lord could dwell among them.

### *David's Day*

For David, the path to the crown was through suffering. He wrote psalms that described his suffering and God's faithfulness.

### *The Major Prophets' Day*

Isaiah proclaimed that Israel (both kingdoms) was unrighteous. He showed the weaknesses of three kings and the need for God's first solution: a future righteous king. He prophesied that Assyria would exile the northern kingdom, and later, Babylon would exile the southern kingdom.

## God's Word to Us

In Isaiah 40–55, the Lord addresses the future exiles from Judah who fear that he has abandoned them because of their sin. Babylon has crushed Assyria and is the new superpower. Isaiah 41:8-10 comforts the exiles with these words:

> But you, Israel, my servant, Jacob, whom I have chosen...you whom I took from the ends of the earth...saying to you, "You are my servant, I have chosen you and not cast you off"; fear not, for I am with you; be not dismayed, for I am your God; I will strengthen you, I will help you, I will uphold you with my righteous right hand.

How will he strengthen and uphold them? The answer is found in four passages called servant songs. It is God's second solution to Israel's sin problem.

 Take a moment to pray for insight as you read God's Word.

1. ♥ Read Isaiah 42:1-9; 49:1-12; 50:4-9; and 52:13–53:12. Note that the Lord called the righteous servant *Israel* in Isaiah 49:3. (a) What stands out to you? Why? (b) Is this the first time you've read the servant songs? ☐ Yes ☐ No

The Israelites feared they weren't good enough to dwell with God.

2. ♥ Have you feared not being good enough to go to heaven? If so, how did that feel?

# A Walk with Christ—Snapshots for Serenity

Photographs capture inspiring moments. In a similar way, snapshots of Scripture and God's goodness will bolster your faith when suffering shatters your tranquility. Spend time revisiting the images of Christ's peace:

**Look to the Cross:** "And let us run with perseverance the race marked out for us, fixing our eyes on Jesus, the pioneer and perfecter of faith" (Hebrews 12:1-2 NIV). When you feel you cannot take another step, retrace Christ's last days, and gain strength for your next steps. Like Jesus, look to the victory ahead and, by faith, write the results you are praying for.

**Look at what you have, not what you don't:** "We are hard pressed on every side, but not crushed; perplexed, but not in despair; persecuted, but not abandoned; struck down, but not destroyed" (2 Corinthians 4:8-9 NIV). This could read: "You are in a vise grip of pressure, but it won't flatten you; you are at a loss to make sense of it all, having doubts but not in utter despair, because God will give an alternative route; you are hunted down and harassed, but God is always with you; you have been thrown to the ground but not killed." It could be worse! List what is going right.

**Look to help others:** "Praise be to the God...the Father of compassion and the God of all comfort, who comforts us in all our troubles, so that we can comfort those in any trouble with the comfort we ourselves receive from God" (2 Corinthians 1:3-4 NIV). List ways God has comforted you. Pass on these to another.

**Look away from pain:** Jesus replied, "No one who puts a hand to the plow and looks back is fit for service" (Luke 9:62 NIV). Christ discerned these people were struggling with doubt about following him. For their own good, they needed to step nearer the Lord to be distracted from their pain. When I am in turmoil, I play a song on repeat which was written by my friend Teresa Muller based on Luke 9:62. It reminds me to keep my hand on the plow and my eyes on Jesus. What ministry assignments require your full focus?

**Look to replenish:** "Elijah did as the LORD told him and camped beside Kerith Brook...The ravens brought him bread and meat each morning and evening, and he drank from the brook" (1 Kings 17:5-6 NLT). God sent his weary prophet away from the battle and his enemies. Plan a holistic treat such as a spa day, nap, healthy meal, fun workout, or a day near water to elevate your mood. To release happy endorphins, do the things that have brought joy in the past to gain joy today. [2]

**Look for purpose in the pain:** When Jesus went to Gethsemane, he said: "'My soul is very sorrowful, even to death; remain here, and watch with me.' And going a little farther he fell on his face and prayed, saying, 'My Father, if it be possible, let this cup pass from me; nevertheless, not as I will, but as you will'" (Matthew 26:38-39). Take extended time away with God to sort out emotions, seek answers, or gain comfort.

**Look for ways to smile and praise:** "Why, my soul, are you downcast? Why so disturbed within me? Put your hope in God, for I will yet praise him" (Psalm 42:5 NIV). When *downcast* (depressed, discouraged, despairing) and *disturbed* (having nagging thoughts), the solution is to praise God. Put on uplifting music and read the Psalms, noting verses that inspire praise.

An expanded version of this devotional, *Verses for Turbulent Times,* is at www.DiscoveringTheBibleSeries.com.

*Pam*

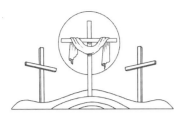

**The Little Details**

*Figure 1: The Fearful Servant, Israel*

Isaiah 40–55 talks about four figures. The first is the future exiled Israelites, whom Isaiah calls Israel. They are frightened because it seems as if the promises of God didn't come through. This was because they held three false beliefs about God's promises.

First, they believed Solomon was the offspring of David whose throne would last forever, despite the Lord's words to Solomon: "If you turn aside from following me, you or your children…I will cut off Israel from the land" (1 Kings 9:6-7).

Second, they believed God wouldn't exile them if they offered sin sacrifices. But those didn't cover most intentional sin, and they ignored Moses's warning that breaking their covenant with God would result in exile.

Third, they thought that Babylon's idols had proved stronger than God since Babylon had defeated them.

# A Future Righteous Servant

Here's the outline of Isaiah that we're using:

    I. The Problem: Israel Is Unrighteous (Isaiah 1–5)

    II. God's First Solution: A Future Righteous King (Isaiah 6–39)

    III. God's Second Solution: A Future Righteous Servant (Isaiah 40–55)

    IV. God's Third Solution: A Future Righteous People (Isaiah 56–66)[3]

We looked at sections I and II already, and we discovered that section II announced that Assyria's exile of the north was just the beginning. One day, Babylon would be a superpower and would exile Judah.

Section III addressed the future frightened exiles and revealed the coming of a future righteous servant. In this section, the northern kingdom no longer exists, and Isaiah uses the names *Jacob* and *Israel* to refer to all the descendants of the man Jacob whom God renamed Israel. These chapters show God's grace through four figures.

1. *The Fearful Servant, Israel.* The future exiled Israelites fear that God has abandoned them forever, and the Lord assures them he has not.

2. *The Gentile Deliverer, Cyrus.* God tells the future exiles that he will call a Gentile named Cyrus to bring them back to the land.

3. *The Fallen Queen, Babylon.* God denounces Babylon's idols as powerless and foretells the fall of the mighty empire as proof.

4. *The Suffering, Righteous Servant.* Four servant songs describe a future righteous servant who will suffer and solve Israel's spiritual problem.

This lesson's sidebars describe how Isaiah develops the first three figures and what each meant to the exiles. Here, we'll look at the fourth figure, the suffering, righteous servant. Since we have a lot to cover, we'll discover how Jesus fulfilled each one as we go.

### Servant Song 1 (Isaiah 42:1-9)

Matthew 12:15-21 quotes Isaiah 42:1-3 and applies it to Jesus.

> **3.** In Isaiah 42:1 below, circle the one whom the Lord beholds. Underline the Lord's reaction to his chosen servant. Box what the Lord puts on his servant.
>
> Behold my servant, whom I uphold,
>     my chosen, in whom my soul delights;
> I have put my Spirit upon him;
>     he will bring forth justice to the nations.

Jesus said he came "not to be served but to serve" (Matthew 20:28), fulfilling the first part of this verse. When he was baptized, he saw "the Spirit of God descending like a dove and coming to rest on him; and behold, a voice from heaven said, 'This is my beloved Son, with whom I am well pleased,'" fulfilling the rest of the verse (Matthew 3:16-17).

Here are a few more ways that Jesus fulfilled the first servant song. The servant would not break a bruised reed; Jesus was tender toward "tax collectors and sinners" (Isaiah 42:3;

Matthew 9:11-12). The servant would be righteous; Jesus was "tempted as we are, yet without sin" (Isaiah 42:6; Hebrews 4:15). The servant would be given as a covenant; Jesus gave himself to inaugurate the new covenant (Isaiah 42:6; Luke 22:20). The servant would open blind eyes; Jesus healed the blind (Isaiah 42:7; Mark 10:46-52).

## Servant Song 2 (Isaiah 49:1-12)

The second servant song's speaker is identified as the Lord's servant in verse 5.

> **4.** (a) Whose attention does the servant want (Isaiah 49:1)? (b) From where did the Lord call and name the servant?

The servant calls to the "coastlands" (Gentiles); Jesus sent his disciples to all the world (Acts 1:8). The Lord called and named the servant before birth, indicating he is an individual and reminding us of two other children the Lord called and named before birth: the child Immanuel (Isaiah 7:14) and the child Mighty God (Isaiah 9:6). Likewise, the Lord called Jesus from the womb of his mother and named him before his birth (Matthew 1:20-21,25; Luke 1:31; 2:21).

> **5.** In Isaiah 49:2 below, circle what the servant's mouth is like. Underline where the Lord hid the servant (lines 2, 4). Box what he made his servant (line 3).
>
> He made my mouth like a sharp sword;
>     in the shadow of his hand he hid me;
> he made me a polished arrow;
>     in his quiver he hid me away.

The servant's weapon is his words. They are judgments that pierce both near ("sword") and far ("arrow"). The collective Israel has unclean lips, but this servant's mouth contains the Lord's judgments. Jesus said the Father gave all judgment to him (John 5:22). Revelation 1:16 depicts the resurrected Jesus as having "a sharp two-edged sword" coming from his mouth. Revelation 19:13,15 calls Jesus "The Word of God" and pictures him with "a sharp sword" coming from his mouth.

> **6.** In Isaiah 49:3 below, circle the servant's name. Underline what he will do.
>
> And he said to me, "You are my servant,
>     Israel, in whom I will be glorified."

Verse 1 indicates the speaker is an individual, so why would the Lord call him "Israel"? We discovered earlier that the Lord called the people Israel "my firstborn son" (Exodus 4:22). Matthew 2:15 revealed that this Israel was a type of God's Son, Jesus.

Something similar happens in the second servant song. Exodus 32:13 calls the man Israel God's servant. Isaiah 41:8 calls the exiles collectively, "Israel, my servant, Jacob." Both were flawed servants who were types of the future righteous servant. Oswalt explains:

> It is important to note that the term *Israel* is used not so much as a name as it is a parallel term to *servant*. It is as though the Lord had said, "You are my Israel, in whom I will be glorified." Thus it is the function, not the identity, of Israel

## The Little Details
### *Figure 2: The Gentile Deliverer, Cyrus*

God assures the frightened future exiles that he will redeem them and bring them back to the land (Isaiah 43:1-6). He tells them, "You are precious in my eyes, and honored, and I love you" (verse 4). He will bring their offspring back from exile (verses 5-6).

The Lord reminds them of the exodus from Egypt, but says, "Remember not the former things" because "I am doing a new thing" in how he will bring them back (43:16-19).

Just the idea of a return from exile is a new thing. In those days, exiles never returned. Conquerors assimilated exiles into their own culture.

The other new thing is that the Lord will anoint a future Gentile named Cyrus to defeat Babylon and send the exiles home to rebuild Jerusalem and the temple (Isaiah 44:28). He says of Cyrus, "I call you by your name, I name you, though you do not know me...I equip you, though you do not know me" (45:4-5).

### Figure 3: The Fallen Queen, Babylon

God denounces Babylon's idols as powerless (Isaiah 46:1-7). Babylon did not conquer Israel because her idols were strong. Babylon conquered Israel because Israel abandoned God (47:6). To prove it, God foretells not only the coming exile, but also the deliverance from exile by Cyrus and the fall of mighty Babylon (48:3-5).

To drive home the point, the Lord presents four cases against idols, arguing for the folly of bowing to wood and metal (41:21-29; 43:8-13; 44:6-20; 45:20–46:7). He declares himself the only God (46:9).

The Lord says he exiled Israel to refine Israel "in the furnace of affliction" (48:10). Israel's sins had profaned God's name; Israel gave God's glory to idols (48:11). Nonetheless, they shall go out from Babylon with a shout of joy, for "The LORD has redeemed his servant Jacob!" (48:20).

- - - - - - - - - - - - - - - -

Although the servant will seem to have labored in vain, in "a day of salvation" the Lord will help him.

- - - - - - - - - - - - - - - -

that is emphasized. This Servant is going to function as Israel. What was Israel's task, as indicated throughout the entire book, from ch. 2 onward? To be the means whereby the nations could come to God. But how could a nation that could not find its own way to God, a blind, deaf, rebellious nation, show anyone else the way? This is the dilemma that the Servant has come to solve. He will be for Israel, and the world, what Israel could not be.[4]

The servant will glorify the Lord (Isaiah 49:3); Jesus glorified the Father on earth and in the crucifixion (Mark 2:12; Matthew 9:6-8; John 21:19).

7. (a) In Isaiah 49:4, how does the servant describe his labor? (b) From whom will come his recompense (reward)?

The servant's work will appear frustrated, as if nothing came of it. But he will trust the Lord to reward him. Isaiah will reveal more about this in later chapters. For now, it suffices to note that Jesus was at times dismayed over his disciples' inability to understand his teaching, particularly about servanthood and his coming death. At Jesus's crucifixion, his disciples wondered if Jesus's work had come to naught.

8. ♥ When we feel as if we've labored in vain, how does it help to take the servant's attitude of waiting for God to reward us?

9. (a) What is the servant's purpose (Isaiah 49:5)? (b) What even greater purpose will he serve (verse 6)?

It is too small a thing for the servant to merely bring Israelites back to the Lord. The servant will bring salvation "to the end of the earth." Acts 13:47 quotes Isaiah 49:6 and applies it to Jesus's mission to the world.

10. (a) How will people treat the servant initially (Isaiah 49:7)? (b) Yet what will kings and princes eventually do? (c) Why?

God will use the righteous servant to redeem Israel. As we discovered previously, many despised and mocked Jesus. But there will come a day when "at the name of Jesus every knee should bow, in heaven and on earth and under the earth, and every tongue confess that Jesus Christ is Lord, to the glory of God the Father" (Philippians 2:10-11).

Although the servant will seem to have labored in vain, in "a day of salvation" the Lord will help him (Isaiah 49:8)—the day of salvation that Jesus's death inaugurated (2 Corinthians 6:2).

## Day 3

# A Future Suffering Servant

Keep in mind that today's passages were written long before Jesus was born. Baylis writes, "No one can claim that the prediction was made after the fact, as we possess copies of Isaiah that are actually older than the birth of Jesus of Nazareth."[5]

### Servant Song 3 (Isaiah 50:4-9)

Isaiah 50:10 identifies the speaker in Isaiah 50:4-9 as the Lord's servant.

11. (a) In Isaiah 50:4, what kind of tongue will the Lord God give the servant? (b) What will he know how to do? (c) What will the Lord God do "morning by morning"? (d) How will the speaker respond (verse 5)?

Fearful servant Israel had unclean lips, but the righteous servant will have a tongue that teaches and sustains. When Jesus at age 12 sat among the teachers at the temple, "all who heard him were amazed at his understanding and his answers" (Luke 2:47). Later, when he set out with the good news, "the crowds were astonished at his teaching, for he was teaching them as one who had authority, and not as their scribes" (Matthew 7:28-29).

12. (a) How will the servant respond to the Lord's teaching (Isaiah 50:5)? (b) Summarize what obedience will involve (verse 6).

Fearful servant Israel turned away from the Lord God's teaching. But the righteous servant would obey, even when it meant suffering. Jesus obeyed the Father, even to death. The devil tempted him just as he tempted the people Israel (see chapter 1 sidebars). But where the collective Israel failed, Jesus prevailed.

The Gospels show how Jesus fulfilled Isaiah 50:6. Pilate had Jesus's back flogged (John 19:1). The Jewish leaders spat on him, struck him, and slapped him (Matthew 26:67). The Roman soldiers struck him and spat on him (Matthew 27:30).

13. In Isaiah 50:7 below, circle who helps the servant. Underline the two things that will not happen to him (lines 2, 4). Double underline what he did with his face (line 3).

> But the Lord GOD helps me;
>     therefore I have not been disgraced;
> therefore I have set my face like a flint,
>     and I know that I shall not be put to shame.

To me, this is one of the most powerful verses in the Old Testament. The Lord God helps

## The Little Details

### Sklar on Sin:

The essence of sin is to break the Lord's laws, instead of keeping them. The results of sin are always catastrophic, both for sinners and for the world: for sinners, because their relationship with the Lord, their King and Creator, is now ruptured, and alienation replaces warm fellowship; for the world, because sin destroys the type of community the Lord intended, one in which people experience his love, joy, peace, goodness and justice. Sin is an acid that mars and destroys whatever it touches. The Lord is not being a killjoy by forbidding sin; he is being a loving Saviour.[6]

---

The righteous servant would obey, even when it meant suffering.

---

## The Little Details
### *Hunter and Wellum on the Old and New Covenants:*

This covenant, often called "the old covenant," although given by God, also points beyond itself to something greater. In itself it was insufficient because it foreshadowed what was necessary to save us, but it did not provide that salvation in full.

...In God's plan, the covenant with Israel through Moses—the old covenant—was intended to be temporary as part of God's unfolding plan...It graciously allowed God to dwell in Israel's midst as their Covenant Lord, but it also revealed the need for a greater covenant tied to a greater mediator and sacrifice. As part of God's plan, the old covenant served several purposes: it revealed the hideous nature of human sin (Rom. 7:13), it unveiled the greatness of God's grace, and it prophetically anticipated the righteousness of God in the gospel (Rom. 3:21) by serving as a guardian to lead us to the promised seed of Adam and the true son of Abraham, Jesus Christ (Gal. 3:19–4:7).[7]

him, so he knows that in the end he will be neither disgraced nor ashamed. He hardens his resolve.

And that is what Jesus did: "When the days drew near for him to be taken up, he [Jesus] set his face to go to Jerusalem" (Luke 9:51). Hebrews 12:2 explains more: "Jesus...for the joy that was set before him endured the cross, despising the shame."

> **14.** (a) In Isaiah 50:8, who is near the servant? (b) Because of that, what does he ask?

Jesus did indeed let his enemies come near him. But he knew that the Lord God would vindicate him in the resurrection and at the judgment.

> **15.** (a) In Isaiah 50:9, who helps the righteous servant? (b) What should that stop others from doing? (c) What will happen to the righteous servant's accusers?

The Pharisees declared Jesus guilty of breaking their laws, of blasphemy, and of claiming to be a king at odds with Rome. They falsely accused him. They are gone.

> **16.** ♥ God speaks in Isaiah 50:10. (a) Do you fear the Lord and obey the voice of his servant, Jesus? (b) If so, what should you do in times of darkness?

### Servant Song 4 (Isaiah 52:13–53:12)

And now we come to the most magnificent of the servant songs.

### *The Servant's Work*

> **17.** In Isaiah 52:13 below, circle how the servant shall act. Underline the result.
>
> Behold, my servant shall act wisely;
>     he shall be high and lifted up,
>     and shall be exalted.

The Hebrew translated "act wisely" or "prosper" means he'll succeed, despite the contrary appearances of Isaiah 49:4. In the end, he will be "high and lifted up," words Isaiah uses elsewhere only of God (Isaiah 6:1).

When the Roman soldiers lifted Jesus on the cross, his mission appeared to have failed. He had not defeated Rome and established an earthly kingdom. But God raised him from the dead and "exalted him at his right hand as Leader and Savior" (Acts 5:31). Because he took "the form of a servant...becoming obedient to the point of death, even death on a cross...God has highly exalted him and bestowed on him the name that is above every name" (Philippians 2:7-9).

**18.** (a) What astonished many (Isaiah 52:14)? (b) What will the servant do (verse 15)?

In Matthew 27:26-31, the soldiers flogged Jesus, which ripped off skin. A crown of thorns pierced his head and face. They beat his head with a staff. Finally, they nailed his wrists and feet to wooden beams. "His appearance was so marred," he did not look like a king.

But his blood sprinkled the earth, just as the priests sprinkled blood in front of the curtain that blocked the way to Most Holy Place (Leviticus 4:6). Kings have shut their mouths in amazement, including the astonished King Festus (Acts 26:19-29) and all kings who have come to God through Christ. Those who previously had not known the things of God understood as the gospel spread (Isaiah 52:15; Romans 15:20-21).

### The Servant's Rejection

Isaiah 53:1-3 describe the servant's rejection. In these verses, "we" is Isaiah and his hearers. "He" and the "arm of the LORD" are the servant.

Isaiah 53:1 reads, "Who has believed what he has heard from us? And to whom has the arm of the LORD been revealed?" The message went out and the servant was revealed, but not all believed. John wrote that the people who saw the signs Jesus did but wouldn't believe in him fulfilled Isaiah 53:1 (John 12:38). Paul wrote that those who heard the gospel but didn't obey it also fulfilled it (Romans 10:16).

**19.** How was Isaiah 53:2 fulfilled in Mark 6:1-3 below?

> He...came to his hometown...Many who heard him were astonished, saying, "Where did this man get these things? What is the wisdom given to him? How are such mighty works done by his hands? Is not this the carpenter, the son of Mary and brother of James and Joses and Judas and Simon? And are not his sisters here with us?" And they took offense at him.

**20.** In Isaiah 53:3 below, underline all the descriptions of the servant.

> He was despised and rejected by men;
>     a man of sorrows, and acquainted with grief;
> and as one from whom men hide their faces
>     he was despised, and we esteemed him not.

The Jews expected a strong, majestic Messiah who would take an earthly kingdom by force. They received a gentle, servant Messiah who gained a heavenly kingdom by dying.

---

**The Little Details**
*Baylis on the Servant's Identity:*

*The servant*, however, is not merely Israel. There is a future Servant who will restore Israel herself and finally succeed at being the light to the nations. The salvation of Yahweh will finally reach to all the earth...This individual Servant is described in detail—his marred and startling appearance, his unlikely beginning, his rejection, his vicarious suffering (52:13–53:12). This Servant is not the whole nation, for "He was pierced for our transgressions, he was crushed for our iniquities" (53:5). Indeed, "We all, like sheep, have gone astray, each of us has turned to his own way; and the LORD has laid on him the iniquity of us all" (53:6). His death is a guilt offering, yet he will see his offspring and prolong his days! Again, the Servant's suffering cannot be Israel's suffering in the exile, because Israel there suffers for her own guilt (cf. 50:1). This final Servant...is...the Davidic King whom they await (55:3-4).[8]

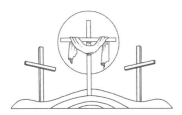

**The Little Details**

*The Ethiopian Eunuch*

Read Acts 8:26-39 to discover how an Ethiopian eunuch came to know Christ from reading Isaiah 53:7-8 and hearing Philip explain that it was "the good news about Jesus."

Day 4

# The Servant's Sacrifice

We'll continue from where we left off on the fourth Servant Song.

## Servant Song 4 (Isaiah 52:13–53:12), *continued*

21. In Isaiah 53:4 below, circle what the servant has borne and carried. Underline how people esteemed him.

> Surely he has borne our griefs
>     and carried our sorrows;
> yet we esteemed him stricken,
>     smitten by God, and afflicted.

22. Write out Isaiah 53:5.

Soldiers pierced Jesus's wrists and feet with nails, and his side with a spear (John 19:34). He carried our sorrows. He bore the punishment we deserved to bring us peace and healing. He healed the sick (Matthew 8:17; Acts 5:16). He is "Jesus our Lord, who was delivered up for our trespasses and raised for our justification" (Romans 4:24-25).

23. (a) What have all of us done (Isaiah 53:6)? (b) Therefore, what did the Lord lay on the servant?

First Peter 2:24-25 explains why:

> He himself bore our sins in his body on the tree, that we might die to sin and live to righteousness. By his wounds you have been healed. For you were straying like sheep, but have now returned to the Shepherd and Overseer of your souls.

### The Apparent Outcome

Isaiah 53:6 portrays humans as sheep gone astray. The next verses describe another sheep.

24. (a) What happened to the servant in Isaiah 53:7? (b) What was his response? (c) What was he like? (d) Again, what was his response?

He bore the punishment we deserved to bring us peace and healing.

We like sheep have gone astray. So he, like a lamb led to slaughter, willingly submitted and "opened not his mouth." Jesus refused to respond to the accusations of the Sanhedrin, Pilate, and Herod (Mark 14:60-61; 15:4-5; Luke 23:8-9). First Peter 2:23 says, "When he was reviled, he did not revile in return; when he suffered, he did not threaten, but continued entrusting himself to him who judges justly."

> 25. In Isaiah 53:8 below, circle by what the servant was taken away. Underline what he was cut off out of. Box what he was stricken for.
>
> By oppression and judgment he was taken away;
>     and as for his generation, who considered
> that he was cut off out of the land of the living,
>     stricken for the transgression of my people?

The Jewish leaders condemned Jesus in an unfair trial: "Many bore false witness against him, but their testimony did not agree" (Mark 14:56). Even Jesus's disciples did not yet rightly consider God's purpose for his death.

> 26. In Isaiah 53:9 below, circle whom his grave and death were with (lines 1-2). Underline why that was unjust (lines 3-4).
>
> And they made his grave with the wicked
>     and with a rich man in his death,
> although he had done no violence,
>     and there was no deceit in his mouth.

Jesus died between two crucified criminals (Mark 15:27). A rich follower put his body in his own tomb (Matthew 27:57-60). Isaiah 53:9 says the servant "had done no violence" and had "no deceit"; 1 John 3:5 says of Jesus, "In him there is no sin."

The confused disciples thought Jesus's mission had failed. The Jewish leaders thought they'd successfully ended the crowd's belief that Jesus was the Messiah. But Jesus's death was not the end of the story.

### The True Outcome

> 27. In Isaiah 53:10 below, circle whose will it was to crush the servant. Box what the servant's soul will make. Underline the two things the servant will do in line 4. Double-underline what will prosper in the servant's hand.
>
> Yet it was the will of the LORD to crush him;
>     he has put him to grief;
> when his soul makes an offering for guilt,
>     he shall see his offspring; he shall prolong his days;
> the will of the LORD shall prosper in his hand.

Isaiah prophesied the death of the servant. The Lord revealed the plan that was in place before the foundation of the world. Though the servant would be cut off without children, his offering for guilt brings children into God's family.

Isaiah 53:10 reads, "He shall prolong his days." How, when he has died (verse 9)? Jesus told us how in John 10:15-18:

**The Little Details**
*Oswalt on "Cut Off" in Isaiah 53:8:*
Thus the sense is that no one has considered that the Servant was left without children in a culture where to die childless was to have lived an utterly futile existence. This...fits in with the concern of the entire book [of Isaiah] for childbearing and childlessness as signs (respectively) of the presence and absence of God's blessing (Isa. 29:23; 54:1-2; 51:18-20; 56:3).[9]

- - - - - - - - - - - - - - - - - - - - - - - - -

The confused disciples thought Jesus's mission had failed.

- - - - - - - - - - - - - - - - - - - - - - - - -

I lay down my life for the sheep. And I have other sheep that are not of this fold. I must bring them also, and they will listen to my voice. So there will be one flock, one shepherd. For this reason the Father loves me, because I lay down my life that I may take it up again. No one takes it from me, but I lay it down of my own accord. I have authority to lay it down, and I have authority to take it up again.

He will lay down his life and take it up again. By so doing, he will bring "other sheep" (Gentiles) into the flock, "so there will be one flock, one shepherd."

> **28.** (a) In Isaiah 53:11 (NIV) below, underline what the servant will see. (b) Circle how the servant will feel. (c) Box what the Lord calls the servant. (d) Double-underline what the servant will accomplish.
>
> After he has suffered,
> > he will see the light of life and be satisfied;
> by his knowledge my righteous servant will justify many,
> > and he will bear their iniquities.

The righteous servant will pass his righteousness to others. Oswalt says, "Somehow this Servant has actually suffered the condemnation of all the sins ever committed, and by virtue of that fact, he is able to declare all those who will accept his offering as righteous, delivered, before God."[10]

> **29.** In Isaiah 53:12 below, underline what the Lord will do for the servant (lines 1-2). Number the four reasons why (lines 3-6).
>
> Therefore I will divide him a portion with the many,
> > and he shall divide the spoil with the strong,
> because he poured out his soul to death
> > and was numbered with the transgressors;
> yet he bore the sin of many,
> > and makes intercession for the transgressors.

Jesus said, "For I tell you that this Scripture must be fulfilled in me: 'And he was numbered with the transgressors.' For what is written about me has its fulfillment" (Luke 22:37). And so he hung on the cross between two crucified criminals while he made "intercession for the transgressors." On the cross, Jesus prayed, "Father, forgive them, for they know not what they do" (Luke 23:34).

From an earthly view, the servant's mission failed with his death. But from a heavenly view, Jesus conquered.

In Luke 24:25-27, the risen Jesus spoke to his followers:

> And he said to them, "O foolish ones, and slow of heart to believe all that the prophets have spoken! Was it not necessary that the Christ should suffer these things and enter into his glory?" And beginning with Moses and all the Prophets, he interpreted to them in all the Scriptures the things concerning himself.

From an earthly view, the servant's mission failed with his death. But from a heavenly view, Jesus conquered.

30. ♥ How have the servant songs helped you understand and appreciate Jesus's sacrifice?

## Day 5

# True Servanthood

We've discovered a lot about the meaning of servanthood in Isaiah.

## God with Us Then

God announced his second solution for the problem of sin: a suffering, righteous servant who will die without offspring but will live and see offspring. He will make unrighteous people righteous.

## The Reveal Continued

### The Second Temple's Day

Zechariah 3:8-9 prophesies, "I will bring my servant the Branch…and I will remove the iniquity of this land in a single day." The Branch is the future royal priest and temple builder, the king descended from David (Zechariah 6:12-14).

### Jesus's Day

People didn't understand that Isaiah's king descended from David (Messiah) and Isaiah's suffering, righteous servant were the same person (Mark 8:31-33). No wonder: How could a king's throne last forever if he's despised, rejected, and killed? All the Jews of the day who looked forward to the coming Messiah expected him to deliver them from foreign rule, reestablish the kingdom of Israel, and rule on earth.

## Jesus the Servant

Two of the disciples hoped to have positions of honor when Jesus was king. So did their mom.

31. Read Matthew 20:20-28. (a) What must anyone who wants to be great be (verse 26)? (b) What must anyone who wants to be first be (verse 27)? (c) What is our example (verse 28)?

When Jesus gathered with his disciples to eat the last supper, no servant washed their dusty feet. Jesus arose from the meal and performed the lowly task.

---

### The Little Details
#### Why the Slow Reveal?

You may be wondering why God revealed his plans slowly. And if you've read the Old Testament prophets, you may wonder why he revealed his plans in sometimes mysterious ways.

First Corinthians 2:7-8 provides a clue: "But we impart a secret and hidden wisdom of God, which God decreed before the ages for our glory. None of the rulers of this age understood this, for if they had, they would not have crucified the Lord of glory." The "rulers of this age" refers to the religious and political leaders who crucified Jesus. They wouldn't have fulfilled God's plan if they'd understood it better.

First Peter 1:10-12 tells us "angels long to look" into the salvation that the prophets predicted. Another reason these things were partially hidden may be that if they weren't, the spiritual rulers may "not have crucified the Lord of glory," either.

---

How could a king's throne last forever if he's despised, rejected, and killed?

---

**32.** (a) What was Jesus to the disciples (John 13:12-13)? (b) What did Jesus want them to do for each other (13:14-15)? (c) What does Jesus want his followers to do (13:15-16)? (d) What does Jesus say will happen if we follow his example (13:17)?

Jesus was a servant, and he wants his followers to be servants too.

**33.** ♥ (a) Consider prayerfully if there's an area of service which you've considered beneath you. (b) In Jesus's time, having someone wash your feet was welcomed and necessary. What is an equivalent welcome and needed service you could do for someone this week? [11]

## The Suffering Servant in Hebrews

Earlier we read that when the servant's labor seemed to be in vain, he looked to God for reward (Isaiah 49:4). If you've been serving others in a way that feels fruitless, here's a comforting verse: "For God is not unjust so as to overlook your work and the love that you have shown for his name in serving the saints" (Hebrews 6:10).

**34.** ♥ Read Hebrews 4:15-16. (a) How do the servant songs help you understand how Jesus sympathizes with our weaknesses (verse 15)? (b) How do the servant songs erase any fear of not being good enough to dwell with God (verse 16)?

## God with Us Still

### God with Us Today
Peter didn't forget the Lord Jesus's lessons about servanthood or how he fulfilled the servant songs.

**35.** Read 1 Peter 2:18-23. (a) How should we act towards bosses, leaders, etc. (verse 18)? (b) What is gracious in God's eyes (verse 20)? (c) What is the example we should follow (verse 21)? (d) Instead of retaliating, how did Jesus respond (verse 23)?

When the servant's labor seemed to be in vain, he looked to God for reward.

### God with Us Forever
Revelation 5 describes a heavenly scene in which a search is made for someone worthy to open the sealed scroll containing God's plan of judgment and redemption. In verse 5, "the Lion of the tribe of Judah" alludes to the

elderly Israel's prophecy that his son Judah was a lion from whom the king's scepter and ruler's staff would not depart (Genesis 49:9-10). Judah's descendant David was the first fulfillment of this, and Revelation 5 describes the ultimate fulfillment. "Root of David" in Revelation 5 alludes to Isaiah's prophecy of a future righteous king from the line of David (Isaiah 11:1,10).

**36.** Read Revelation 5. What encourages you the most? (Stay in Revelation 5.)

*God with Me Now*
Revelation 5 contains three prayers. Praying them is a fitting way to close.

**Pray** the three prayers in Revelation 5:9-10,12,13 to the Lord in worship.

**Praise** God for something you saw of his character this week. **Confess** anything that convicted you. **Ask** for help to do something God's Word calls you to do. **Thank** God for something you learned this week.

# The Heart and Art of Worship

I had recently said "yes" to God…a long overdue surrender after a painful and traumatic chapter of my life. With this surrender came a prompting from God for me to step back into women's ministry. It took everything in me to sign up for the fall Bible study that year. My heart was guarded, knowing I wasn't ready to totally trust again, but I knew this was part of God's plan to bring healing to my heart, and I was ready to experience that.

Just a couple of weeks into the study, the leader asked for a volunteer to set up the coffee and snack table, and again, I felt the nudging of the Lord. God knew it was the perfect place for me to serve. I went in, by myself, before all the other women arrived to set it up…and I stayed, by myself, after all the women left to clean up. I didn't have to talk to anyone, and no one even knew it was me. The only problem was that the table was boring, so I began bringing flowers and decorations from home to dress it up. And still no one knew it was me. No praise. No glory. It was simply God's perfect plan to allow me to serve him and be a blessing to others during that time of healing.

That season, as painful as it was to step out of my comfort zone, brought much healing, and I eventually opened my heart to other women again…some who are still my dearest friends. I know that saying "yes" to God and allowing him to use my talents and abilities to serve him and others played a huge part in my healing. It also was a huge stepping-stone to how God is using my talents today. My hope for you is, that as you color this week's illustration and meditate on how much Christ sacrificed to serve you, you might ask him how he wants to use you…your gifts, talents, and abilities to serve him…and others…and all for his glory.

*Karla*

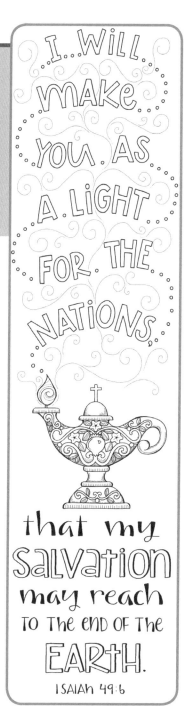

## Chapter 9

# Isaiah 49
## Jesus the Light of the World

The hope of salvation for all nations

## Day 1

## God Is Light

When Rich told Linda and me that we needed to accept Jesus as Lord so that we could have eternal life, he was a light showing the way to Jesus. But neither of us believed him. That night, Linda told her mom what Rich had said and asked if it was true. She said, "Of course it's true! Haven't you paid attention in Sunday school?" So, after we crawled into beds that night, Linda led us in a prayer to receive Jesus as Lord.

But neither of us prayed in belief. I doubted Jesus really saved, and Linda thought the prayer was one more good deed to make sure the good outweighed the bad.

Rich gave Linda a paperback New Testament that she passed on to me. When I read the Gospels, I discovered what they said about Jesus. Then I prayed again for Jesus to save me, this time believing he could. The Bible was the light that guided me to him.

I shared what I was learning from the Bible with Linda. She thought that she was a good person and that the Bible's commands didn't apply to modern times. But one day Linda realized that she couldn't be the judge of what was right and wrong. There had to be a higher authority. When she compared her actions against what the Bible taught, she fell short. When she understood that no one can be good enough on her own to reach God, she turned to Jesus as Savior. That made me a light to my friend.

Both Linda and I came to view Jesus as the true light illuminating the way to God. And that is what the key verse for this chapter tells us he is. The Lord God made the righteous, suffering servant into a light to guide people of all nations to God.

**The Reveal**

*Eve's Day*
God created the sun to light the day, and he created the moon and stars to light the night. He later used the word *light* in metaphors to help people understand him.

*Abraham's Day*
God told Abraham, "You shall be the father of a *multitude of nations*" and "In your offspring shall *all the nations of the earth* be blessed" (Genesis 17:4; 22:18, emphasis added).

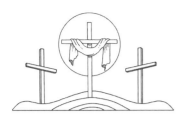

## The Little Details

### Hunter and Wellum on Israel as a Light:

The Law-covenant was God-given and intended to separate Israel from the nations for her own purity and preservation. The goal of the Law was for Israel to be a light to the gentiles, that through her the Messiah would come to bring salvation to the nations. But in her pride Israel took what was good and misused the Law as a means of justifying herself before God and as an excuse to hate the nations. The Law exposed Israel's sin and revealed in a greater way the hideous nature of the human heart.[2]

### Moses's Day

Like most people in Moses's day, the Egyptians worshiped many gods. The plagues that the Lord brought on Egypt showed those gods' powerlessness before the Lord God. For instance, they worshiped the sun god Re. The ninth plague brought darkness that covered their land, but not the land where the Hebrews lived. Thus, God showed *he* had power over light, not Re.

Another way the Lord used light among the Hebrews was by going before them as they traveled "by day in a pillar of cloud to lead them along the way, and by night in a pillar of fire to give them light" (Exodus 13:21).

As for guiding other nations to the Lord, God called the Israelites a kingdom of priests (Exodus 19:5-6). That meant that "they were to represent him to the rest of the world and attempt to bring the rest of the world to him."[1] If they kept the covenant and told the rest of the world about the Lord, then they would fulfill the Lord's promise to Abraham. They would be lights leading people of other nations to the Lord.

### David's Day

David frequently used the word *light* to describe God: "For you are my lamp, O Lord, and my God lightens my darkness" (2 Samuel 22:29); "The Lord is my light and my salvation" (Psalm 27:1); and "You have delivered...my feet from falling, that I may walk before God in the light of life" (Psalm 56:13).

### The Major Prophets' Day

By the time of Isaiah, many Israelites embraced idols. They had forsaken God's light and had stumbled into the darkness of the surrounding nations.

## God's Word to Us

In the last chapter, we saw that the righteous, suffering servant will "make many to be accounted righteous, and he shall bear their iniquities" (Isaiah 53:11). Our first passage comes from the second servant song. Then we'll move to the final section of Isaiah. It presents God's third solution to Israel's unrighteousness: a future righteous people.

Take a moment to pray for insight as you read God's Word.

1. ♥ Read Isaiah 49:6; 59–61:3. What stands out to you? Why?

2. ♥ Who or what in your life functioned as a light illuminating the way to Jesus, the light of the world? Explain.

The Lord God made the righteous, suffering servant into a light to guide people of all nations to God.

# A Walk with Christ—Our Lighthouse

One of my "bucket list" goals is to book a romantic night in a historic lighthouse, not only because Bill and I live on a boat, but because I find lighthouses fascinating. In a storm or on a pitch-black night, the beam from a lighthouse can keep a vessel safely away from a rocky shore and point the way to a safe harbor.

Abbie Burgess is a lighthouse legend. At age 16, she kept the light burning during a treacherous storm at Matinicus Rock Lighthouse for 21 days in 1856. The light, produced by lard oil, was difficult to keep lit and needed tending around the clock. Abbie's mother was an invalid, so as the oldest daughter, Abbie learned to run the light, allowing her father to fish and trap lobsters. One winter day while her father and brother were gone, a tempest hit the shores. In her own words, Abbie tells the perilous tale:

> As the tide arose, the sea made a complete breach over the rock, washing every movable thing away, and of the old dwelling not one stone was left upon another. The new dwelling was flooded, and the windows had to be secured to prevent the violence of the spray from breaking them in. As the tide came, the sea rose higher and higher, till the only endurable places were the light towers. If they stood, we were saved, otherwise our fate was only too certain. But for some reason, I...went on with my work as usual...Though at times greatly exhausted...not once did the lights fail. Under God I was able to perform all my accustomed duties as well as my father's.[3]

Even today, on life's stormy seas, we look to the light in the darkness—Christ.

Wayne Wheeler, founder and chair of the United States Lighthouse Society, shares: "That light was the last thing the sailor saw as he left for foreign shores, and the first thing he sees as he comes home...It offers a shining light against the darkness."[4] This is why, during a heavy season of caring for my elderly in-laws, one feeble of mind and the other feeble of body, I bought a table lamp shaped like a lighthouse. I needed the daily reminder that Christ would be the light we all needed to secure safe harbor in turbulent times.

The Pharos of Alexandria, of ancient Greece, built between 280 and 247 BC, is considered the oldest lighthouse in the world. Which means the concept of a lighthouse existed during the life of Christ. While *lighthouse* is not in the Bible, the reference to Jesus as our light is!

"In him was life, and the life was the light of men" (John 1:4).

"Again Jesus spoke to them, saying, 'I am the light of the world. Whoever follows me will not walk in darkness, but will have the light of life'" (John 8:12).

"While you have the light, believe in the light, that you may become sons of light" (John 12:36).

In addition, we, the church, are called to be beacons of lights: "Let your light shine before others, that they may see your good deeds and glorify your Father in heaven" (Matthew 5:16 NIV).

When I dissected this last verse, I gained vital insights. We are called to shine—like a very brilliant light reflecting God's divine illumination—with our *excellent* and *powerful* works. Our obedience (powered by the Spirit) causes people to pay special attention to God, and the result is people who praise and worship God! What would make your life shine brighter for Jesus? Pray to know where, to whom, and how to shine bright for him.

*Pam*

## The Little Details
### Examine, Confess, Repent

The New Testament teaches the same message as the Old when it comes to the importance of examining our lives, confessing sin, and repenting. Here are examples.

Jesus announced, "The kingdom of God is at hand; repent and believe in the gospel" (Mark 1:15).

Paul asked, "Do you presume on the riches of his kindness and forbearance and patience, not knowing that God's kindness is meant to lead you to repentance?" (Romans 2:4).

Paul instructed people that before taking communion, "Let a person examine himself, then, and so eat of the bread and drink of the cup...But if we judged ourselves truly, we would not be judged. But when we are judged by the Lord, we are disciplined so that we may not be condemned along with the world" (1 Corinthians 11:28-32).

John wrote, "If we confess our sins, he is faithful and just to forgive us our sins and to cleanse us from all unrighteousness" (1 John 1:9).

---

## Day 2

# The Need for Light

All four sections of Isaiah address Israel's need for light and how God addresses the need. Let's discover how the first three sections do so.

### Israel's Need for Light

#### The Problem: Israel Is Unrighteous (Isaiah 1–5)

In his introduction, Isaiah told the people, "O house of Jacob, come, let us walk in the light of the LORD" (Isaiah 2:5). "Walk in the light of the LORD" means to live in accordance with God's words by examining actions and thoughts to see if they're aligned with those words and by turning from any that aren't. The Israelites in Isaiah's day (both the northern kingdom of Israel and the southern kingdom of Judah) had stopped doing this.

3. (a) What were the people doing wrong (Isaiah 5:20)? (b) Why did they do that (verse 21)? (c) What happened to justice (verse 23)?

They no longer followed God's commands. They made their own list of right and wrong that didn't match God's instructions.

4. ♥ What is something you once thought was okay to do, but later discovered the Bible says is wrong (for instance, malice, slander, lies—see Colossians 3:5-9)?

#### God's First Solution: A Future Righteous King (Isaiah 6–39)

This section begins with a story about King Ahaz refusing to trust God. Instead of seeking direction from God, he consulted mediums who claimed to talk to the dead (Isaiah 8:19). In response, Isaiah said, "Consult God's instruction and the testimony of warning. If anyone does not speak according to this word, they have no light of dawn" (verse 20 NIV). He warned that rejecting God's words would result in "distress and darkness, the gloom of anguish" (verse 22).

But there was hope. The future child called Mighty God would rule and be "a great light" on those who dwell "in a land of deep darkness" (Isaiah 9:2,6).

#### God's Second Solution: A Future Righteous Servant (Isaiah 40–55)

The servant songs describe the suffering servant as a light for all people. In the first, the Lord tells the servant, "I will give you as...a light for the nations" (Isaiah 42:6). In the second, he tells Gentiles to listen to the servant and then speaks to the servant about the Gentiles.

5. In Isaiah 49:6 (NIV) below, underline the reason the servant won't restore just the descendants of Israel (first six words). Circle for whom the servant will also be a light. Double-underline why (what follows the last comma).

> It is too small a thing for you to be my servant to restore the tribes of Jacob and bring back those of Israel I have kept. I will also make you a light for the Gentiles, that my salvation may reach to the ends of the earth.

Although Israel in many ways had failed to be the offspring of Abraham who would bless all nations, the suffering servant would succeed.

### God's Third Solution: A Future Righteous People (Isaiah 56–66)

Now we come to the book's climax and God's third solution to Israel's sin problem.

6. (a) What separates the people from God (Isaiah 59:1-2)? (b) What defiles their hands, fingers, lips, and tongues (verse 3)? (c) What has happened in the courts (verse 4)?

In Isaiah 59:3, *blood* includes murder and child sacrifice (Hosea 4:2; 2 Chronicles 28:3).

7. In Isaiah 59:7-8 below, underline the three descriptions of the people's actions and thoughts. Double-underline what's in their highways. Circle the two things they lack.

> Their feet run to evil,
>     and they are swift to shed innocent blood;
> their thoughts are thoughts of iniquity;
>     desolation and destruction are in their highways.
> The way of peace they do not know,
>     and there is no justice in their paths.

Verse 8 goes on to say that they've made their roads crooked, so no one knows peace. Isaiah speaks often of a highway that leads to God, but that's not the highway they're on.

8. In Isaiah 59:9 below, circle the two things the people lack. Box the two things for which they hope. Underline the two things they get instead of what they hope for.

> Therefore justice is far from us,
>     and righteousness does not overtake us;
> we hope for light, and behold, darkness,
>     and for brightness, but we walk in gloom.

They've become like people with no eyes (Isaiah 59:10). When they realize what their actions and thoughts have led to, they confess their sin (verses 12-13).

## The Little Details
### Psalm 82

This psalm is in Book III of the Psalter, which was probably compiled during exile, though the psalmist likely wrote it before the exile. The injustices he describes fit the situation leading to the exile.

In this psalm, God condemns corrupt leaders who don't care for the poor and needy. He calls them *gods*, a word that's often translated *God*, but which also can refer to angels or human leaders.[5]

In verses 2-4, God speaks to the rulers, saying,

> How long will you judge unjustly / and show partiality to the wicked? Selah / Give justice to the weak and the fatherless; / maintain the right of the afflicted and the destitute. / Rescue the weak and the needy; / deliver them from the hand of the wicked.

Though they are "gods," "nevertheless, like men you shall die, / and fall like any prince" (verse 7).

The psalmist then calls on God: "Arise, O God, judge the earth" (verse 8).

## The Little Details
### Baylis on the Divine Warrior:

God has sent his Servant, who has addressed the problem of sin and guilt. Redemption is provided!

Yet, the message goes deeper than that. For in the convergence of themes, we find that not only the servant theme is fulfilled in Jesus, we find that the anticipation of Yahweh himself as conqueror is understood to be fulfilled in Jesus. Just as the New David bears divine names, so *God coming himself to conquer* will be fulfilled in Jesus. It is significant that as Paul lists the Christian's battle armor in Ephesians 6:10-20 he combines the armor of the coming King and the armor of God as conqueror from the book of Isaiah...Even though the final battle that Christ leads at his second coming is still future, Paul believes that Christians may already be suited in Christ's conquering armor to fight spiritual battles today for Christ as his people. The story of Christianity is the story that God himself found "no one to intercede" [Isaiah 59:16] and so himself comes—"The Redeemer will come to Zion" [Isaiah 59:20].[8]

9. In Isaiah 59:14-15 below, circle the four things missing from the land. Underline what happens in such a land to those who try to live rightly.

> Justice is turned back,
>     and righteousness stands far away;
> for truth has stumbled in the public squares,
>     and uprightness cannot enter.
> Truth is lacking,
>     and he who departs from evil makes himself a prey.

All this displeased the Lord, and he was appalled that there was no one to intervene (Isaiah 59:15-16). So "his own arm brought him salvation" (verse 16). Isaiah 53:1-2 identifies the arm of the Lord as the suffering servant.[6]

10. How does the Lord dress for war (Isaiah 59:17)?

The Lord is a Divine Warrior who defeats his enemies (Isaiah 59:18). Oswalt writes that in the context of the previous chapters, the primary enemy is the people's sins.[7] When the Lord defeats sin, then people from the west and east—that is, everywhere—will worship the Lord (verse 19).

11. In Isaiah 59:20 below, circle who will come to Zion. Underline to whom he'll come.

> And a Redeemer will come to Zion,
>     to those in Jacob who turn from transgression.

Just as he redeemed the Israelites from slavery in Egypt, so he will redeem the repentant from slavery to sin.

12. (a) What is the good news for those living in darkness (Isaiah 60:1)? (b) Though darkness continues to cover the earth, what will be seen (verse 2)? (c) What will nations and kings then do (verse 3)?

The light of the Lord will come and arise upon the people. That light will attract people and even leaders from the nations.

13. In Isaiah 60:16-17 below, underline what the people would then know. Circle who their two taskmasters will be.

> You shall know that I, the Lord, am your Savior and your Redeemer, the Mighty One of Jacob...I will make your overseers peace and your taskmasters righteousness.

## Day 3

# The Spirit of the Lord

We left off at an exciting place in the last lesson. The arm of the Lord was completely reversing all that was wrong with Israel.

14. In Isaiah 60:18 below, draw a line through the three things that will be gone. Circle the names of their walls and gates.

> Violence shall no more be heard in your land,
> devastation or destruction within your borders;
> you shall call your walls Salvation,
> and your gates Praise.

15. (a) Instead of the sun and moon, what will give God's people light (Isaiah 60:19)? (b) Who will be their glory (verse 19)? (c) What shall end (verse 20)?

16. In Isaiah 60:21 below, circle what the people will finally be. Box how long they will possess the land. Underline what God calls the people (third line). Double-underline the reason he planted them.

> Your people shall all be righteous;
> they shall possess the land forever,
> the branch of my planting, the work of my hands,
> that I might be glorified.

Finally, the people shall be righteous. When? "In its time I will hasten it" (Isaiah 60:22).

Isaiah 61:1 has a new speaker (and you can probably guess who it is!).

17. In Isaiah 61:1 below, circle who is upon the speaker. Box why (line 2). Underline what the speaker is anointed to do.

> The Spirit of the Lord God is upon me,
> because the Lord has anointed me
> to bring good news to the poor;
> he has sent me to bind up the brokenhearted,
> to proclaim liberty to the captives,
> and the opening of the prison to those who are bound.

The Lord has anointed the speaker. Since kings were called *anointed ones,* this suggests the speaker is a future king.

**The Little Details**

*The Branch*

Isaiah 60:21 calls the now righteous people "the branch of my planting."

*Branch* refers back to Isaiah 11:1: "There shall come forth a shoot from the stump of Jesse, and a branch from his roots shall bear fruit." Jesse was King David's father, so the "shoot from the stump of Jesse" is someone descended from Jesse—a new David. This future king will arise from a stump—from what seems lifeless. He'll bear fruit.

"The Spirit of the Lord shall rest upon him" (Isaiah 11:2), just as he rests on the speaker in Isaiah 61:1. In 61:3, the speaker makes the people righteous.

Jesus later claims to be the Messiah (and therefore the branch in Isaiah 11:1), as well as the speaker in Isaiah 61:1-3. That means the branch from Jesse is the one who enables the people to be "the branch of my planting" and "oaks of righteousness" (Isaiah 60:21; 61:3).

---

The arm of the Lord was completely reversing all that was wrong with Israel.

---

## The Little Details
### *Amos on Social Injustice*

The prophet Amos ministered about a decade before Isaiah. His portrayal of the social injustices in Israel and Judah give us rich insights into conditions there. They also show God's deep displeasure over social injustices and his concern for the poor and needy.

In chapter 1, the Lord judges the nations for slavery, cruelty, and barbarity. Amos 2:6-8 and 5:10-13 judge Israel because the rich oppress the poor, deny justice to the oppressed, abuse girls, and tax the poor. Chapter 6 judges Judah's complacent rich who don't grieve over the ruin of others.

Amos announces the coming exile as God's judgment and declares, "Prepare to meet your God" (4:12). Yet the book ends with the hope of restoration after judgment.

Martin Luther King Jr. quoted Amos 5:24 (NIV) in his "I Have A Dream" speech: "But let justice roll on like a river, righteousness like a never-failing stream!"

---

The speaker will enable the people to be oaks of righteousness whom the LORD will plant.

---

**18.** (a) What will the speaker proclaim (Isaiah 61:2)? (b) What will he do for those who mourn (verse 2)?

**19.** (a) List the three things the speaker will give to mourners (Isaiah 61:3). (b) What will the mourners be called? (c) Why has the Lord done all this?

The speaker will enable the people to be oaks of righteousness whom the LORD will plant. That is God's third solution to Israel's sin problem. He will make his people righteous.

### The Future Exiles Question God

That's all wonderful news. But the Lord isn't done speaking through Isaiah. God knows that those alive just before the exile won't believe Isaiah's message and won't believe God will exile them. Yet once they're exiled, they'll argue that God should forget their sin because "we are all your people" (Isaiah 64:9).

**20.** In Isaiah 63:17, whom will the future exiles blame for their sin?

The future exiles will be in the dark about these questions:

    a. Where is God (Isaiah 63:11)?

    b. Where is God's zeal and might (63:15)?

    c. Why did God make them sin (63:17)?

    d. Is it possible to be saved from long-standing sin (64:5)?

    e. Will God deliver them after the temple is destroyed (64:11-12)?

    f. Will God keep silent (64:12)?

**21.** ♥ Describe a time you asked one of these questions.

### God's Answers

*Where Is God? Why Did God Make Them Sin? Will God Keep Silent?*

God's answers to all these questions would await the future exiles in Isaiah 65.

**22.** In Isaiah 65:1-2 (NIV) below, circle the four actions God took to reach the people. Underline the descriptions of the people (they're in every line except 4 and 5).

> I revealed myself to those who did not ask for me;
> 　I was found by those who did not seek me.
> To a nation that did not call on my name,
> 　I said, "Here am I, here am I."
> All day long I have held out my hands
> 　to an obstinate people,
> who walk in ways not good,
> 　pursuing their own imaginations.

**The Little Details**
*Oswalt on Isaiah 65:17-25's "New Earth":*
Interpreters disagree over the precise reference. There are three main positions: (1) a metaphoric statement about a restored but ideal Jerusalem, and more literal statements about (2) the millennial kingdom, or (3) eternity. Each of these has certain inconsistencies. Whereas the "new heavens and a new earth" (v. 17) most easily speak of eternity (Rev. 21), the references to old age and dying do not accord with that view, nor do they accord with a millennial kingdom. These difficulties have led some to the first interpretation, describing in physical terms the benefits that come to those in fellowship with God: peace, security, abundance, freedom from sorrow and destruction. At the same time…literal fulfillment of some or all of the elements described here perhaps in ways we cannot now imagine should not be ruled out.[9]

God wasn't absent. The Lord didn't make them sin; their own obstinacy was at fault. God wasn't silent but had spoken to them through Moses and the prophets.

### Will God Deliver Us After the Temple Is Destroyed?

The Lord answers that he will finish judging their sin but will not destroy all the exiles (Isaiah 65:6-8). He will bring back a remnant.

### Where Is God's Zeal and Might?

Those who forsake the Lord will perish "because, when I called, you did not answer; when I spoke, you did not listen, but you did what was evil in my eyes and chose what I did not delight in" (Isaiah 65:11-12).

But the destiny of the Lord's servants is different: "My servants will sing out of the joy of their hearts" (Isaiah 65:14 NIV). They will not perish; instead, "his servants he will call by another name" (verse 15).

### Is It Possible to Be Saved from Long-standing Sin?

For the Lord's servants, "the former troubles are forgotten and are hidden from my eyes" (Isaiah 65:16). This doesn't mean God gives up his omniscience: *Remember* means act on, and *forget* means no longer act on.

Their argument that God should forget their sin because they were all his people was based on a false belief. Isaiah 65:11-16 explains that only some of Israel's descendants were servants of the Lord. A day will come when the sins of his servants will no longer count against them, and they will be saved from their long-standing sin, but judgment awaits those who forsake him.

**23.** In Isaiah 65:17,19 below, circle what God will create. Underline what won't be there.

> For behold, I create new heavens and a new earth…No more shall be heard in it the sound of weeping and the cry of distress.

## The Final Word

Isaiah concludes by declaring that people from all nations will worship the Lord—and will see God's final judgment against those who rebelled against him (Isaiah 66:23-24).

## God with Us Then

God spoke to the people through Scripture and prophets, but many didn't listen.

> Their argument that God should forget their sin because they were all his people was based on a false belief.

## The Little Details
### Samaritans

According to Assyrian records, Assyria deported the wealthy and the leaders, but left the poor to work the land.[10] This explains why Hezekiah was able to call on the remaining Israelites to join him in celebrating Passover (2 Chronicles 30:1). It also explains why Josiah was able to bring a revival into the former territories of the north (2 Chronicles 34:6-9).

Assyria settled exiles from other nations into what was formerly Israel (2 Kings 17:24). The Israelites left in the land and the newcomers intermarried, combining religious beliefs. The people of mixed heritage and mixed beliefs became known as Samaritans.

---

Josiah was the last king to be a light showing the way to God.

---

Day 4

# The True Light

Let's discover how Jesus fulfilled these prophecies about the light of the world.

## The Reveal Continued

Assyria exiled Israel's wealthy and leaders but left the poor to work the land. Assyria settled exiles from other nations in Israel. The people of mixed heritage and mixed beliefs eventually became known as Samaritans.

Hezekiah brought Judah back to worshiping God and destroyed the altars used in idol worship. He listened to the prophet Isaiah. He invited the remaining northern Israelites to celebrate Passover in Jerusalem. He was a light that showed people the way to God.

But when he died, his son Manasseh rejected God. He installed altars to idols in God's temple, rebuilt all the places of idol worship his father had torn down, and even burned his son as an offering to an idol. The land plunged into darkness again.

Manasseh's grandson, Josiah, sought the Lord and repaired the temple. During repairs, the high priest discovered the Book of the Law. Discovered! That meant the high priests had neglected their duty to know and teach God's Word.

Josiah led the people to recommit to their covenant with God. He listened to the prophetess Huldah and the prophet Jeremiah. He defiled the valley where people sacrificed children so it could never be used that way again. He extended his reforms into the northern areas controlled by Assyria. He was a light.

Josiah was the last king to be a light showing the way to God. He died in 609 BC. Shortly after, Babylon attacked Judah. Josiah's sons mistreated and imprisoned Jeremiah. The first group of exiles left in 605 BC, the second in 597 BC, and the rest in 586 BC.

### The Second Temple's Day

Just as Isaiah prophesied, the Gentile Cyrus conquered Babylon and permitted the people to return to Jerusalem and rebuild the temple. Psalm 119 probably was added to the book of Psalms around the time the second temple was finished. Verse 105 reads, "Your word is a lamp to my feet and a light to my path."

God's promise that Abraham would be the father of many nations had not happened before the exile. But Zechariah 8:22-23 prophesied that hope remained:

> Many peoples and strong nations shall come to seek the LORD of hosts in Jerusalem and to entreat the favor of the LORD...In those days ten men from the nations of every tongue shall take hold of the robe of a Jew, saying, "Let us go with you, for we have heard that God is with you."

### Jesus's Day

Decades turned to centuries, and the Jews still had no king of their own. A portion of what was previously Israel and Judah became three provinces: Galilee, Samaria, and Judea.

## God with Us in Jesus

The Gospel of John opens by describing Jesus as the Word of God.

> **24.** (a) According to John 1:4, what was Jesus's life? (b) What did it do (verse 5)? (c) To whom does the true light give light (verse 9)? (d) Who rejected him (verses 10-11)?

> **25.** (a) What did the true light give to all who received him (John 1:12)? (b) Who were they born of (verse 13)? (c) What happened to the Word of God (verse 14)? (d) Whose glory did people then see (verse 14)?

The Word of God who was the true light was the only Son from the Father.

> **26.** ♥ Jesus told his followers that they "are the light of the world...Let your light shine before others, so that they may see your good works and give glory to your Father" (Matthew 5:14-16). Describe two ways you can do what Jesus said here.

## The Light Enters the World

Let's jump to Luke to see what happened when the light entered the world he created.

> **27.** When Jesus's parents presented him at the temple, what did Simeon prophesy he would be, according to Luke 2:32?

Later, Jesus went to John the Baptist to be baptized.

> **28.** (a) What opened when John baptized Jesus (Luke 3:21)? (b) Who descended upon him (verse 22)? (c) What did the voice from heaven say (verse 22)?

Isaiah prophesied that the Spirit of the Lord would be on the future king (11:2) and on the person who would make people righteous (61:1,3). Now look at what Jesus announced at the start of his ministry.

**The Little Details**

*Gehenna and Hell*

Isaiah's final verse describes a place of judgment for those who rebel against God: "For their worm shall not die, their fire shall not be quenched" (Isaiah 66:24). Jesus quotes this and identifies the place as Gehenna, which is usually translated *hell* (Mark 9:47-48).

The name Gehenna comes from the valley where the people sacrificed children during the major prophets' day. They burned them at Topheth in the Valley of the Son of Hinnom. God declared that when he avenged the children's death, it would be called the Valley of Slaughter (Jeremiah 7:32).

The kings who sacrificed sons there were Ahaz and Manasseh. Josiah became king just two years after his grandfather Manasseh died. This godly king defiled the valley so that no one could sacrifice a child there again (2 Kings 23:10). Gehenna became a place to burn trash and the bodies of criminals.

In the New Testament, hell is the place of punishment after the last judgment.[11]

## The Little Details

### Carson on the Festival in John 8:12:

"He who has not seen the joy of the place of water-drawing has never in his life seen joy": this extravagant claim stands just before the description of the lighting of the four huge lamps in the temple's court of women and of the exuberant celebration that took place under their light (Mishnah *Sukkah* 5:1-4). "Men of piety and good works" danced through the night, holding burning torches in their hands and singing songs and praises. The Levitical orchestras cut loose, and some sources attest that this went on every night of the Feast of Tabernacles, with the light from the temple area shedding its glow all over Jerusalem. In this context Jesus declares to the people, *I am the light of the world.*[14]

--------------------------------

By using the festival's lights as his setting, Jesus identified himself with the pillar of fire in the exodus to the promised land.

--------------------------------

29. Read Luke 4:16-21. What did Jesus proclaim (verse 21)?

Jesus read Isaiah 61:1-2, the introduction to the prophecy about the person who would make people righteous.

## "I Am the Light"

Let's return to John and follow how he weaves light into his narrative. The setting of John 7–8 is the weeklong celebration called the Feast of Booths. Jews lived in tents and ate unleavened bread to commemorate how God delivered their ancestors from Egypt. By Jesus's day, the ceremony included lighting four huge golden lamps to symbolize the Lord leading the Israelites in a pillar of fire that lit their way.[12] Worshipers sang psalms about God and his word being light.[13] Pious men danced.

30. (a) What did Jesus call himself (John 8:12)? (b) What will those who follow him never do? (c) What will they have?

This is an incredible claim. By using the festival's lights as his setting, Jesus identified himself with the pillar of fire in the exodus to the promised land. "I am the light of the world" linked him to the suffering, righteous servant who would be "a light for the Gentiles" (Isaiah 42:6; 49:6). It also linked him to the king (Messiah) who was "a great light" called "Mighty God" (Isaiah 9:2,6,7). Since following him gave people "the light of life," then to follow him was to "walk before God in the light of life" (Psalm 56:13).

Later, Jesus healed a blind man (John 9:1-7), fulfilling the prophecy that the suffering servant would open blind eyes (Isaiah 42:7). Jesus again claimed, "I am the light of the world" (John 9:5).

## A Light for the Gentiles

John then wrote that Jesus called himself the good shepherd and said, "I have other sheep that are not of this fold. I must bring them also, and they will listen to my voice. So there will be one flock, one shepherd" (John 10:16). The other sheep are the Gentiles.[15]

Soon after, Jesus raised his friend Lazarus from the dead.

31. (a) Why did raising a man from the dead worry the Jewish leaders (John 11:47-48)? (b) What did the high priest Caiaphas say was better to happen (verse 50)? (c) Who was he prophesying that Jesus would die for (verses 51-52)?

Jesus's triumphal entry followed the miracle that worried the leaders. John records next that some Greeks came to Philip, seeking to see Jesus. This began the fulfillment of Isaiah 60:3: "And nations shall come to your light." It also fulfilled Zechariah 8:22-23: People from other nations will say to a Jew, "We have heard that God is with you."

Upon hearing of the Greeks, Jesus said, "The hour has come for the Son of Man to be glorified" (John 12:23). He cried out, "I have come into the world as light, so that whoever believes in me may not remain in darkness" (John 12:46).

## Day 5

## Lights in the World

Why did so many of the Jewish leaders reject Jesus? Jesus had explained the answer to Nicodemus, one of the Pharisee rulers who turned to Jesus.

> **32.** Read John 3:19-21. (a) Why did people love darkness more than light (verse 19)? (b) What does light do (verse 20)? (c) Why does whoever does what's true seek light (verse 21)?

The Pharisees prided themselves on being good and denied their sin, but Jesus told them they were good only on the outside, and that wasn't good enough (Matthew 23:27).

> **33.** ♥ (a) Did you have difficulty coming to Jesus for salvation because you thought you were a good person who didn't need saving? Explain. (b) Do you know people who won't turn to Jesus because they believe they're good enough to go to heaven?

In Jesus's day, most Jews looked down on Samaritans and Gentiles as unclean dogs. But Jesus told his disciples, "You will be my witnesses in Jerusalem and in all Judea and Samaria, and to the end of the earth" (Acts 1:8). Thus, they were to share the gospel with Jews, Samaritans, and Gentiles. Acts 2 describes Peter sharing the good news about Jesus with Jews in Jerusalem. In Acts 8, Philip proclaimed Jesus in Samaria. And in Acts 10, Peter testified about Jesus to Gentiles. They were lights leading people to Jesus.

Paul wrote to Gentile Christians about what Jesus accomplished for them.

> **34.** Read Galatians 3:26-29. (a) Through what did the Galatians become sons of God in Christ Jesus (verse 26)?
> ☐ Circumcision   ☐ Faith   ☐ Sacrifices   ☐ Good deeds
> (b) Is there still a separation between Jews and non-Jews (verse 28)?
> ☐ Yes   ☐ No
> (c) Are Gentile Christians Abraham's offspring (verse 29)?
> ☐ Yes   ☐ No

The Pharisees prided themselves on being good and denied their sin, but Jesus told them they were good only on the outside, and that wasn't good enough.

## The Little Details
### Poythress on "God Is Light":

We still need to bear in mind that the Creator is distinct from all the creatures that he has made. There is a fundamental distinction between God and created light. God is not created. He is not to be confused with created light. When we say that God is light, we mean light at the level of the Creator. Created light *reflects* who God is, but it does so at the level of the creature.[16]

The brightness of the sun, as a created thing, reflects the uncreated, original "brightness" or splendor of God's character.[17]

But we should continue to acknowledge the fundamental distinction between God the Creator and the creation that he has made. God shows himself and reflects his character through created things. But he is never *identical* to those created things.[18]

Through Jesus, God fulfilled his promise to make Abraham "the father of a multitude of nations" (Genesis 17:5). He fulfilled his word concerning the suffering, righteous servant: "I will make you as a light for the nations, that my salvation may reach to the end of the earth" (Isaiah 49:6). And to the ends of the earth the gospel has reached.

## The Light of the World in Hebrews

Isaiah prophesied that the Lord would create new heavens and a new earth, and there God's people would be righteous (Isaiah 65:17). Hebrews speaks of this too.

> **35.** In Hebrews 12:22-24 below, underline what we have come to. Circle how the spirits of the righteous are made.
>
> But you have come to Mount Zion and to the city of the living God, the heavenly Jerusalem, and to innumerable angels in festal gathering, and to the assembly of the firstborn who are enrolled in heaven, and to God, the judge of all, and to the spirits of the righteous made perfect, and to Jesus, the mediator of a new covenant, and to the sprinkled blood that speaks a better word than the blood of Abel.

The blood of Eve's son Abel cried out for vengeance, but the blood of Jesus speaks a better word: the offer of forgiveness. Hebrews 12:28 concludes, "Therefore let us be grateful for receiving a kingdom that cannot be shaken, and thus let us offer to God acceptable worship, with reverence and awe."

## God with Us Still

### God with Us Today

So, how does knowing Jesus is the light of the world affect our actions today?

### We Are Lights to the World

Jesus told his followers, "You are the light of the world...Let your light shine before others, so that they may see your good works and give glory to your Father who is in heaven" (Matthew 5:14-16). We model what it means to follow Jesus so that others can discover our Father through us.

### We Walk in the Light

John wrote about walking in the light.

> **36.** In 1 John 1:5-6 below, circle what God is. Box what is not in him. Underline what a person who claims to fellowship with God while walking in darkness does.
>
> God is light, and in him is no darkness at all. If we say we have fellowship with him while we walk in darkness, we lie and do not practice the truth.

God is light. He is sinless, true, and holy. John is not teaching pantheism, the belief that all is God.[19] In Genesis 1:3-4, God created light and separated light from darkness. Then he used light as a metaphor to teach us about himself, the uncreated and invisible God.

**37.** In 1 John 1:7-9 below, underline the result of walking in the light. Box what those who claim to be sinless are doing. Double-underline what we should do instead of denying sin.

> But if we walk in the light, as he is in the light, we have fellowship with one another, and the blood of Jesus his Son cleanses us from all sin. If we say we have no sin, we deceive ourselves, and the truth is not in us. If we confess our sins, he is faithful and just to forgive us our sins and to cleanse us from all unrighteousness.

To walk in light is to act in accordance with God's good and righteous ways; to walk in darkness is to act in ways God forbids (1 John 1:3-10). Light reveals what is true; what is false hides in darkness so it cannot be seen for what it is. Walking in the light enables us to be lights to the world.

### God with Us Forever

John saw a heavenly vision of the fulfillment of God's promise to Abraham and the prophecies to Isaiah.

**38.** Read Revelation 7:9-17. What stands out to you the most?

### God with Me Now

Psalm 119:105-112 is a prayer about God's words lighting our paths.

Turn to Psalm 119:105-112 in your Bible and read it. **Pray** Psalm 119:105-112 to God. Prayerfully examine your actions and thoughts.

**Praise** God for something you saw of his character this week. **Confess** anything that convicted you. **Ask** for help to do something God's Word calls you to do. **Thank** God for something you learned this week.

To walk in light is to act in accordance with God's good and righteous ways.

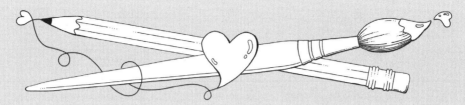

# The Heart and Art of Worship

Can you believe that Jesus, the Light of the world, would entrust you and me...mere humans...to be his light bearers here on earth? And he said, not only would we be lighting up our own neighborhoods, but that he would make us a light for all nations! How can that be, you might wonder, when my light is so small and insufficient and the world is so big and overwhelmingly dark?

Have you ever seen satellite photos of the earth taken from heaven's viewpoint? The pictures taken during the darkest hours of the night are incredible! You can easily pick out the most populated, well-lit cities because they shine like stars on the earth's canvas. What's fascinating is that these "earth stars" are created by multitudes of little lights...street lamps, house lights, business signs, and highway lighting. Each individual light, by itself, would never show up on a satellite image, but working together, they light up the world!

Yes, you and I are just individual little lights...seemingly small and insufficient, but every light matters. I am just one, among many amazingly talented artists, who are using their art to bless others and glorify the Lord. I can sometimes look at their art and think mine doesn't measure up, or they have a bigger sphere of influence—in other words, they shine brighter than I do, so maybe I should just quit. But God says my little light does matter. And so does yours.

As I researched ancient oil lamps for this week's illustration, I thought about how we are all created to be unique vessels of God's light...but none more important than another. The truth is that you are uniquely designed to shine the light and love of Christ in ways and to people my light will never reach. That's why every light matters! And when we're all shining together, we light up the world! So, as you color this week's drawing, ask God to show you how your light—your time, talents, and resources—matters. And let's light up the world together!

*Karla*

I WILL MAKE YOU AS A LIGHT FOR THE NATIONS, that my salvation may reach to the end of the EARTH.

ISAIAH 49:6

## Chapter 10

# Jeremiah 31
## Jesus the Covenant Mediator

The hope of a new and better covenant

behold, the days are coming, declares the LORD when I will make a new covenant

JEREMIAH 31:31

## Day 1

### The Covenants

Initially when I launched my business as a computer programmer, I relied on verbal agreements. I thought contracts would make prospective clients feel like I didn't trust them. That changed the first time a client tried to cheat me. After that, I attached contracts to proposals. Both my client and I signed the contract to show we accepted it.

To my surprise, clients appreciated contracts. They liked the project parameters, time estimates, and costs spelled out. It made them feel that they could trust me.

In earlier chapters, we discovered that God made covenants with people. Covenants are like contracts in that they involve people and agreed-upon obligations. The difference is that contracts are mostly about obligations, while covenants are mostly about relationship. For example, rental agreements are contracts, while marriage vows are covenants.[1]

**The Reveal**

#### Abraham's Day
God made a covenant with Abraham in which he promised to give Abraham's descendants land. To show acceptance of this covenant, all Abraham's male descendants underwent circumcision.[2] This is called the *Abrahamic covenant.*

#### Moses's Day
After the Lord rescued the Israelites from slavery in Egypt, he led them to Mount Sinai. There he offered them a covenant to establish a relationship with him in which he would be their God and they would be his people.

On Mount Sinai, God appeared in a theophany (divine manifestation) of thunder, lightning, smoke, and trumpet blasts. The people were terrified and asked Moses to represent them before God. Moses became the mediator of the covenant; that is, he was the go-between (Exodus 20:18-19). This covenant is called the *Mosaic covenant.*

God gave the people the Ten Commandments and other commands. Some of the commands provided ways they could be cleansed from impurity and sin so that they could approach God (Leviticus 16:30).

The people showed their acceptance of the covenant in two ways. The first was a onetime act to initiate the covenant. Moses told the people the terms of the covenant and asked

## The Little Details
### *Jeremiah and Ezekiel*

In the book of Jeremiah, the prophet Jeremiah describes not just the messages the Lord gave him for others, but also his own prayers and God's personal messages to him. He gives us an intimate look into what it was like to be a prophet with a message people didn't want to hear.

Sadly, one of the wicked kings burned the original scroll containing Jeremiah's prophecies (Jeremiah 36:23). He had to dictate them again to his assistant. That may be one of the reasons the messages are arranged topically rather than chronologically.

The prophet Ezekiel wrote the book bearing his name entirely from exile. He recorded the dates he received messages. He records several spectacular visions as well as the more usual messages for people. The Lord always addresses him as "son of man."

---

The second way they showed they accepted the Mosaic covenant was by making the final day of the week a day of rest.

---

them to choose whether they accepted the terms. They responded, "All that the LORD has spoken we will do, and we will be obedient" (Exodus 24:7). Then Moses sprinkled them with blood, saying, "Behold the blood of the covenant that the LORD has made with you in accordance with all these words" (Exodus 24:8).

The second way they showed they accepted the Mosaic covenant was by making the final day of the week a day of rest. That day—Friday sundown to Saturday sundown—was called the Sabbath. God said, "You shall keep my Sabbaths, for this is a sign between me and you" (Exodus 31:13). So keeping the Sabbath as a day of rest was the sign of accepting the covenant (much like signatures are the sign of accepting a contract today).

God described his covenant relationship with the Israelites in this way: "For you are a people holy to the LORD your God, and the LORD has chosen you to be a people for his treasured possession, out of all the peoples who are on the face of the earth" (Deuteronomy 14:2). *Holy* means "set apart."

### *David's Day*

God made a covenant with David in which he promised that a descendant of his would sit on the throne forever. This is the *Davidic covenant.*

### *The Major Prophets' Day*

When King Ahaz rejected God, Isaiah prophesied that the Lord would give his righteous, suffering servant as a covenant that would include both Jews and Gentiles (Isaiah 42:6; 49:6-8). With God's covenant of peace, all "shall be taught by the LORD" (Isaiah 54:10,13). Ahaz's son, King Hezekiah, listened to Isaiah and brought religious reform, but his son Manasseh followed in the footsteps of Grandpa Ahaz. He installed idols in the Lord's temple, burned his son as a sacrifice to an idol, and murdered many, angering God. Jewish tradition says Manasseh sawed Isaiah in half (see Hebrews 11:37). After he died, the Lord spoke through the three prophets we'll read from today.

### God's Word to Us

In today's reading, *Chaldeans* (ESV) is another name for *Babylonians* (NIV). *Chaldea* (ESV) is also called *Babylonia* (NIV) and *Babylon* (the capital city and its province).

>  Take a moment to pray for insight as you read God's Word.

> 1. ♥ Read Habakkuk 1:1-6; Ezekiel 37:24-28; Jeremiah 31:31-37; and 2 Kings 25:1-21. What stands out to you? Why?

> 2. ♥ Has anyone broken a contract, relationship agreement, or significant promise with you? If so, how did that make you feel?

# A Walk with Christ—The Wedding

Do you love weddings? One is coming that will outshine anything you have ever experienced: the marriage supper of the Lamb!

> "Let us rejoice and exult
>             and give him the glory,
>     for the marriage of the Lamb has come,
>             and his Bride has made herself ready;
>     it was granted her to clothe herself
>             with fine linen, bright and pure"—
> for the fine linen is the righteous deeds of the saints...
> "Blessed are those who are invited to the marriage supper of the Lamb" (Revelation 19:7-9).

Our Bridegroom, Christ, is calling us to prepare ourselves by our *righteous deeds*. Unlike the contemporary wedding industry's persuasion to consider extravagant events, Christ asks his bride to simply "walk worthy of the calling" (Ephesians 4:1 HCSB).

Christ, celebrating the Passover ceremony with his disciples, instituted a new covenant:

> And he [Jesus] took bread, gave thanks and broke it, and gave it to them, saying, "This is my body given for you; do this in remembrance of me." In the same way, after the supper he took the cup, saying, "This cup is the new covenant in my blood, which is poured out for you" (Luke 22:19-20 NIV).

We have a responsibility when taking communion:

> For whenever you eat this bread and drink this cup, you proclaim the Lord's death until he comes. So then, whoever eats the bread or drinks the cup of the Lord in an unworthy manner will be guilty of sinning against the body and blood of the Lord. Everyone ought to examine themselves before they eat of the bread and drink from the cup. For those who eat and drink without discerning the body of Christ eat and drink judgment on themselves (1 Corinthians 11:26-29 NIV).

Communion is a time of reflection, so we, his bride, should ask, "Does my life reflect a heart thankful for the epic sacrifice Christ made?"

"Search me, God, and know my heart; test me and know my anxious thoughts. See if there is any offensive way in me and lead me in the way everlasting" (Psalm 139:23-24 NIV).

In *7 Simple Skills for Every Woman*, I give seven reflections that help us live honest before our Bridegroom.

## A Bride's Renewal

**Acknowledge God as the giver of mercy:** "I will have mercy on whom I will have mercy" (Exodus 33:19 NIV). Review God's traits and see if you have an unclear view of any of God's attributes. Choose a trait of God to investigate that will help you see God and your life clearer.

**Acknowledge your sin** (the sinful choice, rebellious act or attitude): "Whoever conceals their sins does not prosper, but the one who confesses and renounces them finds mercy" (Proverbs 28:13 NIV). Don't make excuses or rationalize. Confess.

**Ascertain your identity in Christ:** Is your view of yourself matching God's view of you? Look at the mirror list online, then stand in front of a mirror and complete this sentence: "God says I am _____."

**Amend your mistakes as much as possible:** If you hurt another, apologize, correct the mistake, and make amends to try to restore the relationship.

**Actively pursue accountability:** Create a weekly time for life-giving friendships.

**Advance a forward plan:** Pray and ask God whether you should stay put or restart somewhere else. Bring those you love with you onto the redeemed path.

**Alter your heart:** Hate the darkness and love the light. Living in the light brings the freedom to become a beautiful bride!

Write a love note to your Bridegroom:

 At www.DiscoveringTheBibleSeries.com I have posted an expanded *7 Steps of Renewal* interactive as well as *God's Mirror: Your Identity in Christ* devotional worksheets.

*Pam*

---

## Day 2

## God's Plan to Stop Evil

Merely giving people right laws and a government designed to implement those laws does not change the fundamental human problem: a sinful heart. In Israel, kings arose who viewed God's commands as unneeded restraints. People who felt likewise reveled in such kings and took advantage of what they saw as freedoms.

### God's Plan Revealed in the Mosaic Covenant

The covenant God made with the Israelites on Mount Sinai had contingencies. If the people followed the terms of the covenant, God would pour blessings on them. If they didn't, God would send curses as warnings. If they continued to break the covenant, he would scatter them and their king among other nations (Deuteronomy 28:36,52,64).

But even in exile, there was hope. If the people returned to God with all their heart and soul, the Lord would have mercy on them and would bring them back (Deuteronomy 30:1-3). They would get a do-over. But what good is a do-over if the problem's source isn't fixed?

> 3. In Deuteronomy 30:6 below, underline what else God would do.
>
> And the LORD your God will circumcise your heart and the heart of your offspring, so that you will love the LORD your God with all your heart and with all your soul, that you may live.

### God's Law Forgotten

But even in exile, there was hope.

Ahaz was one of the evil kings who led the people away from God. So was his grandson Manasseh. Under them, violence, oppression, corruption, and child sacrifice spread like California wildfires. Victims cried to God for help. The prophet Habakkuk asked why God allowed evil.

4. (a) What was Habakkuk's frustration in Habakkuk 1:2's first line? (b) What evils did he see (verses 3-4)?

The Lord replied that he was about to end the evil by sending the dreaded Babylonians to invade, just as he said previously through Isaiah. The Babylonians had conquered Assyria and emerged as the new superpower. God spoke a similar message to Jeremiah, who prophesied about the same time as Habakkuk.

But the people didn't listen to Moses, Isaiah, Habakkuk, or Jeremiah. Why not?

## Why People Ignored God's Message

Let's turn to Jeremiah to discover the reasons because they're instructive to us today.

### Reason 1

5. (a) In Jeremiah 7:2, where did the Lord tell Jeremiah to prophesy? (b) How could the people avoid exile (verses 5-7)? (c) What were they trusting (verse 8)? (d) What did the people say in the temple even though they were sinning freely (verses 9-10)?

The people thought they could sin freely, offer temple sacrifices, yet stand forgiven and safe. Unfortunately, many people misinterpreted God's promise to David of an offspring with an everlasting throne to mean Solomon's dynasty would never end; therefore, God would never exile them. They reasoned that they could live how they pleased without fearing consequences if they simply offered sacrifices at the temple.

But the temple sacrifices were never designed to cover unrepentant, intentional rebellion. Plus, the Lord told David, "If your sons pay close attention to their way, to walk before me in faithfulness with all their heart and with all their soul, you shall not lack a man on the throne of Israel" (1 Kings 2:4).

6. (a) What had they turned the temple into (Jeremiah 7:11)? (b) What would the Lord do to the temple (verse 14)? (c) What particularly angered the Lord (verse 31)?

Jeremiah mentions Shiloh. There, ungodly priests treated the ark of the covenant as an amulet with magical powers to guarantee victory in war (1 Samuel 4). Now the people were treating the temple the same way. They should have known better because at Shiloh, the enemy temporarily captured the ark.

## The Little Details
### Habakkuk

Habakkuk was a contemporary of Jeremiah and Zephaniah. He wrote his prophecy during Babylon's initial meteoric rise to power.

In his prophecy, Habakkuk is upset over the evil he sees in Judah and asks God why he allows it. God reveals that he is about to end the injustices disturbing Habakkuk. He will do so by sending Babylon.

Habakkuk is shocked. He tells God that surely he would not discipline his people by sending such a cruel and wicked people to invade Judah. God replies that yes, he would, but whatever evil Babylon commits will come back on her.

Habakkuk ends with a prayer, his initial cry for justice tempered by intercession: "In wrath remember mercy" (Habakkuk 3:2).

Habakkuk determines to wait quietly for calamity to come on Babylon, no matter how bad things get meanwhile. He prays, "Yet I will rejoice in the LORD, I will take joy in the God of my salvation" (Habakkuk 3:18).

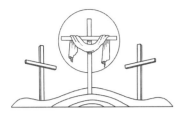

## The Little Details
### Why Not Sin Freely?

After Jesus's resurrection, some Gentile Christians made a mistake similar to what the Jews in Jeremiah's day made. They wondered why they shouldn't sin freely since their sins were forgiven. Paul wrote, "What shall we say then? Are we to continue in sin that grace may abound? By no means! How can we who died to sin still live in it?" (Romans 6:1-2). He told his readers not to let sin reign, but instead to present their bodies to God as instruments of righteousness (Romans 6:12-14).

---

The second reason people ignored the prophets is that humans tend not to listen to what they don't want to hear.

---

### Reason 2

7.  (a) What did the Lord tell Jeremiah to say he was bringing (Jeremiah 19:3)? (b) Why (verse 4)? (c) Why didn't the people listen to God (verse 15)?

The second reason people ignored the prophets is that humans tend not to listen to what they don't want to hear. Not many people like to be told what they're doing is wrong.

### Reason 3

8.  What did Pashhur the priest do when he heard Jeremiah (Jeremiah 20:1-2)?

The third reason the people ignored the prophets is that ungodly religious leaders told them to. Many religious leaders were worshiping other gods in the Lord's temple (Ezekiel 8:10-12). And the priests had stopped publicly reading the words of Moses.[3] There was a dearth of godly leadership and instruction.

### Reason 4

9.  (a) How were most of the prophets living (Jeremiah 23:14)? (b) What did the Lord instruct Jeremiah to tell the Israelites not to do (verse 16)? (c) Why (verse 16)? (d) Who were the lying prophets comforting (verse 17)?

The fourth reason the Israelites didn't repent is that most of those who called themselves prophets weren't. They told people what they wanted to hear instead of what they needed to hear. The conflicting messages confused people.

### Summary

Let's summarize. The Israelites ignored the Lord's prophets because (1) they misinterpreted God's covenant promises and thought temple sacrifices without repentance kept them safe; (2) they didn't like the true prophets' messages; (3) ungodly religious leaders told them to ignore the true prophets; and (4) false prophets misled them.

The Lord told Jeremiah to tell the priest who beat him that the Lord called Pashhur *Terror on Every Side*, for he, all his house, and all the people he had misled through false prophesies were going to captivity (Jeremiah 20:3-6).

The time for repentance was over. Judgment was on its way.

10.  ♥ Read 2 Timothy 4:3-4. How can you avoid the four mistakes the people of Jeremiah's day made?

## Day 3

# The Glory of the Lord

Godly King Josiah listened to Jeremiah, but his sons and grandson didn't.

- In 609 BC, King Josiah died. He was the last righteous king. His son reigned three months before a Pharaoh exiled him to Egypt and enthroned his brother.
- In 605 BC, Babylon invaded Judah and exiled some of the royal family, including a young man named Daniel. Daniel became a government leader serving the Babylonian king in the palaces (2 Kings 24:1-4; Daniel 1:1-6).
- In 597 BC, Babylon invaded Judah after she rebelled. Babylon took Judah's king, military, skilled workers, and leaders into exile in Babylon near a river close to Ur (where Abraham came from). Babylon enthroned the exiled king's uncle in Judah. This exile included young Ezekiel (2 Kings 24:10-14).

God didn't abandon his exiled people but called both Daniel and Ezekiel as his spokespersons in different places in Babylon while Jeremiah continued ministering in Jerusalem.

### The Glory of the Lord Leaves the Temple

We discovered earlier that the Lord showed he accepted the wilderness tabernacle and Solomon's temple by a visual display of his presence in the form of a cloud. The glory of the LORD filled both at their dedications (Exodus 40:34-35; 1 Kings 8:10-11). After Babylon invaded, God showed one of the exiles another display of his glory.

After being in exile five years, Ezekiel turned 30, the age at which he would have entered the priesthood if he were back in Judah. Babylon ripped away his professional expectations. But God had other plans for him.

One day he saw the heavens open to display winged cherubim below a throne. Upon the throne sat the glory of the Lord (Ezekiel 1). The Lord told him he was sending him to speak to the exiles on his behalf, and he should be neither afraid of nor dismayed at the people's reaction (Ezekiel 2). The Lord gave him a message for the exiles.

About a year later, the Lord took Ezekiel's spirit into the Jerusalem temple. Ezekiel saw religious leaders, men, and women all using God's temple to worship idols (Ezekiel 8).

11. In Ezekiel 9:3, what did Ezekiel see the glory of the Lord doing?

The glory of the Lord had rested on the man-made cherubim in the Most Holy Place

---

The Lord's goal had always been relationship with people.

---

(Numbers 7:89). Ezekiel watched the glory of the Lord lift on heavenly cherubim and depart to the temple's entrance (Ezekiel 10:18-19). The Lord took Ezekiel to the east gate of the temple and gave him a message of judgment and of hope. Jerusalem would fall and the rest of the people would be exiled, but then he would bring them back (11:9,17).

> **12.** (a) What would God one day give his people (Ezekiel 11:19)? (b) What would he remove (verse 19)? (c) What would they then do (verse 20)?

With that, the glory of the Lord departed (Ezekiel 11:23).

## The Hope of a New Covenant

Back in Jerusalem, the Lord spoke through Jeremiah a similar message.

> **13.** (a) How long would the people be exiled in Babylon (Jeremiah 29:10)? (b) Why was God sending them into exile (verse 11)?

To the people, God's plans didn't seem good. But their exile was the only way to give Abraham's descendants a future and a hope: "Have I any pleasure in the death of the wicked, declares the Lord GOD, and not rather that he should turn from his way and live?" (Ezekiel 18:23).

> **14.** (a) What was the Lord going to make with the Israelites (Jeremiah 31:31)? (b) What had the Israelites done with the covenant God made with them when he brought them out of Egypt (verse 32)? (c) This time, where would the law be written (verse 33)? (d) What relationship will finally happen (verse 33)?

The Lord's goal had always been relationship with people. Now everyone could see that good laws weren't enough to bring that. Let's return to Ezekiel.

> **15.** (a) What would God do for his people, according to Ezekiel 36:25? (b) What would he give them (verse 26)? (c) What would he remove from them (verse 26)? (d) What would he put in them (verse 27)? (e) What would this enable (verse 27)?

Here God says he will cleanse people. In an earlier chapter, we discovered that God would give the suffering servant as a covenant and as an offering for guilt (Isaiah 49:8; 53:10). That guilt offerings brought cleansing suggests the Isaiah and Ezekiel passages may be speaking of the same cleansing event (we'll see later that this is what Jesus will teach).

So, God would put his own Spirit within people, and his Spirit would move them to obey him. But that couldn't happen yet. First, they needed cleansing—a better cleansing than what the sacrificial system in the Mosaic covenant offered.

> 16. Read Ezekiel 37:23-28 and describe one thing that stands out to you and why you believe it's important.

This oracle prophesies the fulfillment of all the covenants. The Lord will fulfill the Abrahamic covenant by giving his people land in which to dwell with him. He will fulfill the Mosaic covenant by making people righteous and clean. He will fulfill the Davidic covenant by setting a descendant of David over his people to reign forever. And he will offer a new covenant that comes with a new heart and his own Spirit.

> 17. ♥ The exile seemed bad, but God said it would bring good. Describe a difficulty in your life that seemed bad but later proved to be good. What did God teach you?

## Jerusalem's Fall

Judah's last king ignored Jeremiah's warning and rebelled against Babylon. Babylon's mighty forces invaded and in 586 BC tore down Jerusalem's walls, burned the temple, and deposed Judah's king (2 Kings 25:6-10). The kingdom of Judah existed no more.

But the prophets promised hope: hope of restoration, hope of a new covenant—and hope of resurrection: "And many of those who sleep in the dust of the earth shall awake, some to everlasting life, and some to shame and everlasting contempt" (Daniel 12:2).

## God with Us Then

God was with his people wherever they were—even in exile. He was never limited to the tabernacle or temple. His offer of hope revealed his continuing plan to dwell with people.

## The Reveal Continued

### The Second Temple's Day

As God promised, the exile was temporary. A remnant later returned and rebuilt the temple under Zerubbabel's guidance and governance. But the second temple's dedication was not accompanied by a visible display of the glory of the Lord returning.

Meanwhile, the Jewish sect called Pharisees developed oral traditions meant to be a hedge around God's law so that the people would never experience exile again. These traditions interpreted what, for instance, was allowed on the Sabbath. Though intended for good, they still addressed only external actions, not the heart.

🖥 For more about God's omnipresence, go to www.DiscoveringTheBibleSeries.com.

## The Little Details
### What the Exile Accomplished

1. It removed bad leaders who looked out for themselves instead of for the people (Ezekiel 34:1-10; Jeremiah 23:1-2).

2. It stopped the rich and powerful from oppressing the poor and weak (Ezekiel 34:17-20).

3. It brought judgment on the wicked, while sparing the righteous whom the Lord marked (Ezekiel 9:4-6).

4. It destroyed the defiled temple (Ezekiel 8:10-12).

5. It taught discipline so that people would fight sin instead of saying, "It's no use" (Jeremiah 18:12).

6. It showed the need for God's rule (Ezekiel 34:15).

7. It showed God hates evil (Habakkuk 1:3).

8. It showed victims that God cares (Habakkuk 1:2).

9. It showed grace by allowing a do-over (Ezekiel 11:17).

-------------------------

But the prophets promised hope: hope of restoration, hope of a new covenant—and hope of resurrection.

-------------------------

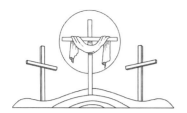

### Jesus's Day

By Jesus's day, the Pharisees elevated their oral traditions above written Scripture (Matthew 15:3-7). Most Jews highly regarded Pharisees for their piety.

# Jesus Offers a New Covenant

Both Moses and Jesus taught on what it meant to live in covenant relationship with God.

## Jesus Teaches on Kingdom Living

Moses taught on kingdom living at Mount Sinai. Jesus taught on kingdom living on another mountain in a message known as the Sermon on the Mount.

### The Beatitudes

Just as Moses explained what actions God would bless, so did Jesus. These actions are called the beatitudes.

> 18. ♥ Read the beatitudes in Matthew 5:3-12. (a) Which one gives you the most comfort? Why? (b) Which one is the most challenging? Why?

Notice that the blessings include being in the kingdom of heaven and heavenly rewards.

### The Law and the Prophets

What we now call the Old Testament, Jesus called the Law and the Prophets.

> 19. What did Jesus say about the Old Testament (Matthew 5:17)?

*Fulfill* means to "bring it to its intended goal."[5] Jesus fulfilled the Old Testament in several ways. First, he fulfilled promises and prophecies by carrying them out. Second, he fulfilled types by living out what significant Old Testament people, institutions, and events foreshadowed. Third, he fulfilled commands by expressing their complete intent and by following them perfectly.

Jesus warned, "Unless your righteousness exceeds that of the scribes and Pharisees, you will never enter the kingdom of heaven" (Matthew 5:20). This was radical because the people considered the Pharisees with their extra rules to be the epitome of righteousness. Jesus explained why they weren't by interpreting six commandments as being matters of the heart, not just actions (Matthew 5:21-48). For instance, the sixth commandment prohibited murder; Jesus said God also judges anger (verse 22). The seventh prohibited adultery; Jesus said God also judges lust (verse 28).

---

**The Little Details**

*Hunter and Wellum on the Law:*

When we think of the Law-covenant, we're tempted to think only of the Ten Commandments. While these commands are given first to highlight their importance, the Law as an entire covenant package includes far more. For example, the Law includes commands concerning how members of the community are to relate with one another in their daily life together, laws for the priesthood and a system of sacrifices, and laws concerning Israel's civil life. People often divide the Law into three parts: civil laws that govern Israel's life as a nation, ceremonial laws that regulate Israel's religious life tied to the sacrificial system, and moral laws such as the Ten Commandments. This is a helpful way to think of how different laws functioned in the nation's life, but ultimately it is best to think of the Law as a single covenant unit or package.[6]

---

Jesus fulfilled the Old Testament in several ways.

---

20. ♥ Pick *one* of the following, read the related verses in Matthew 5, and explain how you can apply Jesus's words to a current situation: anger (verses 21-26); lust (27-30); divorce (31-32); oaths (33-37); retaliation (38-42); or love (43-48).

**The Little Details**
*The Torah*
Professor Daniel I. Block writes that the word *Torah* originally applied to just the speeches of Moses. Later, the word was used to refer to the Book of Deuteronomy. By New Testament times, it referred to the entire Pentateuch (the first five books of the Old Testament).[7]

*Torah* can be used more generally in the sense of instruction: "Receive instruction from his mouth" (Job 22:22). It is sometimes translated *teaching*: "The teaching of kindness is on her tongue" (Proverbs 31:26). Professor Allen P. Ross writes that in Psalm 1:2, "The psalmist is thinking of meditation on divine revelation, beginning with the Law."[8]

By teaching that righteousness was a matter of the heart, not just outward actions, Jesus accomplished two things. He helped his followers interpret God's commands correctly, and he let them know that no one was righteous enough for God's kingdom yet.

Jesus warned against hypocrisy, such as asking for God's forgiveness without forgiving others (Matthew 6:1-18). He instructed people to lay up treasures in heaven rather than on earth (verses 19-21). Like Moses, he warned against false prophets (Matthew 7:15).

Jesus then summed up the Old Testament teachings: "Whatever you wish that others would do to you, do also to them, for this is the Law and the Prophets" (Matthew 7:12). When he finished teaching, "the crowds were astonished…for he was teaching them as one who had authority, and not as their scribes" (Matthew 7:28-29).

## Jesus Teaches on God's Kingdom

Earlier we read in Ezekiel 36:25-27 that God promised to cleanse his people with water, give them new hearts and spirits, and put his Spirit in them so they could obey him. Jesus explained what this meant to Nicodemus, a ruler and Pharisee.

21. (a) Why did Nicodemus and other Jewish leaders at that time think Jesus came from God (John 3:2)? (b) What did Jesus say is required to see the kingdom of God (John 3:3)? (c) All people have been born of a human parent, or *flesh*; of whom do they also need to be born (verse 6)?

This surprised Nicodemus who expected to enter God's kingdom because he was a good person who obeyed both the Law of Moses and the oral traditions.

Jesus said, "Unless one is born of water and the Spirit, he cannot enter the kingdom of God" (John 3:5). Let's discover more about rebirth and the Holy Spirit.

22. (a) To whom did Jesus give the right to become children of God (John 1:12)? (b) Of whom are the children of God born (verse 13)?

*Born again* is the same thing as *born of God* and *become a child of God*. We don't start out as God's children, but being born again of God's Spirit makes us children of God.

23. In John 16:7-8 below, underline why it was to the disciples' advantage to have Jesus leave them. Circle the word that describes the action the Holy Spirit—the Helper—will take concerning sin.

    It is to your advantage that I go away, for if I do not go away, the Helper will not

> By teaching that righteousness was a matter of the heart, not just outward actions, Jesus accomplished two things.

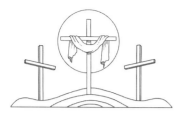

**The Little Details**

*D.A. Carson and Andrew David Naselli on Water and Spirit:*

The most plausible interpretation of "born of water and the Spirit" is the purifying and transforming new birth. Since Jesus expects Nicodemus to understand what he means (vv. 7,10), the background to the concept is previous Scripture. Water in the OT often refers to renewal or cleansing, and the most significant OT connection bringing together water and spirit is Ezek. 36:25-27, where water cleanses from impurity and the Spirit transforms hearts. So "born of water and the Spirit" signals a new birth that cleanses and transforms.[9]

One of the things the Holy Spirit does for those he indwells is convict them of sin, the false ways they pursue righteousness, and the false ways they judge righteousness.

come to you. But if I go, I will send him to you. And when he comes, he will convict the world concerning sin and righteousness and judgment.

Jesus had to leave his disciples by dying for their sins. That cleansed them so that the Holy Spirit could come into them. One of the things the Holy Spirit does for those he indwells is convict them of sin, the false ways they pursue righteousness, and the false ways they judge righteousness.

> **24.** In John 14:26 below, underline two additional tasks of the Holy Spirit.
>
> But the Helper, the Holy Spirit, whom the Father will send in my name, he will teach you all things and bring to your remembrance all that I have said to you.

The Father sends the Holy Spirit into his people so that he can help them live the way God wants, as Jeremiah 31:31-34 said would happen with the new covenant.

Jesus paraphrased Isaiah 54:13 and said it was fulfilled whenever someone comes to him: "No one can come to me unless the Father who sent me draws him. And I will raise him up on the last day. It is written in the Prophets, 'And they will all be taught by God.' Everyone who has heard and learned from the Father comes to me" (John 6:44-45).

## Jesus Brings the New Covenant

Let's look again at Jesus's last meal with his disciples. His words show that the crucifixion inaugurated the new covenant and fulfilled two more Old Testament types. First, recall that when the Israelites agreed to the covenant that came through Moses, Moses sprinkled them with blood, saying, "Behold the *blood of the covenant* that the LORD has made with you" (Exodus 24:8, emphasis added).

> **25.** In Matthew 26:27-29 below, underline the phrase that Jesus used that is the same as what Moses said above. Circle the two-word phrase that describes what will happen to his blood. Double-underline why (last five words of the first sentence). Box where Jesus will next drink wine with them (last three words of the second sentence).
>
> And he took a cup, and when he had given thanks he gave it to them, saying, "Drink of it, all of you, for this is my blood of the covenant, which is poured out for many for the forgiveness of sins. I tell you I will not drink again of this fruit of the vine until that day when I drink it new with you in my Father's kingdom."

By using the same phrase *blood of the covenant*, Jesus showed that Moses's inauguration of the Mosaic covenant was a type of Jesus's inauguration of the new covenant. When he said his blood "is *poured out* for many," he identified himself as the suffering servant who "*poured out* his soul to death and was numbered with the transgressors; yet he bore the sin of many (Isaiah 53:12, emphasis added). By offering a covenant for the forgiveness of sins, he showed his crucifixion was the fulfillment of Jeremiah's new covenant that would bring forgiveness (Jeremiah 31:31-34). By telling them he would drink wine with them in his Father's kingdom, he placed the fulfillment of Ezekiel's covenant in which the Messiah rules forever and God dwells with man in the afterlife (Ezekiel 37:22-27). Hallelujah!

## Day 5

# The New Covenant Today

Let's read some highlights about the Mosaic and new covenants from Hebrews 8–10.

### The Covenant Mediator in Hebrews

Hebrews 8:6 says the new covenant is better than the old. The old covenant was limited in what it could accomplish and prepared the way for the new covenant. Hebrews 8:8-12 quotes the passage in Jeremiah that we read about the new covenant.

> **26.** In Hebrews 8:13 below, circle the status of the first covenant.
>
> In speaking of a new covenant, he makes the first one obsolete.

Hebrews 9:1-14 explains how Jesus's blood purifies completely, while the Old Testament sacrifices made people only "outwardly clean" (verse 13 NIV).

> **27.** (a) Why did Jesus mediate a new covenant (Hebrews 9:15)? (b) What does his death do?

Verses 16-22 describe how Moses inaugurated the first covenant by sprinkling the tabernacle with blood. Verse 23 reads, "The copies of the heavenly things [were] purified with these rites, but the heavenly things themselves with better sacrifices than these."

> **28.** (a) Where did Christ enter (Hebrews 9:24)? (b) How often did the high priest enter the earthly Most Holy Place to offer sacrifices (verse 25)? (c) How often did Jesus have to offer himself (verse 26)?

The earlier sacrifices couldn't accomplish the final work. Just as the earthly "holy places made with hands" were copies (types) of "heaven itself," so the high priests' offerings were copies (types) of Jesus's offering of himself.

> **29.** (a) What was the law, according to Hebrews 10:1? (b) What couldn't it do?

Hebrews 10:4 reads, "It is impossible for the blood of bulls and goats to take away sins." The law was "but a shadow"—that is, a type. The animal sacrifices cleaned outwardly so people could draw near to God in the tabernacle, but they didn't clean inwardly or permanently (see sidebar on next page for an excellent analogy).

Hebrews 10:18 concludes about sins, "Where there is forgiveness of these, there is no longer any offering for sin." Indeed, in AD 70, Rome destroyed the temple and all other sacrifices ceased.

---

**The Little Details**
*Sklar on Sacrifice as Grace:*

The ability of guilty sinners to ransom their lives by means of sacrificial lifeblood was a gracious gift from the Lord...Sacrifice was indeed something the Israelites gave to the Lord, but it was first and foremost something he granted to them, in his grace, as a means of atoning for sin and achieving the forgiveness they so desperately desired...

This is seen with even greater clarity in Jesus' sacrifice, for here it is no longer guilty sinners presenting an atoning sacrifice to ransom themselves, but the offended King who has himself provided the atoning sacrifice to ransom guilty sinners, all because of his love for them: "But God demonstrates his own love for us in this: while we were still sinners, Christ died for us" (Rom. 5:8; cf. John 3:16). Sinners do not earn this salvation; they receive it from God as a gift of his grace, mercy and love.[10]

---

The old covenant was limited in what it could accomplish and prepared the way for the new covenant.

---

**The Little Details**

*Sklar on Atoning Sacrifice in the Old Testament:*

Atoning sacrifice in the Old Testament may be compared to writing a cheque...The purpose of the cheque was to cover the debt of sin. The form of the cheque was an animal sacrifice, whose lifeblood was given in place of the sinner's (see at Lev. 17:11). The Lord in his grace received the cheque and declared the debt paid, graciously assuring forgiveness to the offeror. But he did not cash it. In the grand scheme of things, it is not possible for the lifeblood of an animal to fully ransom the lifeblood of a human. To return to the analogy, the cheque would have bounced. So why did the Lord receive it as payment at the time? Because he knew that there would one day be money in the account to cover the debt: namely, when Jesus gave his lifeblood as the perfect and final ransom for the lifeblood of sinners (Heb. 10:10,12-14).[12]

---

Our resurrected bodies will have never sinned or been sinned against.

---

## God with Us Still

### God with Us Today

Christians show they partake of the new covenant with two signs. The first is water baptism. The second sign we repeat regularly: communion.[11]

> **30.** In Ephesians 1:13-14 (NIV) below, circle the time period mentioned first (the first three words). Box what you were marked with. Underline who the seal is. Double-underline what he guarantees.
>
> When you believed, you were marked in him with a seal, the promised Holy Spirit, who is a deposit guaranteeing our inheritance until the redemption of those who are God's possession.

That leads us back to Ezekiel's prophecy that God would put his Holy Spirit in people.

### The Holy Spirit Indwells

After Jesus rose from the dead, he breathed on his disciples and said, "Receive the Holy Spirit" (John 20:22). He told them to stay in Jerusalem until they were baptized with the Holy Spirit (Acts 1:5).

> **31.** (a) What would they receive when the Holy Spirit came on them (Acts 1:8)?
> (b) What would they then be able to be?

Acts 2:2-4 (NIV) describes what happened on the Jewish holiday called Pentecost:

> Suddenly a sound like the blowing of a violent wind came from heaven and filled the whole house where they were sitting. They saw what seemed to be tongues of fire that separated and came to rest on each of them. All of them were filled with the Holy Spirit and began to speak in other tongues as the Spirit enabled them.

The people nearby heard them speaking in their own languages. Peter arose and preached a sermon. Three thousand people believed in Jesus.

That was power indeed.

Just as God's presence filled the tabernacle and temple visibly when they were brought into service, so God's Holy Spirit filled Jesus's followers who were now Jesus's body and the temple of the living God (1 Corinthians 3:16).

> **32.** ♥ Describe a time the Holy Spirit convicted you, reminded you about Scripture, or helped you share the gospel.

### God with Us Forever

On this earth, we won't obey perfectly, but in the new heaven and earth, Jesus will send angels to remove all causes of sin (Matthew 13:41-43). This world and all its desires will pass away (1 John 2:16-17).

**33.** ♥ Read Revelation 20:10-15. What stands out to you the most?

Jesus will also resurrect our bodies (1 Corinthians 15:35-54). Our resurrected bodies will be imperishable, glorious, and powerful, like Jesus's resurrected body. Perhaps even better, our resurrected bodies will have never sinned or been sinned against.

### God with Me Now
Psalm 116 is another of the Hallel psalms that Jesus likely sang with his disciples at the last supper. With its theme of gratitude over being rescued from death, it's a perfect way to end this chapter.

Turn to Psalm 116 and read it. **Pray** the psalm to the Lord in worship.

**Praise** God for something you saw of his character this week. **Confess** anything that convicted you. **Ask** for help to do something God's Word calls you to do. **Thank** God for something you learned this week.

## The Heart and Art of Worship

There are some things we really want to remember, aren't there? And then there are memories we want to forget. And then again, there are things we'd like to remember but can't. Memories are a funny thing.

That's why we take a zillion photos, buy souvenirs, and create keepsakes. That's why some of us like to document our faith in creative ways. We want and need visual reminders of the mile markers and monumental moments in our lives. And not just for ourselves but as a way to share those memories with future generations.

It makes me think of when God rolled back the waters of the river Jordan so the Israelites could enter the promised land. He told them to pick up stones from the bottom of the river as they were crossing over and stack them up on the other side. God did this so they would have a visual reminder for all generations of not only what he had done, but also as a testimony of his faithfulness to fulfill his promises.

God also promised mankind, from the very beginning of time, to send a Messiah who would save us from sin and allow us to enter into eternity with him. And he did. He sent Jesus to give his life for ours. And he doesn't want us to forget. So instead of piling rocks, this time he gave us bread and wine...a visual and tangible way to remind us of how Jesus died for us on the cross.

As you color this week's illustration, consider setting your table with more than color pencils or crayons. Take the time to break some bread and pour yourself a little wine or juice as you color. Allow the truth of these creative symbols to soak into your soul and spirit. Give yourself time to think about some of your mile marker moments...including your salvation. Ask God to show you how you might creatively document those moments as reminders of his love...and give him praise!

*Karla*

## Chapter 11

# Daniel 7
## Jesus the Son of Man

The hope of Jesus's return

**Day 1**

## It's Not As Good As It Gets

I have some good news. This life is not as good as it gets. Jesus said he's coming to take us away—away from this world with its suffering, injustices, and evil. He's taking us to be with him in the kingdom he rules. No one who rejects his rule will be there. Neither will there be anything that causes sin. There will be no more suffering, weeping, or death. We'll be with the one who loved us enough to die to give us eternal life.

**The Reveal**

The themes of exile and exodus resonate throughout the Old and New Testaments.

### Eve's Day
***Humanity's Exile.*** Adam and Eve enjoyed fellowship with God in a garden that provided for their every need. When they rebelled, they were exiled from the garden. God still visited some of their children, but when Cain murdered his brother, God exiled him completely out of his presence and away from the land he had worked.

### Abraham's Day
***Israel's First "Exile" and Exodus Announced.*** When God made his covenant with Abraham, he said, "Know for certain that your offspring will be sojourners in a land that is not theirs and will be servants there, and they will be afflicted for four hundred years" (Genesis 15:13). But later there would be an exodus from the land: "They shall come back here in the fourth generation" (verse 16).

### Moses's Day
***Israel's First "Exile" and Exodus.*** Abraham's descendants left the land promised to Abraham's descendants and went to live in Egypt to escape a famine. Though they left voluntarily, later prophets describe it as the start of their first exile.[1] Eventually, the Egyptians enslaved them. God sent Moses to lead them in an exodus from Egypt to the promised land. Moses warned them that if they broke their covenant with God, God would exile them from the promised land.

## The Little Details
### Daniel

Daniel 1–6 describe events in Babylon's palaces. Daniel 7–12 contain four visions that are apocalyptic, like the book of Revelation. Daniel received the first two visions (chapters 7 and 8) between the court narratives described in chapters 4 and 5. Here are dates to help you understand the reading.

***605:*** King Nebuchadnezzar of Babylon makes Judah's king his vassal and takes Daniel to Babylon.

***586:*** Nebuchadnezzar demolishes Jerusalem.

***562:*** Nebuchadnezzar dies.

***556:*** Nabonidus becomes king of Babylon.

***~553-550:*** Nabonidus makes his son Belshazzar coregent and leaves him to rule in Babylon while he travels.

***539:*** Cyrus conquers Babylon, kills Belshazzar, and tells the Jews they can return to Jerusalem and rebuild the temple. The events of Daniel 5 take place immediately before Cyrus comes (Darius the Mede is probably another name for either Cyrus or his governor Gubaru).

*The Major Prophets' Day*

***Israel's Second Exile and Exodus.*** When the Israelites and their kings rebelled against God as their King of kings, the second exile began. First, Assyria exiled the people of the northern kingdom of Israel who hadn't fled to Judah for safety. Later, Babylon exiled the people of Judah and burned down the temple. The major prophets foretold the exile and the eventual return (exodus) from it.

Isaiah likened the exile in Egypt to the exile in Assyria and Babylon (Isaiah 10:24-26; 11:16; 52:4). He said Cyrus would enable the exodus from Babylon just as Moses enabled the exodus from Egypt. But he made plain that Cyrus would not be like Moses: He would be a Gentile and a foreign ruler who would not know God. The exodus wouldn't fix the problems that led to exile: human sin. That task would fall to the righteous, suffering servant.

After Jerusalem fell and news of it reached the exiles with Ezekiel, they gathered around him, now thinking he was a true prophet. They gathered to hear him—but not to do what he said (Ezekiel 33:30-31). The exiles were despondent and didn't know how to process what had happened because it seemed as if all the promises of God had failed (Psalm 89:34-39). Through Ezekiel, God spoke words of hope. He would revive the nation, not because of the people's goodness, but because of his mercy. He would bring the people back so that they and the surrounding nations would know that he was God.

Meanwhile, back in Jerusalem, the book of Lamentations helped the people process grief. In the Babylonian palaces, Daniel recorded visions.

### God's Word to Us

The Babylonians (Chaldeans) exiled Judah in three deportations. The book of Daniel covers the time period beginning with the first deportation and ending with Babylon's fall. It isn't chronological, so I've put key dates in the sidebar to help you follow the readings. The events in the first reading below happen while King Nebuchadnezzar rules Babylon. Those in the next two passages happen under Belshazzar's reign.

For timelines, go to www.DiscoveringTheBibleSeries.com.

> Take a moment to pray for insight as you read God's Word.

> 1. ♥ Read Daniel 1:1-6 (605 BC); Daniel 7 (~550 BC); Daniel 5 (539 BC); 2 Chronicles 36:22-23 (539 BC). What stands out to you? Why?

> 2. ♥ What is something you're glad will be missing from the afterlife? Explain.

# A Walk with Christ—Fully ALIVE

I live near a military base, so each day at exactly 8:00 a.m., I hear "The Star-Spangled Banner" and the "Reveille" trumpet call. This morning ritual reminds soldiers of their mission and motivation—and I have been using it to do the same for me. To kick-start my day, I hold my planner and ask, "What do you have for my day, Lord? You are the commander of my heart. Help me march to the beat of your heart."

Elisa Morgan, in her book *The Prayer Coin*, looks at Christ's Gethsemane prayer, "Father, if you are willing, take this cup from me; yet not my will, but yours be done" (Luke 22:42 NIV). Elisa explains, "Prayer is like a two-sided coin, minted in the heat and pressure of life and spent in the bent-knee practice."[2]

Can you imagine how different each of us and this world would be if we gave God the pen to write in the planner of our life?

I am a personal planner enthusiast. I believe God wants us to be good stewards of our time here on earth. Christ calls us to estimate the cost of building a tower (Luke 14:28). Paul reminds in Ephesians 5:15-17 (NIV): "Be very careful, then, how you live—not as unwise but as wise, making the most of every opportunity, because the days are evil...understand what the Lord's will is."

I love the thrill of opening a new planner whether it's January or September. Seeing the open days and months ahead conjures up feelings of possibility. God wants us to plan, and he also wants us to allow the Creator to design our day while giving us power to walk it out:

"The heart of man plans his way, but the LORD establishes his steps" (Proverbs 16:9).

"The LORD makes firm the steps of the one who delights in him" (Psalm 37:23 NIV).

No matter what scheduling app or planner you use, in the end, it is a vital daily decision to say, "Your will, your way, your day, Lord." Some days, his plan for you will look exactly like what you have written; however, on other days, God wants to give us something better than our agenda. On these days, he offers us an experience that will draw us nearer to his heart; an assignment where our only path to success is complete dependence on God's power; an inter-action that will bless and build us or encourage and equip another. Sometimes, we are asked to just get in the boat, not to simply get to the other shore, but to see Christ come walking on water!

Dr. Ken Nichols shares the key to being A.L.I.V.E.:

**A**lways
**L**iving
**I**n
**V**iew of
**E**ternity

Dr. Nichols explains: "An eternal perspective cultivates confidence, courage and commitment as we navigate the unexpected events in life. Seeing life through the grid of Bible truth is the single most important contributor to emotional, relational, physical and spiritual fulfillment."

God's Word influences my perspective.
My perspective influences my response.
My response influences the outcome...
100% of the time.[3]

"We, however, are free citizens of Heaven, and we are waiting with longing expectation for the coming from Heaven of a Saviour, the Lord Jesus Christ" (Philippians 3:20 WNT).

Live with your eyes on the Savior, heaven in your heart, and your feet on earth accomplishing God's purpose. "Since, then, you have been raised with Christ, set your hearts on things above, where Christ is, seated at the right hand of God. Set your minds on things above, not on earthly things" (Colossians 3:1-2 NIV).

Keep your gaze upward by placing a reminder of heaven in your planner or on your smartphone screen saver.

 At www.DiscoveringTheBibleSeries.com you'll discover a *Living Love-Wise* time planning worksheet to help you discern your priorities and daily schedule with a more heavenly mindset.

*Pam*

---

## *Day 2*

# The Everlasting Kingdom

Isaiah began prophesying around 740 BC. He foretold that Babylon would exile Judah, but the exile would be temporary. Let's take a look.

> **3.** In Isaiah 44:24,27-28 below, the Lord calls himself the exiles' Redeemer. Box what he'll do to rivers. Circle the name of the shepherd (king) who will fulfill the Lord's purpose. Underline what that shepherd will say.
>
> Thus says the LORD, your Redeemer…
>
> who says to the deep, "Be dry;
>     I will dry up your rivers";
> who says of Cyrus, "He is my shepherd,
>     and he shall fulfill all my purpose";
> saying of Jerusalem, "She shall be built,"
>     and of the temple, "Your foundation shall be laid."

At that time, returning from exile was unheard-of, so this was an amazing prophecy. The Lord goes on to say to Cyrus, "I call you by your name, I name you, though you do not know me" (Isaiah 45:4). Cyrus would be a Gentile, not a Jew. God called Cyrus by name more than a century ahead of time so that all people would know he is "the LORD, and there is no other" (Isaiah 45:6).

### God Places Daniel in the Babylonian Courts

Let's jump ahead a little over a century and meet Daniel.

> **4.** (a) In Daniel 1:3-4, what kind of people did King Nebuchadnezzar bring to Babylon? (b) What name did the official give Daniel (verse 7)?

## The Little Details
### *Was Daniel a Eunuch?*

Ashpenaz was the official over Daniel and his friends. The ESV calls him the king's "chief eunuch," while the NIV calls him "chief of his court officials (Daniel 1:3). According to Stephen R. Miller in the New American Commentary, the Hebrew word *sārîs* could be translated either way. Genesis 37:36 uses the term to describe Potiphar, who was married. Since Daniel and his friends were "without any physical defect" (Daniel 1:4 NIV), they probably were not eunuchs.[4]

God called Cyrus by name more than a century ahead of time so that all people would know he is "the LORD, and there is no other."

The official gave Daniel and his friends Babylonian names, a common practice there. About a year later, King Nebuchadnezzar had a disturbing dream. He asked his wise men and astrologers to tell him the dream and interpret it. When they said that was impossible, he ordered all the wise men executed, including Daniel. Daniel and his friends prayed for God to reveal the dream, and that night Daniel saw the dream in a vision.

Daniel went to the king. When the king asked if he could interpret the dream, Daniel said, "No wise men, enchanters, magicians, or astrologers can show to the king the mystery that the king has asked, but there is a God in heaven who reveals mysteries, and he has made known to King Nebuchadnezzar what will be in the latter days" (Daniel 2:27-28).

Daniel told the king the dream and explained that it meant that Nebuchadnezzar's kingdom was the first of four kingdoms.

5.  (a) In the time of the fourth kingdom, what would God set up (Daniel 2:44)? (b) How long would that kingdom last?

In this vision, God revealed that when Cyrus ended the exile, the reign of the king descended from David wouldn't start immediately.

Daniel told the king, "A great God has made known to the king what shall be after this" (Daniel 2:45). Daniel rightly credited God for the dream and its interpretation. The king said, "Truly, your God is God of gods and Lord of kings, and a revealer of mysteries, for you have been able to reveal this mystery" (verse 47). "Then the king gave Daniel high honors and many great gifts, and made him ruler over the whole province of Babylon and chief prefect over all the wise men of Babylon" (verse 48).

6.  ♥ What's a way you can follow Daniel's example of humility this week?

## Daniel Sees One Like a Son of Man

About four decades later, King Nebuchadnezzar died. Nabonidus eventually took his place, making his son Belshazzar coregent. While traveling, he left Belshazzar in charge in Babylon. During Belshazzar's first year, the aging Daniel had a vision of four beasts.

7.  (a) Who took his seat among thrones (Daniel 7:9)? (b) When the court was seated, what was opened (verse 10)? (c) What happened to the fourth beast (verse 11)?

White clothing depicts righteousness. This theophany has a court scene, fire, and angels.

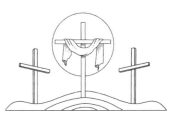

## The Little Details
### Nebuchadnezzar's Dreams

In Nebuchadnezzar's first dream, he is the head of gold. The kingdoms that follow him are of silver, bronze, and iron mixed with clay. After Daniel interprets the dream, Nebuchadnezzar makes a giant gold image and demands everyone to bow down to it (Daniel 3:1,6). It is as if he defies the dream and intends his kingdom to last forever.

In Nebuchadnezzar's second dream, he is a tree that is cut down, leaving a stump bound with iron and bronze (Daniel 4:15). The interpretation is that he will be driven mad for a time, until he acknowledges that the Most High gives kingdoms to whomever he wishes.

In Daniel 5, his successor Belshazzar ignored what Nebuchadnezzar learned and arrogantly used the goblets taken from Judah's temple in a banquet, all the while praising the gods of gold, silver, bronze, and iron. Cyrus's men killed him that night and ended Babylonian rule.

**8.** (a) Who came in the clouds of heaven (Daniel 7:13)? (b) To whom was he presented? (c) What was he given (verse 14)? (d) For how long (verse 14)?

## The Little Details
### Psalm 89

Exiled psalmists penned psalms to help the people grieve. They provide insight into what the exiles thought and felt.

In Psalm 89, Ethan lamented over what appeared to be God breaking his covenant with David. He poetically states his understanding of the Davidic covenant and his confusion:

> Of old you spoke in a vision to your godly one, and said…"Once for all I have sworn by my holiness; / I will not lie to David. / His offspring shall endure forever, / his throne as long as the sun before me"…But now you have cast off and rejected; / you are full of wrath against your anointed. / You have renounced the covenant with your servant; / you have defiled his crown in the dust…Lord, where is your steadfast love of old, / which by your faithfulness you swore to David? (Psalm 89:19,35-36,38-39,49).

This vision assured the exiles that God still planned to bring an everlasting kingdom. *Son of man* usually means "human being," so the person Daniel saw was like a human being. "Coming with the clouds" (NIV) suggests divinity, yet he was presented to the Ancient of Days.

Daniel approached someone—probably one of the angels previously mentioned—and asked for the interpretation. The interpreter said the four beasts were four kingdoms. One of the kings of the fourth kingdom would devour the earth, speak against the Most High, and oppress God's holy people.

**9.** (a) What will happen to this force of evil (Daniel 7:26)? (b) What will be given to the holy people of the Most High (verse 27)?

## God Judges Belshazzar

Another decade passed. In 539 BC, Babylon's economy was in shambles, but King Belshazzar threw a big party. He served wine in the gold goblets from the Jerusalem temple and praised the gods of gold and silver.

Suddenly, a hand appeared and wrote on the wall. But Belshazzar didn't understand the message. He promised to make anyone who could interpret it the third ruler in the land, after his father Nabonidus and himself. But none of the wise men and astrologers could do it. The queen (either his mother or grandmother) told him about Daniel. Belshazzar called for Daniel, promising him great rewards.

**10.** (a) What's the gist of why God was judging Belshazzar (Daniel 5:22-23)? (b) What was the judgment (verse 28)? (c) What happened that night (verses 30-31)?

*Darius the Mede* is another name for either Cyrus or someone Cyrus left in charge.

According to the ancient historian Herodotus, the troops of Cyrus—the king of Media and Persia—diverted the Euphrates River and invaded Babylon without a fight,[5] fulfilling Isaiah 44:27: "I will dry up your rivers." Belshazzar died that night. The invasion was relatively bloodless. When Cyrus arrived two weeks later, the Babylonians welcomed him as a liberator. He exiled Nabonidus.[6] The kingdom of Babylonia existed no more.

## Day 3

# Coming Home

"Son of man." That's how God addressed Ezekiel when he called him to be his prophet (Ezekiel 2:1). It's how the angel Gabriel addressed Daniel (Daniel 8:17). The Hebrew is *bēn 'ādām*. It could also be translated more personally, *Son of Adam*. Or less personally, *human*.

It's also how Daniel described what he saw: "Behold, with the clouds of heaven there came one like a son of man...his dominion is an everlasting dominion" (Daniel 7:13-14).

## Daniel's Prayer

In Cyrus's first year, Daniel opened Jeremiah's scroll.

**11.** (a) How long would the exile last, according to Jeremiah (Daniel 9:2)? (b) What did Daniel do next (verse 3)?

Daniel had been in Babylon around 66 years. Daniel confessed the sins of his people and sought mercy from the Lord.

**12.** (a) Since the calamity that befell them matched Deuteronomy's curse for breaking the covenant, Daniel felt remiss that the people hadn't done three things that Deuteronomy called for; what were they (Daniel 9:13)? (b) What did he confess that the people had done (end of verse 15)?

Daniel implored, "O Lord, hear; O Lord, forgive. O Lord, pay attention and act. Delay not, for your own sake, O my God, because your city and your people are called by your name" (Daniel 9:19).

**13.** (a) While Daniel was praying, who came to see him (Daniel 9:21)? (b) Why did he come to Daniel (verse 22)? (c) When did word go out for Daniel (verse 23)? (d) Why (verse 23)?

With that, the angel Gabriel gave Daniel the answer to his prayers. He explained that everlasting righteousness was coming. So was an anointed one.

## Cyrus's Decree

Isaiah prophesied that Cyrus would say "of Jerusalem, 'She shall be built,' and of the temple, 'Your foundation shall be laid'" (Isaiah 44:28). In Cyrus's first year, he put this proclamation in writing, as recorded in Ezra 1:2-4:

Thus says Cyrus king of Persia: The LORD, the God of heaven, has given me all

---

**The Little Details**

*The Four Kingdoms in Daniel 2*

Interpretations of the four kingdoms vary, but a common one is that they represent the Babylonian Empire, the Medo-Persian Empire, the Greek Empire, and the Roman Empire. Professor of biblical theology, James M. Hamilton Jr., explains: "Each of these four kingdoms will control the land of promise, three of the four are named, and though the fourth kingdom is not overtly identified as Rome, Rome is the kingdom in control in the land of promise between the third kingdom, identified as Greece, and the inauguration of God's kingdom through Jesus of Nazareth."[7]

Other interpreters separate the Medes and Persians into two kingdoms and end with the Greeks. Others think the statue parts may represent not specific kingdoms, but many evil human kingdoms.[8]

---

Gabriel explained that everlasting righteousness was coming. So was an anointed one.

---

## The Little Details
### *Psalm 80*

Asaph wrote Psalm 80 from exile. It's a prayer for restoration and repeats the refrain three times, each time building on God's name: "Restore us, O God; / let your face shine, that we may be saved!" (verse 3); "Restore us, O God of hosts; / let your face shine, that we may be saved!" (verse 7); "Restore us, O LORD God of hosts; / let your face shine, that we may be saved!" (verse 19).

Asaph begins with a lament: "How long will you be angry with your people's prayers?" (verse 4). He recounts how God took Israel from Egypt and planted it like a vine in the promised land. He pleads, "Have regard for this vine, the stock that your right hand planted, and for the son whom you made strong for yourself" (verses 14-15). He reminds God that he called the people his son. But as to the vine now, "They have burned it with fire; they have cut it down" (verse 16).

He prays for the king: "But let your hand be on the man of your right hand, / the son of man whom you have made strong for yourself!" (verse 17). He promises repentance.

the kingdoms of the earth, and he has charged me to build him a house at Jerusalem, which is in Judah. Whoever is among you of all his people, may his God be with him, and let him go up to Jerusalem, which is in Judah, and rebuild the house of the LORD, the God of Israel—he is the God who is in Jerusalem.

Cyrus returned temple furnishings and provided funds to rebuild the temple (Ezra 6:8).

## The Kingdom to Come

Daniel described four visions about the future. The last one has a fascinating tidbit. A heavenly figure told Daniel that after a time of great trouble, there would be a deliverance of those whose names are written in a book.

> **14.** (a) In Daniel 12:2, what shall happen to "those who sleep in the dust of the earth" (the dead)? (b) What will happen to those who are wise (verse 3)? (c) What about those who turn others to righteousness (verse 3)?

Daniel introduced kings and officials to the mighty God. He lived by faith according to God's commands. He recorded what he learned from God. These are ways of turning people to righteousness.

> **15.** ♥ What can you do today to turn someone to righteousness?

## God with Us Then

The temple was gone, but God was still with the exiles.

## The Reveal Continued

A remnant returned to Jerusalem. Under Zerubbabel's leadership, they built the second temple (Ezra 5:2; 6:15).

### *The Second Temple's Day*

Esther married the Persian king Ahasuerus (Xerxes NIV). His son Artaxerxes sent Ezra to Jerusalem to teach the people from the Law of Moses (Ezra 7). He also sent Nehemiah to build walls around the city (Nehemiah 2).

### *Jesus's Day*

Jesus referred to himself as "Son of Man." Since the phrase can mean "human," people didn't initially suspect a link to Daniel's prophecy. Let's discover five significant ways Jesus used "Son of Man."

## Jesus, the Son of Man
### *A Son of Man Does What Only God Can Do*

Jesus went to Capernaum, and a great crowd came to the house he was at to hear him. Four men brought a paralytic but couldn't get near Jesus. They climbed up to the roof, made an opening, and lowered the man to Jesus.

**16.** Read Mark 2:1-12. (a) What did Jesus say to the paralytic (Mark 2:5)? (b) Why did that anger some of the scribes (verses 6-7)? (c) What did Jesus ask them (verses 8-9)?

Jesus knew what the paralytic needed most was not physical healing but God's forgiveness. The text doesn't tell us why he needed forgiveness. Jesus also perceived what the scribes were questioning in their hearts. His perception was a sign that God was with him: "For you, you only, know the hearts of all the children of mankind" (1 Kings 8:39).

Since the scribes believed only God could forgive sins, they thought it blasphemy for a mere human to say a person's sins were forgiven. Indeed, the Old Testament says the Lord is the one who forgives sins (Psalms 25:18; 32:5; 130:4; Isaiah 43:25; 55:7). Jesus asked them what was easier to do and named two humanly impossible things.

**17.** (a) What did Jesus want everyone to know (Mark 2:10)? (b) What did he call himself (verse 10)? (c) What happened when he told the paralytic to rise and walk (verses 11-12)? (d) Whom did everyone glorify (verse 12)?

If Jesus had blasphemed, God wouldn't have allowed him to heal the paralytic. If Jesus didn't have authority to forgive sins, God wouldn't have allowed him to support what he said by such a sign.

In the process of all this, he called himself *Son of Man*, showing that a human being had come who could do what only God could do. He was preparing them to see the truth about who he really was.

In the next lesson, we'll see four more ways Jesus used the title Son of Man.

## Day 4

# The Son of Man Revealed

In the last lesson, we discovered Jesus revealed himself as a Son of Man who could do what only God could do. Let's discover four more ways he used the phrase.

### Jesus, the Son of Man, *continued*

#### A Son of Man Who Must Suffer

Once his disciples began to realize that Jesus was the Messiah—the Christ, the one to be anointed king—Jesus began preparing them for what was to come.

He called himself *Son of Man*, showing that a human being had come who could do what only God could do.

**18.** (a) What did Jesus tell his disciples must happen to the Son of Man (Mark 8:31)?
(b) How did Jesus say the Son of Man would come (verse 38)?

Suffering and dying tied into Isaiah's suffering servant (Isaiah 53:8-9). The "Son of Man" coming "in the glory of his Father" referred to Daniel 7:13-14: "With the clouds of heaven a son of man...came to the Ancient of Days" and "was given...glory and a kingdom...which shall not pass away." Thus, Jesus alluded to his being both Isaiah's suffering servant and Daniel's son of man.

Jesus was changing expectations. He knew the Jews didn't realize that the prophets' king descended from David (Messiah), Isaiah's suffering servant, and Daniel's son of man were all one person. The Jews wanted a messiah to deliver them from Rome and be their king on earth. Jesus tried to help his disciples change their expectations to match the whole of what the Old Testament taught about God's eternal plan.

### A Son of Man Who Comes in Glory

Later, Jesus told his disciples that the temple and surrounding buildings would be destroyed. Peter, James, and John asked him about signs of when that and other things would come. He told them there would be wars, earthquakes, and famines. He said they would be persecuted, but the gospel must be proclaimed to all nations. After a time of tribulation, the sun and moon would be darkened. Then he alluded to Daniel.

**19.** (a) In Mark 13:26, who would people see coming in clouds? (b) With what would he come? (c) What would he then send his angels to do (verse 27)?

Jesus again applied Daniel 7:13 to himself but said it wouldn't be fulfilled until after the gospel was preached to all the nations (Mark 13:10).

### A Son of Man Seated at the Right Hand of Power

Now we'll jump ahead to Jesus's trial before the Sanhedrin (the highest Jewish court). In Mark's Gospel, this is Jesus's first public acknowledgment that he is the Messiah. Appropriately, he does so before the chief priest.

**20.** Read Mark 14:55-64. (a) Why was the council seeking testimony against Jesus (verse 55)? (b) What did the high priest ask Jesus in verse 61? (c) What two-word reply did Jesus give (verse 62)?

*Son of the Blessed* is another way of saying *son of God*. All kings descended from David had two titles: *anointed one* and *son of God* (2 Samuel 7:14; Psalm 2:7). In verse 61, the high priest asked if Jesus was the anointed one (Greek *Christos*, which the ESV translates *Christ* and the NIV translates *Messiah*). When used as a title, *son of God* isn't a reference to deity, but to God's promise to be a father to anointed kings on David's throne.

Likewise, Jesus's reply—"I am"—may have alluded to the name of God: "I AM." The context isn't clear.[13] But, the next part of Jesus's reply certainly riled the high priest.

> **21.** In Mark 14:62 below, circle *you*. Underline where Jesus said they would see him seated. Box what he will come with.
>
> And Jesus said, "I am, and you will see the Son of Man seated at the right hand of Power, and coming with the clouds of heaven."

*You* is plural—Jesus spoke to all of them. "Seated at the right hand of Power" comes from Psalm 110:1 (NIV): "The LORD says to my lord: 'Sit at my right hand until I make your enemies a footstool for your feet.'" This psalm was a prophecy about the Christ, called *lord* in this verse. "Son of Man…coming with the clouds of heaven" comes from Daniel 7:13-14. Jesus's answer to the high priest was a claim that he was *both* Psalm 110's lord *and* Daniel 7:13-14's "one like a son of man."

But Psalm 110's lord sits at the LORD God's right hand while God defeats the lord's enemies. Since they were Jesus's enemies, Jesus was saying that they will see him sitting in judgment of them, the tables turned.[14] Also, the Ancient of Days gave Daniel 7's "one like a son of man…dominion and glory and a kingdom, that all peoples, nations, and languages should serve him" (verses 13-14). Jesus claimed to be the one participating in this heavenly court scene who traveled in the clouds like the LORD God.[15]

Those were problems for the chief priest. He cried, "You have heard his blasphemy," and the Sanhedrin voted to condemn Jesus to death. Just as Pharaoh refused to believe Moses came from God despite miraculous signs, so these Jewish leaders refused to believe Jesus came from God despite miraculous signs.

## A Son of Man Who Ascended into Heaven

Jesus died. But he rose from the grave. He showed himself to his disciples and told them to tell others he was alive. Acts 1:9-11 describes what next happened:

> And when he had said these things, as they were looking on, he was lifted up, and a cloud took him out of their sight. And while they were gazing into heaven as he went, behold, two men stood by them in white robes, and said, "Men of Galilee, why do you stand looking into heaven? This Jesus, who was taken up from you into heaven, will come in the same way as you saw him go into heaven."

Jesus ascended into heaven, disappearing in a cloud. In the same way, he'll return.

> **22.** ♥ How does the thought of Jesus returning make you feel?

## The Son of Man in Hebrews

Hebrews 2:5-12 quotes Psalm 8:4-6 and explains how it applies to Jesus as Son of Man.

### The Little Details
#### *James M. Hamilton Jr. on the Son of Man as Priest:*

Jesus identified the son of man from Daniel 7:13 with the Davidic king, and at the same time he asserted that the Davidic king is David's Psalm 110 Lord…The reference to the Son of Man coming on the clouds of heaven is clearly drawn from Daniel 7:13, and the fact that he is seated at the right hand of Power brings in Psalm 110:1. Jesus declared to the wicked high priest of Israel that he was indeed the Christ, the Son of God, and at the same time Jesus asserted himself to be the Son of Man who would come on the clouds of heaven to receive everlasting dominion (Dan. 7:13) as the Melchizedekian high priest (Ps. 110:4). Naturally, the rebel holding the role would not appreciate Jesus declaring himself the true high priest king of Israel.[16]

Jesus ascended into heaven, disappearing in a cloud. In the same way, he'll return.

## The Little Details
### *Poythress on Looking to Christ:*

Spiritually speaking, we are to look on the reality of Christ's rule in heaven:

> If then you have been raised with Christ, seek the things that are above, where Christ is, *seated at the right hand* of God. *Set* your minds on things that are above, not on things that are on earth. (Col. 3:1-2)

By the Spirit we see heavenly realities. The eyes of our heart are opened to know Christ (Eph. 1:18). In a broad sense, this kind of experience of sight is like the human experience of a theophany, but it takes place spiritually rather than by physical sight.

The mind that spiritually understands heavenly reality receives its consummate form of understanding when Christ appears openly:

> When Christ who is your life *appears,* then you also will *appear* with him in *glory* (Col. 3:4).

In the consummation, we ourselves will reflect the glory associated with glory theophanies, such as the appearance of glory on the Mount of Transfiguration.[17]

23. In Hebrews 2:6-8 (NIV) below, circle whom the Lord is mindful of and cares for. Box whom he is a little lower than.

> What is mankind that you are mindful of them,
>    a son of man that you care for him?
> You made them a little lower than the angels;
>    you crowned them with glory and honor
>    and put everything under their feet.

What's translated *son of man* here is often translated *humankind.* God's original plan for humans was that they rule the earth and have everything subject to them.

24. (a) At present, what's not happening (Hebrews 2:8)? (b) Who was made lower than angels in verse 9? (c) Why has he now been crowned with glory and honor (verse 9)? (d) What did he taste for everyone (verse 9)?

Jesus has begun to bring humans back to their original purpose. He shared in their humanity, a position that was lower than angels.

25. (a) Whom is God bringing to glory (Hebrews 2:10)? (b) How did he make the founder or pioneer of salvation perfect?

Suffering as a Son of Man made Jesus the perfect high priest, the perfect sacrifice, the one who makes others holy. Hebrews 2:17-18 (NIV) explains why Jesus became Son of Man:

> For this reason he had to be made like them, fully human in every way, in order that he might become a merciful and faithful high priest in service to God, and that he might make atonement for the sins of the people. Because he himself suffered when he was tempted, he is able to help those who are being tempted.

## Day 5

# The Son of Man in the Clouds

The apostles wrote letters to the churches in which they encouraged their readers to put their hope in the King and the kingdom to come rather than in this world.

### God with Us Still

*God with Us Today*
Let's discover what Paul wrote about what's to come.

26. Read 1 Corinthians 15:20-23. (a) What word does Paul use to describe the resurrected Christ (verse 20)? (b) What did Adam bring (verses 21-22)? (c) What did Christ bring (verses 21-22)? (d) When will those who belong to Christ be made alive (verses 22-23)?

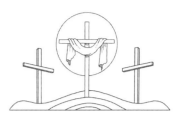

## The Little Details
### *Alexander on God Dwelling with People:*

The next significant development in the biblical meta-story is the coming of Jesus. As the opening chapter of John's Gospel affirms, Jesus, as God, tabernacles among human beings (John 1:14). The incarnation is a further development of the concept of God living on the earth. For this reason Jesus can speak of his own body as a temple, as in his comment "Destroy this temple, and in three days I will raise it up" (John 2:19).[18]

While the ever-expanding church replaces the Jerusalem temple as God's residence on earth, the biblical meta-story records one further development before the process of God inhabiting the whole earth reaches completion. As the book of Revelation reveals, there is yet to come a time when all that is evil will finally be removed from the present earth. At that stage, when God makes all things new, his presence and glory will fill a rejuvenated earth. This is what John sees in his vision recorded in Revelation 21–22.[19]

*Firstfruits* is the first part of every harvest. Jews offered it to the Lord. So, Jesus was the first part of the harvest of the dead, the first to be resurrected. Those who belong to him will be made alive when he comes again.

27. What will Christ destroy (1 Corinthians 15:24-26)?

The first man Adam brought death to the sons of man. Christ, the Son of Man, brought life and will destroy death.

While we await Christ's return to bring us to the heavenly promised land, the New Testament likens our lives on earth to living in exile.

28. In 1 Peter 2:11-12 below, circle the two words that describe believers. Underline from what we should therefore abstain. Box what those things do. Double-underline why we should keep our conduct honorable among unbelievers.

> Beloved, I urge you as sojourners and exiles to abstain from the passions of the flesh, which wage war against your soul. Keep your conduct among the Gentiles honorable, so that when they speak against you as evildoers, they may see your good deeds and glorify God on the day of visitation.

Paul also wrote about remembering this world isn't our true home.

29. Read Colossians 3:1-4. (a) What should we seek (verse 1)? (b) On what should we set our minds (verse 2)? (c) On what should we not set our minds (verse 2)? (d) What will happen when Christ appears (verse 4)?

When we're abandoned on this earth, we can reflect on how we will be with the God who will never abandon us. When we're falsely accused, we can think about what it will be like to be with the God who reveals truth and knows all truth. When we lose a loved one, we can reflect on being in a kingdom in which death is absent and on the joy of reuniting with God's family. When our bodies fail us, we can reflect on our resurrected bodies, the tree of life, and its leaves of healing.

**The Little Details**

*More Allusions to Daniel's Son of Man*

And he said, "Behold, I see the heavens opened, and the Son of Man standing at the right hand of God" (Acts 7:56).

And in the midst of the lampstands one like a son of man, clothed with a long robe and with a golden sash around his chest. The hairs of his head were white, like white wool, like snow. His eyes were like a flame of fire, his feet were like burnished bronze, refined in a furnace, and his voice was like the roar of many waters (Revelation 1:13-15).

30. ♥ (a) What is something of this earth that you think about often? (b) What is its counterpart in the coming kingdom of God? (c) Does thinking on things above bring you more peace, joy, or contentment? Explain.

 *God with Us Forever*

Earlier we read that Jesus's resurrection was the firstfruits of the harvest of God's people. Matthew 24:30-31 describes it:

Then will appear in heaven the sign of the Son of Man, and then all the tribes of the earth will mourn, and they will see the Son of Man coming on the clouds of heaven with power and great glory. And he will send out his angels with a loud trumpet call, and they will gather his elect from the four winds, from one end of heaven to the other.

Revelation 14 describes the Son of Man and two harvests. The first harvest may be the gathering of the elect, while the second is clearly the gathering of the wicked.

31. ♥ Read Revelation 14:14-20. What encourages you the most?

Revelation 22 finishes with Jesus promising to return.

32. ♥ Read Revelation 22:6-21. What encourages you the most?

 *God with Me Now*

Psalm 8 is a glorious praise psalm. It celebrates God's majesty and wonders at what God has done with humankind. In the second half of verse 4, the ESV translates the Hebrew *bēn 'ādām* literally as "son of man," while the NIV translates it "human beings." Ponder both how it applies to people in general and how it applies to Jesus. Jesus became a Son of Man, a human being, to bring us to glory with him. How he loves us.

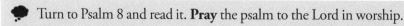

Turn to Psalm 8 and read it. **Pray** the psalm to the Lord in worship.

**Praise** God for something you saw of his character this week. **Confess** anything that convicted you. **Ask** for help to do something God's Word calls you to do. **Thank** God for something you learned this week.

# The Heart and Art of Worship

As I thought about Jesus coming back in the clouds, I was reminded of one of my life's "aha" moments from years ago. It was a gloomy spring day here in the Pacific Northwest, which is not at all uncommon. I was taking an art class at my local community college, and our teacher decided it was the perfect day for a life lesson, so he led us outside the building, told us to look up, and asked what color the sky was. It seemed like such a dumb question at the time, and we, almost all, answered in unison...gray! The sky was gray. Duh. He shook his head and told us to look again...and to keep looking. Slowly, one by one, the colors began to emerge. First, the pinks; then a soft, lovely turquoise; and finally, a few wisps of pale yellow. Wow! I was so surprised! In that moment, I realized all those years I had been looking at clouds without actually seeing them...in all their glory. It was so inspiring and life changing.

That day was significant for me for two reasons. You see, I wasn't a painter in those days. I was content with black and white. Happy with my #2 pencil, a dip pen, and a bottle of ink. But that day changed me. I didn't immediately become a painter, but I did become overwhelmingly aware and in awe of the beauty and vastness of the colors that surround us in our everyday lives. And I believe that awareness also brought me one step closer to knowing and falling in love with the One who created this colorful world we live in.

I also learned that day how easily we can move through life...rushing from one thing to another...looking but not seeing...not allowing God's creative handiwork to influence our own. So with this week's lesson in mind, I encourage you to slow down and look up. Soak in the colors that surround you, and use them in this week's illustration as you worship the coming King!

*Karla*

## Chapter 12

# Zechariah 9
## Jesus the Kingdom Deliverer

The hope of a new heaven and earth

Zechariah 9:10

**Day 1**

## Persevering Through Disappointment

Clay and I walked every day. We hiked our favorite hill twice a week, Clay watching the trail for rattlesnakes while I scanned eucalyptus trees for Anna's hummingbirds, palm trees for orioles, and meadows for deer. We drove to the beach to climb stairs with ocean vistas. We scrambled up hilly neighborhoods nearby.

Every day, that is, until the morning in November 2016 that I bent to pick up a bag of Epsom salts, twisted, and felt a vertebra in my lower back slide with a grinding noise. A few days later, the vertebra above it slid the opposite direction. All told, over ten days, five vertebrae slid. I couldn't lift my right foot off the ground, and I could lift my left foot only a few inches. I couldn't lift a glass of water with my right hand.

My physical therapist told me the new rules. Until all was healed, no more hills, no more slopes. No more weights or sitting without back support. Weakness or pain meant stop lest I make things worse. I followed her orders, did the exercises she gave me, and prayed for a speedy recovery.

I awoke one morning in early March feeling down, but unsure why. When the sadness persisted through the morning, I took it to God in prayer. I asked God to show me what was behind the sadness and prayed the refrain from Psalm 42: "Why are you cast down, O my soul?" A scene popped into my mind that I had viewed from the car the day before: mustard grass dying by a freeway ramp.

Then I knew. We had had exceptional winter rains, which meant spectacular wildflowers on our favorite trail. I had asked God to heal my back before they died. The faded mustard grass meant it was too late.

Immediately, I thanked God for all the years of hiking trails and viewing wildflowers and vistas. I thanked him that I could still walk level ground. I prayed for people who didn't live near beautiful sites, who'd never been able to walk, and who couldn't walk now at all. My sadness left, and I was grateful for all God had given me in the past, all I still had now, and all the wonders that he will give us in the new heavens and earth with resurrected bodies that won't age and fail.

I was (and still am) determined to persevere through disappointment. God has tasks for me that currently don't include hiking hills. My goal is to see what they are and do them.

I was (and still am) determined to persevere through disappointment.

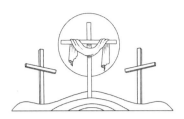

## The Little Details
### *Ezra and Nehemiah*

In the Hebrew Bible, Ezra and Nehemiah are one book and consist of lists, edicts, letters, and personal stories. Together they chronicle three groups of people returning to Jerusalem over approximately a century. They provide fascinating glimpses into the difficult life people faced in the early restoration.

It's a lesson I've gleaned from the lives of the godly people we're reading about in this chapter. They persevered through disappointment, and they helped others do the same.

We can follow their example because Jesus is coming to take us into his kingdom: "Then comes the end, when he delivers the kingdom to God the Father after destroying every rule and every authority and power" (1 Corinthians 15:24). He is the kingdom deliverer.

## The Reveal

### *David's Day*

When the prophet Samuel anointed David as future king, what excitement must have flowed through the shepherd boy's veins. When he married King Saul's daughter, he probably thought that was the path to the crown. He faced bitter disappointment when Saul sought to kill him and gave his wife to another man. But David persevered and became the king whose offspring would rule forever.

### *The Major Prophets' Day*

Exile ripped Daniel and Ezekiel from their homes. They lost their intended professions. But they endured and embraced the new lives God planned for them.

When God first called young Jeremiah to be a prophet, God's words delighted him (Jeremiah 15:16). But painful persecution dismayed him, and he protested. The Lord told him if he repented, God would both strengthen and deliver him (verses 19-21). Jeremiah obeyed and grew into a man able to deliver God's messages no matter the cost.

### *The Second Temple's Day*

The Persian king Cyrus conquered Babylon and announced that all the nations whom Babylon had exiled could return to their homelands. He provided funds and materials for them to rebuild temples. But only a small remnant returned to Jerusalem to rebuild. The work to be done overwhelmed them, and enemies tried to stop them, sometimes successfully.

## God's Word to Us

 Take a moment to pray for insight as you read God's Word.

1. ♥ Read Ezra 3:8-13; Haggai 2:1-9; and Zechariah 9:9-16. What stands out to you? Why?

2. ♥ Describe a time God acted in a way you didn't expect. What did you learn?

# A Walk with Christ—Faith Greater than Fear

We live in a world filled with trials, tribulations, and turmoil. Underline what and who brings peace:

"You will keep in perfect peace those whose minds are steadfast, because they trust in you" (Isaiah 26:3 NIV).

"I have told you these things, so that in me you may have peace. In this world you will have trouble. But take heart! I have overcome the world" (John 16:33 NIV).

"Now may the Lord of peace himself give you peace at all times and in every way. The Lord be with all of you" (2 Thessalonians 3:16 NIV).

"For he himself is our peace" (Ephesians 2:14 NIV).

Peace is readily available through Christ, but to get peace, we need to pursue peace: "A future awaits those who seek peace" (Psalm 37:37 NIV).

The week the U.S. embassy was opened in Israel, Bill and I were leading a tour of the Holy Land. We heard many miraculous stories of the provision and protection *Yahweh* gave Israel from the time of the Old Testament up through the Israel's reinstatement as a nation, on to today in their promised land. We traversed to the home of messianic Jews and asked a few residents, "How do you muster the courage to live in a neighborhood where you can see the weapons of your enemies aimed at you from the mountains overlooking your home?" Their reply: *worship*. We were reminded that peace is the choice to look not at the face of your enemies but into the face of God. Developing a vibrant personal faith with *Yeshuea* (Jesus, the Messiah) moved them (and us) from fear to faith. Our cup of faith was full as we made our way to the hotel.

Just after midnight, Bill and I were startled by booming explosions. We jumped from bed and looked out the window to see bombs bursting directly in front of us. We are mindful of the Iron Dome covering Israel's airspace, but keenly aware that people die daily around the world. As we stood hugging each other, we gazed into the night aglow with missiles intercepting the weapons coming from Iran, over Syria. I turned to my husband and asked, "Are you afraid?"

"I probably should be, but not really. I sense God's powerful presence here. I feel supernatural peace."

I replied, "It feels like the 'good hand of God' expressed in the Old Testament is covering us. If it's my time to enter heaven, I know I've been obedient to do all God has asked of me. We have a legacy of love and faith in the lives of our family and in our Love-Wise ministry. I feel compelled to pray for others here to have this same peace only God can give." By this time, the missiles ceased. After praying, we went back to bed and slept in peace. At dawn, as we dressed for our Golan Heights tour, we heard on the news that 20 missiles had been launched at Israel, and no casualties had occurred.[1]

Christ gifts us with *internal* peace now and peace in heaven as we exit this life. There's a day coming when he will also give us *external* peace in a new heaven and new earth. On paper, write down the Hebrew word for peace, *Shalom*, and list areas in which you need God's peace. Personalize and pray Psalm 29:11 (NIV): "The LORD gives strength to _____; the LORD blesses _____ with peace."

*Pam*

# The New Temple

The last chapter ended with King Cyrus telling the exiles they could return home. In this chapter, we'll look at how Jesus fulfilled some of the prophecies that came during the time of the second temple. Then we'll step back in time to look at an amazing prophecy I saved for the end.

## The Little Details

### Haggai, Zechariah, and Malachi

Three second temple prophets wrote the last three books of the Minor Prophets.

Haggai and Zechariah encouraged the governor Zerubbabel and the high priest Joshua to build the temple. Haggai encouraged the people to remember the blessings and curses of the Mosaic covenant.

The New Testament quotes only Isaiah more than Zechariah. Zechariah has many themes related to Isaiah's prophecies, and so it is sometimes called the Little Isaiah.

Malachi ministered after the completion of the second temple. His audience was disillusioned and disappointed that the restoration was anything but glorious.

### Building the Temple

About 50,000 Jews returned to the ruins of Jerusalem and surrounding villages in what was now the Persian province of Judah. It was part of a larger territory called Beyond the River or Trans-Euphrates (NIV). The returned exiles first built a new altar so that the priests could offer sacrifices again.

3. (a) Who are the two people named in Ezra 3:8 who worked on the temple? (b) What happened when they laid the foundation (verses 10-11)? (c) What did those old enough to remember the first temple do (verse 12)?

Zerubbabel descended from David through the exiled king. Joshua (also spelled *Jeshua*) was the high priest. Together, they started rebuilding the temple. They began enthusiastically, but the difficult work and limited resources slowed progress. Enemies in neighboring provinces opposed them and bribed officials to stop them. To their disappointment, the building project halted (Ezra 4:24).

### The Glory of the Lord

Two discouraging decades passed. Then the Lord sent the prophets Haggai and Zechariah to spur the people on to finish the temple.

4. In Haggai 2:4-5 below, circle Zerubbabel's and Joshua's names. Underline what the Lord tells them to do. Double-underline why they should work. Box where God's Spirit is.

   Yet now be strong, O Zerubbabel, declares the LORD. Be strong, O Joshua...the high priest. Be strong, all you people of the land, declares the LORD. Work, for I am with you, declares the LORD of hosts, according to the covenant that I made with you when you came out of Egypt. My Spirit remains in your midst. Fear not.

5. In Haggai 2:7-9 below, circle the word *glory* wherever it appears. Underline which glory shall be greater. Box what the Lord will give the place (the temple or Jerusalem).

   I will fill this house with glory, says the LORD of hosts...The latter glory of this house shall be greater than the former, says the LORD of hosts. And in this place I will give peace, declares the LORD of hosts.

They began enthusiastically, but the difficult work and limited resources slowed progress.

Here, *latter* modifies *glory*.[2] The glory that will enter the second temple at a later time will exceed the glory that entered the first temple.

Two months after Haggai began prophesying, so did Zechariah. He called the people to return to the Lord so that the Lord would return to them (Zechariah 1:3).

6.  (a) Why shouldn't Zerubbabel worry about opposition and lack of resources (Zechariah 4:6)? (b) What did the Lord promise Zerubbabel (verse 9)? (c) Why (verse 9)?

The Spirit of the Lord of hosts would see the project through to the end, and then they would know that God was indeed with them. Zerubbabel gathered the people to start building again. When the head governor of Beyond the River questioned them, they told him about Cyrus's decree. The new Persian king, Darius, located Cyrus's edict.

7.  In Ezra 6:7-8 below, underline what King Darius told the head governor of Beyond the River to do (first two sentences). Double-underline what the governor was to provide (last sentence).

    Let the work on this house of God alone. Let the governor of the Jews and the elders of the Jews rebuild this house of God on its site. Moreover, I make a decree regarding what you shall do for these elders of the Jews for the rebuilding of this house of God. The cost is to be paid to these men in full and without delay from the royal revenue, the tribute of the province from Beyond the River.

### Zerubbabel Finishes the Temple

Discouragement fled, and the people worked with all diligence (Ezra 6:13).

8.  In Ezra 6:14 below, underline what happened through the prophesying of Haggai and Zechariah. Double-underline what the people did (first four words of second sentence). Circle the four names of people who decreed the work.

    And the elders of the Jews built and prospered through the prophesying of Haggai the prophet and Zechariah the son of Iddo. They finished their building by decree of the God of Israel and by decree of Cyrus and Darius and Artaxerxes king of Persia.

They completed the temple in 516 BC, 70 years after its destruction in 586 BC. Then they joyfully celebrated (Ezra 6:16-17).

9.  ♥ (a) Describe a time someone encouraged you to finish something when you wanted to give up. (b) What traits do you admire in that person? (c) Is there someone you can encourage today? Explain without using names.

## The Little Details
### Jeremiah's 70-Year Exile

Daniel read Jeremiah's prophetic scroll and saw that the exile was to last 70 years (Daniel 9:2). Daniel was among the first group of exiles that left in 605 BC. The first group to return from exile arrived in 538 BC, 67 years after the first exiles departed. Some understand Jeremiah's 70 years as a round number for this 67-year period.

Others count the 70 years from 586 BC, when Babylon burned the temple and destroyed Jerusalem, to 516 BC, when Zerubbabel finished the temple. Zechariah 1:12 speaks of this 70-year period.

It's possible Jeremiah's words had a double intention. The first exiles hoped to return in 70 years, and the last exiles hoped for a new temple and reinstated worship in 70 years.

- - - - - - - - - - - - - - - - - - - - -

Discouragement fled, and the people worked with all diligence.

- - - - - - - - - - - - - - - - - - - - -

## The Little Details

### The Shepherd Rejected for 30 Pieces of Silver

The Lord told Zechariah to "shepherd the flock marked for slaughter" (Zechariah 11:4 NIV). The flock symbolized the nation sent into exile. Their earthly shepherds (kings, priests, and prophets) had not protected them, but instead used their positions to get rich (Zechariah 11:5).

The flock detested him, so he stopped shepherding them (Zechariah 11:7-9). The sheep dealers insulted him with paltry payment:

> And they weighed out as my wages thirty pieces of silver. Then the LORD said to me, "Throw it to the potter"—the lordly price at which I was priced by them. So I took the thirty pieces of silver and threw them into the house of the LORD, to the potter (Zechariah 11:12-13).

In Jesus's day, the chief priests paid Judas 30 pieces of silver (Matthew 26:14-16). Judas regretted betraying Jesus and threw the money into the temple. The chief priests bought a potter's field with it and called it the Field of Blood (Matthew 27:3-10). Matthew said all of this fulfilled Zechariah 11:12-13 and Jeremiah 19:1-13; 32:6-9.

## Zechariah Prophesies About the Messiah

After the temple's completion, Zechariah received more oracles.

### The King Riding on a Donkey

We looked at Zechariah 9:9 already, but let's see it in its context. Verses 1-8 describe judgment against the Jews' enemies. They foretell a time when the Lord will encamp in his house so that no enemy will ever again attack.

> **10.** (a) Why should Zion rejoice greatly (Zechariah 9:9)? (b) What will the king be like? (c) What will he ride?

He will differ from the wicked and arrogant kings who brought Jerusalem's fall. *Lowly* means humble or afflicted, like Isaiah's suffering righteous servant who was afflicted for people's sins (Isaiah 53). He will ride a donkey like David rode when exiled from Jerusalem (2 Samuel 16:2).

> **11.** (a) What will the king cut off (Zechariah 9:10)? (b) What shall he speak? (c) Where shall he rule?

He will end war and will speak peace, like the child who will be called the Prince of Peace and who will sit on David's throne (Isaiah 9:6-7). Because of the blood of his covenant with the people, he will set prisoners free and restore to them double (Zechariah 9:11-12).

> **12.** (a) How will the LORD appear (Zechariah 9:14)? (b) What will the LORD their God do on that day (verse 16)? (c) What will his people be like in his land (verse 16)?

His appearance will be like his appearance on Mount Sinai (Exodus 19). He will shield his people, who will overcome their enemies like David overcame Goliath with a stone in a sling. He will save his people as a good shepherd saves his flock. *On that day* his people will shine in his land like jewels shine in a crown.

That's a clue about what *on that day* means, for Daniel prophesied that the wise and righteous will shine in everlasting life (Daniel 12:3).

## Day 3

# Jesus in the Second Temple Prophecies

Let's discover a couple more prophecies about Jesus.

### Him Whom They Have Pierced

In the next chapters in Zechariah, *on that day* means the day "the LORD will be king over all the earth" (Zechariah 14:9).

13. In Zechariah 12:10 below, underline the two descriptions of the one whom they will look at (they follow the second and third occurrences of the word *on*). Box the two phrases describing what the people will do when they look on the one pierced. Circle *only child* and *firstborn*.

   And I will pour out on the house of David and the inhabitants of Jerusalem a spirit of grace and pleas for mercy, so that, when they look on me, on him whom they have pierced, they shall mourn for him, as one mourns for an only child, and weep bitterly over him, as one weeps over a firstborn.

This prophecy links to Isaiah. Isaiah 44:3-5 foretold that God would pour out his Spirit. The suffering servant would be rejected and pierced (Isaiah 53:3,5).

### The Shepherd Struck

14. (a) How does the Lord describe the one whom the sword will strike (Zechariah 13:7)? (b) What will happen to the sheep when the shepherd is struck? (c) Who are they to God (last sentence of verse 9)?

The Lord calls for the sword to strike, just as it was the Lord's will to strike the suffering servant (Isaiah 53:4,10). The shepherd is close to God. The metaphor shifts from sheep to silver and gold refined in fire. The phrase *my people* describes a covenant relationship.

### The Day of the Lord

After the temple's completion, reality didn't match the glorious restoration of which the prophets had spoken. Disappointment set in. Some of the returned exiles sought God, but others were cynical about living under foreign rule. This latter group refused to tithe and offered blemished and stolen sacrifices. Apathetic priests accepted the improper sacrifices. Into this milieu, God called one more prophet.

15. (a) Whom will the Lord send and why (Malachi 3:1)? (b) Who will come to the temple? (c) What will the day of his coming be like (verse 2)? (d) What will offerings then be like (verses 3-4)?

## The Little Details
### The Chronology of Ezra 4

Journalists often compare current situations to situations under the Bush and Obama administrations. The references aren't confusing to those familiar with the leaders and when they led.

The author of Ezra assumed readers were familiar with rulers and when they led. Chapter 3 ends with laying the temple's foundation in 538 BC. Verse 4:5 describes the opposition that led to halting construction after the foundation was laid until Darius's reign. Verses 6-23 describe similar opposition during the reigns of later kings. Ezra 4:24 resumes with Darius's reign.

The books of Ezra and Nehemiah were originally one book that described three leaders who each brought a group of exiles to Jerusalem and overcame grave opposition.

*538 BC:* Zerubbabel arrived and under Cyrus and Darius built the altar and temple.

*458 BC:* Ezra arrived and under Artaxerxes built the people's spiritual lives.

*445 BC:* Nehemiah arrived and under Artaxerxes built Jerusalem's wall.[3]

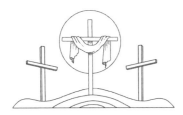

## The Little Details
### *More Fulfillments*

Zechariah 12:10 records that "they shall mourn for him, as one mourns for an only child...a firstborn." This was fulfilled when Jesus's loved ones mourned his death as God's only and firstborn son. Jesus said that "God...gave his only Son," referring to himself (John 3:16). Romans 8:29 says that Jesus is "the firstborn among many brothers." Those who are born again are his later-born brothers and sisters.

Zechariah 13:1 reads that a fountain will open to cleanse from sin and uncleanness. This is fulfilled by the Holy Spirit washing those who belong to Christ (Titus 3:4-7).

------------------------

Nehemiah taught them to persevere and support each other.

------------------------

Malachi called the people to repentance. But they needed more than a prophet.

## Ezra and Nehemiah

The great teacher Ezra led another group of exiles to Jerusalem. He studied and followed Moses's law. The Persian king told him to teach God's ways to all the province of Beyond the River (Ezra 7:25). He gave him several tons of silver and other supplies. Ezra was dismayed to learn of the returned exiles' sins and called them to repent.

A decade later, Nehemiah led a third group of exiles back. Despite great opposition and danger, he inspired the people to rebuild Jerusalem's wall so they had protection from enemies. Nehemiah taught them to persevere and support each other.

Ezra and Nehemiah gathered all the people together. Ezra read Moses's law to the people and explained its meaning (Nehemiah 8–9). Ezra brought spiritual revival.

## God with Us Then

Zerubbabel built the second temple as God commanded. The prophets said the latter glory in that temple would surpass the glory in the first temple. But on the dedication of the temple, the glory of the Lord did not appear.

## The Reveal Continued

Malachi is the last book of the Old Testament. Four hundred years passed waiting for the Messiah. Persia fell to Greece. Greece fell to Rome. And then...the promised one came.

### *Jesus's Day*

Jerusalem was in the Roman province of Judea. Herod began remodeling the temple two decades before Jesus's birth. He covered it in white marble and gold.

## The Fulfillments

### *The Glory of the Lord*

Haggai prophesied, "The latter glory of this house shall be greater than the former...And in this place I will give peace" (Haggai 2:9). When Jesus's parents brought him as a child to the temple, the prophet Simeon said that seeing Jesus was seeing "a light...for glory to your people Israel" (Luke 2:32).

> **16.** In John 1:14 below, circle what people saw when the Word (Jesus) became flesh.
>
> The Word became flesh and dwelt among us, and we have seen his glory, glory as of the only Son from the Father, full of grace and truth.

A cloud theophany of glory filled the tabernacle and the first temple. Jesus, the glory of God incarnate, entered the second temple. This latter glory was greater than the glory of the earlier theophanies. In fact, the word translated *dwelt* could be translated *tabernacled*[4] or "pitched his tabernacle."[5] Professor Vern S. Poythress explains:

> The Greek word for *dwell* in [John 1:14] (*skēnoō*) is not the most common one, but one linked to the Old Testament tabernacle. The word for *glory* has links with the glory of God that appears in the cloud, the cloud that settles on the tabernacle (Ex. 40:34-38).[6]

Haggai 2:9 reads, "And in this place I will give peace."

> **17.** In Romans 5:1 below, circle what we have with God through Jesus.
>
> We have peace with God through our Lord Jesus Christ.

## Him Whom They Have Pierced

Zechariah recorded the Lord's words as "when they look on *me,* on *him* whom they have pierced, they shall mourn for *him*" (12:10, emphasis added). This closely associates the Lord God with the one pierced, just as the New Testament reveals (John 1:1,14).

> **18.** (a) What did the soldier do while Jesus's body was on the cross (John 19:34)?
> (b) Why did this happen (verses 36-37)?

Those present at the crucifixion fulfilled Zechariah 12:10, but there is a future fulfillment as well: "Behold, he is coming with the clouds, and every eye will see him, even those who pierced him, and all tribes of the earth will wail on account of him" (Revelation 1:7). Jesus said that after a time of tribulation, "Then will appear in heaven the sign of the Son of Man, and then all the tribes of the earth will mourn, and they will see the Son of Man coming on the clouds of heaven with power and great glory" (Matthew 24:30). In fact, the New Testament describes the day Zechariah wrote about as starting with the first coming of Jesus and lasting through his second coming.[7]

## The Shepherd Struck

Zechariah 13:7-9 spoke of striking God's shepherd who is close to him, causing the sheep to scatter. That's followed by establishing a covenant between them and God.

At the last supper, Jesus took the cup and said, "This is my blood of the covenant, which is poured out for many" (Mark 14:24). Then he quoted Zechariah 13:7, saying, "You will all fall away, for it is written, 'I will strike the shepherd, and the sheep will be scattered'" (Mark 14:27). He was arrested, his disciples scattered, and Jesus poured out his blood, inaugurating the new covenant between people and God.

## The Day of the Lord

In Malachi 3:1, the Lord said he would send his messenger to prepare the way, and "then suddenly the Lord...will come to his temple; the messenger of the covenant" (NIV). Matthew 11:10 and Luke 7:27 quote this passage and reveal the messenger was John the Baptist, who announced that Jesus was the Messiah. The Lord came to the temple numerous times, and he inaugurated the covenant of which the prophets spoke.

> **19.** ♥ In this study, we've discovered Jesus in many Old Testament scriptures (and we have more to come). What is one that really stood out to you? Why?

### The Little Details
### *Elijah and John the Baptist*

Malachi 4 tells us more about the day of the Lord. Verses 1-2 read that the day of the Lord will set evildoers "ablaze," while "the sun of righteousness shall rise with healing" for those who revere the name of the Lord. John the Baptist's father prophesied that John would prepare the way "whereby the sunrise shall visit us from on high," alluding to Malachi 4:2 (Luke 1:76,78).

Malachi 4:4-6 speaks of Elijah coming before the "great and dreadful day of the LORD comes. And he will turn the hearts of fathers to their children and the hearts of children to their fathers." An angel told John the Baptist's father that this would be fulfilled by John: "He will go before him in the spirit and power of Elijah, to turn the hearts of the fathers to the children, and the disobedient to the wisdom of the just, to make ready for the Lord a people prepared" (Luke 1:17). In Matthew 11:14, Jesus said John the Baptist "is Elijah who is to come."

## The Little Details

### Signs and Wonders

True prophets spoke words of exhortation, judgment, and hope. They sometimes foretold the future. If all they foretold came to pass, that was a sign they were from God. If anything did not come to pass, that was proof they were not from God. Thus, when Jerusalem fell, the people could know that all the false prophets who predicted it would never happen were not from God. It was evidence that Jeremiah and Ezekiel were true prophets.

At key times, God also used miracles to show that a prophet was from him. For instance, when a queen killed or exiled most God worshipers in the northern kingdom of Israel, God called Elijah and Elisha to miraculously demonstrate his power over the queen's god (1 Kings 17–2 Kings 13). They called down fire and raised a dead child to life. These signs gave a wayward king and nation evidence that they should reject the queen's god and follow the true God, even though doing so meant risking one's life.

# The Prophet like Moses

We're going to jump back to Moses's day to discover one more incredible promise.

The book of Deuteronomy contains Moses's final words to the Israelites as they prepared to enter the promised land under Joshua's leadership.

> **20.** Read Deuteronomy 18:15-19. (a) Who was the LORD going to raise up (verse 15)? (b) Why did the LORD speak through the prophet Moses instead of directly to the people (verse 16)? (c) What will this prophet like Moses do (verse 18)? (d) What will happen to anyone who refuses to listen to this prophet (verse 19)?

The last chapter of Deuteronomy tells what happened after Moses died.

> **21.** (a) What does Deuteronomy 34:10 say had not yet happened? (b) How did the LORD know Moses (verse 10)? (c) What did Moses do (verse 11)? (d) What had no one else done (verse 12)?

Moses said that the office of prophet would continue, and God would hold people responsible for listening to or rejecting prophets. At the time that another inspired author added the final 12 verses to Deuteronomy, there had not yet come a prophet equal to Moses. All were like him in some ways, but none were his equal—until Jesus.

## Ways Jesus Is like Moses

Let's discover how Jesus was like, but surpassed, Moses in abilities, roles, and experiences.

### Attested To by Signs and Wonders

God worked signs and miracles through Moses so that the people would know he had sent Moses. They needed evidence before they risked their lives following him. For instance, Moses parted the Red Sea (Exodus 4:1-9; 14:26-31).

> **22.** In Exodus 14:31, what happened when the people saw God's miraculous deliverance through Moses at the Red Sea?

God likewise worked signs and miracles through Jesus so that people would know he had sent Jesus. The early disciples needed evidence before they risked their lives following him.

**23.** (a) In John 2:11, what did John call the turning of water into wine? (b) What did it manifest? (c) What did this cause the disciples to do?

The signs' purpose was to show people they could trust Moses and Jesus. Here are more.

***Showed power over nature:*** Moses parted the Red Sea (Exodus 14). Jesus walked on water and calmed a storm with a word (John 6:16-21; Matthew 8:26). Jesus did not bring plagues in his first coming, but when he hung on the cross offering himself as the firstborn son, darkness filled the land. These were reminders of the ninth plague of darkness and the tenth plague of the death of the firstborn sons (Mark 15:33; Luke 2:7; Romans 8:29; Colossians 1:15,18).

***Showed power over a serpent:*** Moses turned a serpent into a shepherd's staff (Exodus 4:3-4). Jesus cast out demons, showing power over the serpent, Satan (Mark 1:25-26).

***Healed miraculously:*** God answered Moses's prayers to heal Miriam of leprosy and the people of snake venom (Numbers 12:13; 21:9). Jesus healed leprosy (Mark 1:42), but he went beyond that and healed all diseases (Mark 1:34). He even raised the dead (Mark 5:35-42; Luke 7:11-17; John 11:38-44).

***Fed people miraculously:*** When Moses led the people through the desert to the promised land, the Lord miraculously fed the people with bread from heaven, which they called manna (Exodus 16). Jesus fed a crowd of 5000 with five barley loaves and two fish. The people said, "This is indeed the Prophet who is to come into the world!" (John 6:14). They thought he was *the* prophet like Moses. The next day, Jesus linked this feeding to manna, saying, "I am the bread that came down from heaven" (John 6:25-41).

***Gave water:*** Moses gave the Israelites water from a rock (Exodus 17). Jesus offered living water (John 4:10-14; John 7:37-38). The crowds replied, "This really is the Prophet" (John 7:40)—meaning the prophet like Moses. By living water, Jesus meant the Holy Spirit, who came upon his followers visibly at Pentecost (John 7:39; Acts 2:1-3).

***Transfigured before witnesses:*** When Moses descended Mount Sinai, "the skin of his face shone because he had been talking with God" (Exodus 34:29). When Jesus ascended a high mountain, "He was transfigured before them, and his face shone like the sun, and his clothes became white as light" (Matthew 17:2).

***Spoken to from a cloud by God:*** At Mount Sinai, God appeared in a cloud and spoke so that the people would trust Moses (Exodus 19:9,16-20; 20:1-17). At Jesus's transfiguration, a "bright cloud overshadowed them, and a voice from the cloud said, 'This is my beloved Son, with whom I am well pleased; listen to him'" (Matthew 17:5).

## Priestly Duties

***Mediated God's covenant:*** Moses mediated God's covenant with the Israelites. Jesus mediated the new covenant with people from all nations.

***Performed priestly duties:*** Moses was a priest outside of Aaron's priesthood (Psalm 99:6). He consecrated the altar, tabernacle, and the people with animal blood, anointed Aaron and his sons as priests, and taught God's commands (Exodus 24:6-8; Leviticus 8:1-13; Deuteronomy 4:1). Jesus was a priest outside of Aaron's priesthood (Hebrews 7:16-17). He

## The Little Details
### The Suffering Servant as a Prophet like Moses

Isaiah spoke of the return from exile as if it were another exodus, like the one Moses led out of Egypt. But, Isaiah said that God would use the Gentile Cyrus for the exodus from Babylon, not someone like Moses.

Isaiah, however, portrayed the suffering, righteous servant as a prophet like Moses. He would be a prophet (Isaiah 49:1-2; 50:4). He would function as a king, and other kings would bow to him (42:1,4; 49:7). He would function as a priest, teaching, sprinkling the nations, bearing iniquity for the people, offering his own soul for their guilt, and making intercession for transgressors (50:4; 52:15; 53:6,10,12). He would establish justice and be a lawgiver (42:1,3,4). He would bring healing (53:5).

Whereas Moses mediated God's covenant with Israel, God would give the suffering, righteous servant "as a covenant for the people" (Isaiah 42:6; 49:8).

consecrated the heavenly holy places with his own blood, anoints his followers as priests, and taught God's commands (Hebrews 9:15-26; 1 Peter 2:5; Matthew 5)

***Built a dwelling place for God:*** Moses built a tabernacle for God (Exodus 25:9). Jesus is building his followers into a living temple of the Holy Spirit (1 Peter 2:5).

***Created a kingdom of priests:*** Moses brought the people to God to be a kingdom of priests (Exodus 19:6). Jesus is making his followers a kingdom of priests (Revelation 1:6).

***Interceded for God's people:*** Moses interceded for the people (Numbers 14:13-19). Jesus interceded for us on earth and intercedes now (John 17; Romans 8:34).

***Freed from slavery:*** Moses freed the Israelites from slavery in Egypt (Deuteronomy 5:15). Jesus frees all who trust him from slavery to sin (John 8:34-36).

### Led an exodus from exile

Moses led the Israelites from Egypt to the promised land. He led them in battles, just like a king, though he was not called a king. The Father has crowned Jesus as King forever (Hebrews 1:8; Revelation 19:16). He is bringing us to God's kingdom in the heavenly promised land (Hebrews 11:16).

### Summary

Moses said that when God raised up a prophet like him, "it is to him you shall listen" (Deuteronomy 18:15). To Jesus's disciples, God said, "Listen to him"—the same command. But whereas the voice from the cloud called Moses to receive the commandments, this time the voice from the cloud said, "This is my beloved Son, with whom I am well pleased" (Matthew 17:5). Jesus was not merely a prophet like Moses: He was God's beloved Son. Moses knew God face-to-face, but Jesus came from God (John 1:18). Moreover, Moses was a prophet who proclaimed God's words (Deuteronomy 34:10). Although godly people called Jesus a prophet, he was more than that. He was the Word of God himself (John 1:1).

24. ♥ What part of Jesus being a prophet like Moses stands out to you the most? Why?

## The Kingdom Deliverer in Hebrews

25. Read Hebrews 3:1-6. (a) Who has greater glory (verse 3)? (b) What were Moses's and Jesus's roles in God's house (verses 5-6)? (c) Who is God's house (verse 6)?

Although godly people called Jesus a prophet, he was more than that. He was the Word of God himself.

## Day 5

## God's Way and Human Ways

In Exodus 16, God provided the Israelites with manna and quail. But soon after, "they tested the LORD by saying, 'Is the LORD among us or not?'" (Exodus 17:7).

Mark's Gospel shows this happening to Jesus too. In Mark 8, Jesus fed a mostly Gentile crowd, this time 4000 with seven loaves and a few small fish (Mark 7:31; 8:1-9). Soon after, Pharisees came and argued with him.

> 26. (a) What did the Pharisees want from Jesus (Mark 8:11)? (b) Why?

Just as many of the Israelites refused to accept the evidence of the signs God gave them through Moses, so many of the Jews in Jesus's day refused to accept the evidence of the signs God gave them through Jesus.

When Jesus asked his disciples who they said he was, Peter replied, "You are the Christ" (Mark 8:29). Peter recognized correctly that Jesus was the Christ—the Messiah. But Jesus wanted him to see more. He taught them that he must suffer, die, and rise.

> 27. (a) How did Peter respond to Jesus (Mark 8:32)? (b) On what had Peter been setting his mind (verse 33)? (c) On what should he have set his mind (verse 33)?

Peter didn't recognize that the Messiah was also the suffering, righteous servant. "For my thoughts are not your thoughts, neither are your ways my ways, declares the LORD. For as the heavens are higher than the earth, so are my ways higher than your ways and my thoughts than your thoughts" (Isaiah 55:8-9). Indeed. Like most Jews of the day, Peter thought the Christ would throw off Roman rule and sit on an earthly throne.[8] If Jesus did that, Peter and the other disciples would have exalted positions with him.

Peter set his mind on things of men, not things of God. That made him choose human ways over God's ways. Jesus explained how God's ways should impact him (and us).

> 28. (a) What should followers of Jesus do (Mark 8:34)? (b) Why (verses 35-36)?

In those days, bearing a cross was a mark of shame. It meant Rome had condemned you as a criminal deserving death. It meant losing everything of any worth in this life.

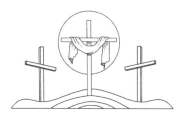

**The Little Details**

*Psalm 72*

This week we'll worship with Psalm 72. We're skipping the last three verses because they aren't part of the psalm. Verses 18-19 are the doxology to Book II of the Psalter (Psalms is divided into five books, each of which has a doxology). Verse 20 is an editorial comment.

**God with Us Still**

*God with Us Today*

Jesus calls us to deny ourselves and set our minds on God's ways. We can do this if we know what's coming in the next life.

29. In 2 Corinthians 4:16-18 below, underline the reason we shouldn't despair when our physical bodies give way. Double-underline what our sufferings prepare for us. Box what we should look to. Circle what the unseen things are.

So we do not lose heart. Though our outer self is wasting away, our inner self is being renewed day by day. For this light momentary affliction is preparing for us an eternal weight of glory beyond all comparison, as we look not to the things that are seen but to the things that are unseen. For the things that are seen are transient, but the things that are unseen are eternal.

Consider memorizing 2 Corinthians 4:16-18.

Throughout this study, we've discovered many ways in which the Lord God revealed his plan of salvation through Jesus the Messiah and then brought that plan to be.

30. ♥ How has discovering God's ability to bring his plans to fruition increased your ability to persevere through disappointment?

James 1:17 reads, "Every good gift and every perfect gift is from above, coming down from the Father of lights with whom there is no variation or shadow due to change." God does not change.

"God is love" (1 John 4:16). He always has been love, and he always will be love. Because he loves us, he will remove all causes of evil and bring us into his kingdom, where we will dwell with him forever.

31. ♥ How has discovering God's unchanging nature and eternal plan affected you?

*God with Us Forever*

Revelation 21–22 tell us more about the new heaven and earth. It describes the New Jerusalem as a perfect cube. Alexander writes, "the proportions of the city match those of the Holy of Holies, the inner sanctuary of the temple, the only other cube specifically mentioned in the Bible."[9]

32. Read Revelation 21:1–22:5. What stands out to you the most? Why?

"God is love" (1 John 4:16). He always has been love, and he always will be love.

*God with Me Now*

Psalm 72:1-17 is a royal psalm that Solomon wrote as a prayer for the monarchy. Israel reached its greatest size under Solomon, but no king ruled over the entire earth, as verse 8 asks. Zechariah 9:10 quotes verse 8 and applies it to Jesus. Verse 17 of Psalm 72 tells us that the perfect king would fulfill God's covenant with Abraham, blessing all nations through him. This didn't happen under any of the kings before Jesus, but it anticipates the coming of the perfect king who will reign forever and be a light to all nations.

Turn to Psalm 72:1-17 and read it. **Pray** the psalm to the Lord in worship.

**Praise** God for something you saw of his character this week. **Confess** anything that convicted you. **Ask** for help to do something God's Word calls you to do. **Thank** God for something you learned this week.

# The Heart and Art of Worship

Wow! We've come to the end of our adventure together—exploring the Old Testament and discovering the signposts God planted all along our path...signs of prophecies and promises all pointing us to Jesus, our Savior and soon-coming King. I feel like we should celebrate...throw sprinkles of confetti in the air, or maybe even do a happy dance. Not because the study is over but because we leave our time together with our eyes on Jesus and the glory that is ours when he returns!

But for now, we wait...not with idle hands, but with renewed passion to stir up the gifts that dwell within us...the spiritual gifts, artistic talents, and natural abilities that God wove into the fiber of our being before we were even born. With greater zeal, we use those God-given gifts to glorify his name and proclaim his praises whenever, wherever, and however he leads us while we wait.

The Bible says you are God's handiwork, created in Christ Jesus, to do good works...to be his hands, his heart, and his voice in this world, and he's given you everything you need—including your gifts, talents, and abilities—to do it. You see, you are one of a kind by God's design, and he has planted you right where you are for a purpose and for such a time as this for a reason. There are people in your neighborhood, your church, your office, and especially your home, who need to see Jesus living in you and through you...to see his truth, his love, and his character being lived out in very real and practical ways. Try asking God every morning to give you an opportunity to bring him glory and be a special blessing to someone that day. Stay alert and you might just be surprised at how creative God can be at setting up divine appointments.

And as you color this last illustration, take some time to celebrate our soon-coming King and maybe even get up, turn on some music, and do that happy dance in his honor!

*Karla*

# Appendix

## Creative Ideas

Engage with Scripture through the arts! Visit www.DiscoveringTheBibleSeries.com for info on items marked 🖥.

### Visual Arts Options

- Find techniques for expressing Scripture with art in Karla's The Heart and Art of Worship offerings.
- Color the bookmarks at the start of each chapter and the full-page illustrations at the end of each chapter.
- Write a verse in calligraphy.
- Create an art journal: sketch, paint, and affix photos and words from magazines.
- 🖥 Overlay a verse on top of a photograph.
- Create a diorama or sculpture or piece of jewelry.
- Create fabric art using cross-stitch, embroidery, or appliqué.
- 🖥 Scan the bookmark, use photo editing software to color it, and print it on printable fabric to use as is or to embroider.
- Create greeting cards or T-shirts to encourage others.
- 🖥 In a journaling Bible, pick one verse to illuminate in the wide margin.

### Performing Arts Options

- 🖥 Find a musical version of passages to play or sing.
- Act out a passage as you read or recite it aloud to music (spoken Word poetry).
- Write music and lyrics based on a passage.

### Literary Arts Options

- Form a passage's message into a poem of any type you like.
- Write an encouraging letter to someone based on a verse.

### Culinary Arts Options

- Celebrate a Christian holiday with a feast in which you talk about the meaning of the holiday.
- Celebrate answered prayer with a meal in which you publicly give thanks.

### Sharing Options

- Share your creations with your small group.
- 🖥 Post recordings, writings, and pictures in the Facebook group, "Discovering Jesus in the OT."
- Also share on Facebook, Instagram, and Twitter with #DiscoveringJesusInTheOT.

# Notes

## Chapter 1—Genesis 3: Jesus the Serpent Crusher

1. Albert H. Baylis, *From Creation to the Cross: Understanding the First Half of the Bible* (Grand Rapids: Zondervan, 1996), 26.

2. Ibid.

3. Ibid., 30.

4. Ibid., 43-44.

5. R.B. Chisholm Jr., "Theophany," T. Desmond Alexander and Brian S. Rosner, eds., *New Dictionary of Biblical Theology* (Downers Grove, IL: InterVarsity, 2000), 817.

6. Clay Jones, *Why Does God Allow Evil?* (Eugene: Harvest House, 2017), 31-32.

7. T. Desmond Alexander, *From Eden to the New Jerusalem: An Introduction to Biblical Theology* (Grand Rapids: Kregel, 2008), 15.

8. C. Hassell Bullock, "Introduction to Job," D.A. Carson, ed., *NIV Zondervan Study Bible* (Grand Rapids: Zondervan, 2015), 903.

9. "This term 'anointed'...refers to the chosen king. The anglicized pronunciation is 'messiah' or when referring to the greatest and final one, 'the Messiah.'" Allen P. Ross, *A Commentary on the Psalms*, 3 vols. (Grand Rapids: Kregel, 2011–2016), 1:204.

10. For consistency, all dates are from Carson, *NIV Study Bible*. Where the 1985 Zondervan Old Testament Chronology and New Testament Chronology conflict with the study notes, the notes take precedence.

11. G.K. Beale and Sean M. McDonough, "Revelation." In G.K. Beale and D.A. Carson, eds., *Commentary on the New Testament Use of the Old Testament* (Grand Rapids: Baker Academic, 2007), 1125-26.

12. William L. Lane, *Hebrews 1–8*, eds. David A. Hubbard and Glenn W. Barker, Word Biblical Commentary (Nashville, TN: Thomas Nelson, 1991), 47A:61.

## Chapter 2—Genesis 22: Jesus the Sacrificed Son

1. "Yet the issue of human mortality in 6:1-4, as we have seen it in continuum with the garden *tôlĕdôt* (2:7, 17; 3:6, 17-24), recommends we take the 120 years as the shortening of life. Since 6:3 concerns God's judgment against all humanity (*'ādām*) and a period of grace would affect only one generation, it is better to take the 120 years as a reference to human life span." Kenneth A. Mathews, *Genesis 1–11:26: An Exegetical and Theological Exposition of Holy Scripture*, ed. E. Ray Clendenen, New American Commentary (Nashville, TN: Broadman & Holman, 1996), 1a:334, WORD*search* CROSS e-book.

2. One of the most startling excavations from Ur is the so-called "Royal Cemetery" with pits containing human sacrifices, most of them adults. One pit had over 70 human sacrifices elaborately arrayed. Laerke Recht, "Symbolic Order: Liminality and Simulation in Human Sacrifice in the Bronze-age Aegean and Near East," *Journal of Religion and Violence* (Academic Publishing, ISSN 0738-098X, 2014), 2:3, 413-14.

3. Ibid., 2:3, 404.

4. John Day, *Molech: A god of human sacrifice in the Old Testament* (Cambridge: Cambridge University Press, 1989), 62-63.

5. Henrietta Mears, quoted in Earl R. Roe, *Dream Big: The Henrietta Mears Story* (Ventura, CA: Regal, 1990), 57, quoted in Pam Farrel, *Woman of Influence* (Downers Grove, IL: InterVarsity, 2006), 71-72.

6. Billy Graham, quoted in "When Billy Graham Overcame Doubt at Forest Home," Forest Home, March 6, 2018, https://www.for esthome.org/a-small-moment-in-the-amazing-legacy-of-billy -grahams-ministry/.

7. Kenneth A. Mathews, *Genesis 11:27–50:26: An Exegetical and Theological Exposition of Holy Scripture*, ed. E. Ray Clendenen, New American Commentary (Nashville, TN: Broadman & Holman, 2005), 1b:171.

8. Trent Hunter and Stephen Wellum, *Christ from Beginning to End: How the Full Story of Scripture Reveals the Full Glory of Christ* (Grand Rapids: Zondervan, 2018), 55.

9. Recht, "Symbolic Order," 413-14.

10. Laerke Recht, "Human sacrifice in the ancient Near East," *Trinity College Dublin Journal of Postgraduate Research* (Dublin: Brunswick Press, 2010), 9:171. Recht says, "The tradition of human sacrifice appears to have continued at Ur into the Ur III period, as shown by the evidence from the Mausoleum of King Shulgi and Amarsin, where one tomb chamber belonged to the king, and another contained a number of human skeletons, interpreted as sacrificial victims."

11. Andreas J. Köstenberger, "John." In Beale and Carson, *New Testament Use of Old Testament*, 420-22.

12. Paul Copan, *Is God a Moral Monster?: Making Sense of the Old Testament God* (Grand Rapids: Baker, 2011), 47.

13. Vern S. Poythress, *Theophany: A Biblical Theology of God's Appearing* (Wheaton: Crossway, 2018), 417.

14. Jay Sklar, *Leviticus: An Introduction and Commentary*, ed. David G. Firth, Tyndale Old Testament Commentaries (Downers Grove, IL: InterVarsity, 2014), 3:50.

15. D.A. Hagner, "PHARISEES," ed. Merrill C. Tenney, *The Zondervan Pictorial Encyclopedia of the Bible*, 2nd printing (Grand Rapids: Zondervan, 1977), 4:745-52.

16. J.E.H. Thomson, "PHARISEES," *The International Standard Bible Encyclopedia*, ed. James Orr (Chicago: Howard-Severance Co., 1915), s.v. "PHARISEES," WORD*search* CROSS e-book.

17. D.A. Hagner, "SADDUCEES." In Tenney, *Zondervan Encyclopedia*, 5:211-16.

18. Köstenberger includes John 3:16 as an allusion to Genesis 22:2,12,16 in his chart of "verifiable OT allusions and verbal parallels in John's Gospel." He writes that his list "is conservative; only those passages have been included that can be determined with a reasonable degree of confidence to have been intended by the Fourth Evangelist as allusions or verbal parallels to specific OT texts." Köstenberger, "John." In Beale and Carson, *New Testament Use of Old Testament*, 419-22.

19. D.A. Carson, *The Gospel According to John* (Grand Rapids: Wm. B. Eerdmans, 1991), 205.

20. Mathews, *Genesis 11:27–50:26,* 283.

21. Ibid., 302.

22. Mathews, *Genesis 11:27–50:26,* 293.

23. Mathews, *Genesis 11:27–50:26,* 303.

24. Augustine, *The City of God,* trans. Marcus Dods (New York: Random House, 1950), 554-56.

25. The five promises are in Genesis 12:3; 18:18; 22:18; 26:4; and 28:14. Paul probably combines 12:3 and 18:18. Douglass J. Moo, *Galatians,* eds. Robert W. Yarbrough and Robert H. Stein, Baker

Exegetical Commentary on the New Testament (Grand Rapids: Baker Academic, 2013), 218.

26. Hunter and Wellum, *Christ from Beginning to End*, 123-24.

27. Mathews, *Genesis 11:27–50:26*, 303.

28. D.M. Lloyd-Jones, *Romans: An Exposition of Chapter 8:17-39: The Final Perseverance of the Saints* (Grand Rapids: Zondervan, 1975), 389, 396-97.

## Chapter 3—Exodus 12: Jesus the Sacrificed Lamb

1. "Although the text does not specify that animals were slain to provide these coverings, it is a fair implication and one that likely would be made in the Mosaic community, where animal sacrifice was pervasive. Since the garden narrative shares in tabernacle imagery, it is not surprising that allusion to animal sacrifice is found in the garden too." Mathews, *Genesis 11:27–50:26*, 253.

2. Sklar, *Leviticus*, 9.

3. Nancie Carmichael, *The Unexpected Power of Home* (Sisters, OR: Deep River Books, 2018), 14-15.

4. Paul M. Hoskins, *That Scripture Might Be Fulfilled: Typology and the Death of Christ* (Xulon, 2009), 89-90.

5. Baylis, *Creation to the Cross*, 107.

6. Exodus 12:5-8. Moses interspersed instructions about the annual ceremony with the actual telling of the story.

7. They arrive at Mount Sinai "on the first day of the third month after the Israelites left Egypt" (Exodus 19:1 NIV). They depart "on the twentieth day of the second month of the second year" (Numbers 10:11-12 NIV).

8. Hunter and Wellum, *Christ from Beginning to End*, 138.

9. Eugene H. Merrill, *Kingdom of Priests: A History of Old Testament Israel*, 2nd ed. (Grand Rapids: Baker, 2008), 98-99.

10. Alexander, *Eden to New Jerusalem*, 32-34.

11. Hunter and Wellum, *Christ from Beginning to End*, 142.

12. Allen P. Ross, *Recalling the Hope of Glory: Biblical Worship from the Garden to the New Creation* (Grand Rapids: Kregel, 2006), 198-204.

13. Craig L. Blomberg, "Matthew." In Beale and Carson, *New Testament Use of Old Testament*, 8.

14. Kevin DeYoung, "Sin," Carson, *NIV Study Bible*, 2644.

15. Hunter and Wellum, *Christ from Beginning to End*, 144.

## Chapter 4—Psalm 22: Jesus the Afflicted One

1. Hoskins, *That Scripture Might Be Fulfilled* (Xulon, 2009), 55.

2. Ross, *Psalms*, 1:534.

3. Sklar, *Leviticus*, 39-49.

4. Ibid., 1:544.

5. Ibid., 1:546.

6. Hoskins, *That Scripture Might Be Fulfilled* (Xulon, 2009), 47.

7. Ross, *Psalms*, 1:536.

8. William D. Edwards, Wesley J. Gabel, and Floyd E. Hosmer, "On the Physical Death of Jesus Christ," *JAMA: The Journal of the American Medical Association*, 1986, 255:1455-63.

9. Ibid.

10. Ibid.

11. Though scholars offer many views as to what exactly happened when Jesus uttered this cry, at the least it was a separation of the sense of the Father's presence.

12. In Luke 2:24, Mary offered "a pair of doves or two young pigeons" for her purification, which the law permitted for mothers who could not afford a lamb. Carson, *NIV Study Bible*, s.v. "Luke 2:24."

## Chapter 5—2 Samuel 7: Jesus the King Forever

1. Alexander, *From Eden to New Jerusalem*, 43.

2. Great kings are called suzerains. The kings who served them were called vassals. David's son would be a vassal of the Lord God.

3. Robert D. Bergen, *1, 2 Samuel: An Exegetical and Theological Exposition of Holy Scripture*, ed. E. Ray Clendenen, New American Commentary (Nashville, TN: Broadman & Holman, 1996), 7:375, WORD*search* CROSS e-book.

4. Alexander, *Eden to New Jerusalem*, 41.

5. Ibid., 43.

6. Ibid., 16.

7. Carson, *NIV Study Bible*, s.v. "Ezra 6:15."

8. Ross, *Psalms*, 3:442.

9. Carson, *NIV Study Bible*, s.v. "Luke 21:5."

10. T. Whitelaw, "TEMPLE," James Orr, ed., *The International Standard Bible Encyclopedia*, (Chicago: Howard-Severance Co., 1915), s.v. "TEMPLE," WORD*search* CROSS e-book.

11. Ross, *Psalms*, 3:453.

12. G.K. Beale and Benjamin L. Gladd, *Hidden But Now Revealed: A Biblical Theology of Mystery* (Downers Grove, IL: IVP, 2014), 293-94.

13. Compare with 2 Kings 9:12-13.

14. Ross, *Psalms*, 3:453-54.

15. Carson, *John*, 182.

16. Ross, *Psalms*, 3:443.

17. Ibid., 3:442.

18. Ibid., 3:457.

## Chapter 6—Psalm 110: Jesus the High Priest Forever

1. "All Time Box Office," *Box Office Mojo*, https://www.boxofficemojo.com/alltime/adjusted.htm (accessed 3/6/2019).

2. Carson, *NIV Study Bible*, s.v. "Psalm 110."

3. Ross, *Psalms*, 3:345.

4. Ibid.

5. Outline adapted from Warren C. Wiersbe, *The Wiersbe Bible Commentary: Old Testament* (Colorado Springs: David C. Cook, 2007), 995-96.

6. Ross, *Psalms*, 3:343.

7. Ibid., 3:346.

8. Ibid., 3:350.

9. Ibid., 3:346-347.

10. Ibid., 3:352.

11. Ibid., 3:353.

12. Ibid., 3:357.

13. Ibid.

14. Mark F. Rooker, *Leviticus: An Exegetical and Theological Exposition of Holy Scripture*, ed. E. Ray Clendenen, New American Commentary (Nashville, TN: Broadman & Holman, 2000), 3a:86, WORD*search* CROSS e-book.

15. A. Rainey, "SCRIBE, SCRIBES." In Tenney, *Zondervan Encyclopedia*, 5:301.

16. Ibid., 4:745-52.

17. Ibid., 5:211-16.

18. Ibid., 1036-37.

19. Alexander, *Eden to New Jerusalem,* 130.

20. Ross, *Psalms,* 3:53-54.

21. Baylis, *Creation to the Cross,* 154.

22. Ross, *Psalms,* 3:359.

23. William L. Lane, *Hebrews 9–13,* eds. David A. Hubbard and Glenn W. Barker, Word Biblical Commentary (Nashville, TN: Thomas Nelson, 1991), 47b:284.

24. Alexander, *Eden to New Jerusalem,* 25.

25. Sklar, *Leviticus,* 52.

## Chapter 7—Isaiah 9: Jesus the Mighty God

1. The outline of Isaiah is based on John N. Oswalt, *The Book of Isaiah: Chapters 1–39,* eds. R.K. Harrison and Robert L. Hubbard Jr., The New International Commentary on the Old Testament (Grand Rapids: Eerdmans, 1986), 54-64.

2. Ibid., 205.

3. Ibid., 203.

4. Carson, *NIV Study Bible,* s.v. "Isaiah 7:14."

5. Oswalt, *Isaiah: Chapters 1–39,* 222.

6. "That Hezekiah was twenty-five years old at his accession in 516 (2 Kings 18:2) means that he was born in 741, at least six years before these events." Ibid., 212.

7. Oswalt, *Isaiah: Chapters 1–39,* 220.

8. Oswalt, *Isaiah: Chapters 1–39,* 227.

9. Ibid., 245.

10. Baylis, *Creation to the Cross,* 275.

11. Blomberg, "Matthew." In Beale and Carson, *New Testament Use of Old Testament,* 18-19.

12. NIV mg., "Matthew 1:21."

13. Blomberg, "Matthew." In Beale and Carson, *New Testament Use of Old Testament,* 5.

14. Oswalt, *Isaiah: Chapters 1–39,* 247.

15. Ibid.

16. George H. Guthrie, "Hebrews." In Beale and Carson, *New Testament Use of Old Testament,* 951.

17. Poythress, *Theophany,* 382.

## Chapter 8—Isaiah 52–53: Jesus the Suffering Servant

1. Baylis, *Creation to the Cross,* 287.

2. Ephrat Livni, "Blue mind science proves the health benefits of being by water," Quartz, August 5, 2018, https://qz.com/1347904/blue-mind-science-proves-the-health-benefits-of-being-by-water/.

3. The outline of Isaiah is based on Oswalt, *Isaiah: Chapters 1–39,* 54-64.

4. John N. Oswalt, *The Book of Isaiah: Chapters 40–66,* ed. Robert L. Hubbard Jr., The New International Commentary on the Old Testament (Grand Rapids: William B. Eerdmans, 1998), 291.

5. Baylis, *Creation to the Cross,* 294.

6. Sklar, *Leviticus,* 42.

7. Hunter and Wellum, *Christ from Beginning to End,* 58-59.

8. Baylis, *Creation to the Cross,* 292.

9. Oswalt, *Isaiah: Chapters 40–66,* 395.

10. Ibid., 405.

11. The early church treated foot washing as a good deed, not a universal rite: "The heart of Jesus's command is a humility and helpfulness toward brothers and sisters in Christ that may be cruelly parodied by a mere 'rite' of foot washing that easily masks an unbroken spirit and haughty heart." Carson, *John,* 468.

## Chapter 9—Isaiah 49: Jesus the Light of the World

1. Douglas K. Stuart, *Exodus: An Exegetical and Theological Exposition of Holy Scripture,* ed. E. Ray Clendenen, New American Commentary (Nashville, TN: Broadman & Holman, 2006), 2:423, WORD*search* CROSS e-book.

2. Hunter and Wellum, *Christ from Beginning to End,* 227.

3. Abbie Burgess, quoted in "Abbie Burgess, Teenaged Heroine of Matinicus Rock Light," New England Historical Society, updated 2018, http://www.newenglandhistoricalsociety.com/abbie-burgess-16-year-old-heroine-matinicus-rock-lighthouse/.

4. Wayne Wheeler, quoted in "On stormy seas, we still look to the light in the darkness," The Trust for Public Land, August 2, 2016, https://www.tpl.org/blog/lighthouses#sm.00001moanfmrpofo3zgi87yvehzwl.

5. Carson, *NIV Study Bible,* s.v. "Psalm 82:1."

6. Oswalt, *Isaiah: Chapters 40–66,* 382.

7. Oswalt, *Isaiah: Chapters 40–66,* 527.

8. Baylis, *Creation to the Cross,* 295.

9. Carson, *NIV Study Bible,* s.v. "Isaiah 65:17-25."

10. See 2 Kings 17; 2 Chronicles 30; 34. "Exile of the Northern Kingdom" (chart). In Carson, *NIV Study Bible,* 687.

11. R.E. Davies, "GEHENNA." In Tenney, *Zondervan Encyclopedia,* 2:670-72.

12. Borchert, *John 1–11,* 294.

13. Carson, *John,* 337-38.

14. Ibid., 337.

15. Ibid., 388.

16. Poythress, *Theophany,* 156.

17. Ibid., 169.

18. Ibid., 167.

19. Ron Rhodes, "The New Age Movement (Pantheism and Monism)," Bodie Hodge and Roger Paterson, *World Religions and Cults: Moralistic, Mythical and Mysticism Religions* (Green Forest, AR: Master Books, 2016), 2:22.

## Chapter 10—Jeremiah 31: Jesus the Covenant Mediator

1. Hunter and Wellum, *Christ from Beginning to End,* 55.

2. Ibid., 116.

3. The high priest who served during Josiah's reign found the Book of the Law while repairing the temple (2 Kings 22:8-13). He and Josiah read it and appear surprised at what it said, even though the priests were supposed to read it publicly every seven years at the Feast of Booths (Deuteronomy 31:10-11).

4. Alexander, *Eden to New Jerusalem,* 56-57.

5. Hunter and Wellum, *Christ from Beginning to End,* 136.

6. Craig L. Blomberg, *Matthew: An Exegetical and Theological Exposition of Holy Scripture,* ed. David S. Dockery, New American Commentary (Nashville, TN: Broadman & Holman, 1992), 22:101, WORD*search* CROSS e-book.

7. Daniel I. Block, *The Triumph of Grace: Literary and Theological*

*Studies in Deuteronomy and Deuteronomic Themes* (Eugene: Cascade, 2017), 44, Kindle.

8. Ross, *Psalms*, 1:189.

9. Carson, *NIV Study Bible*, s.v. "John 3:5."

10. Sklar, *Leviticus*, 53-54.

11. Hunter and Wellum, *Christ from Beginning to End*, 231.

12. Sklar, *Leviticus*, 72.

## Chapter 11—Daniel 7: Jesus the Son of Man

1. The Assyrian/Babylonian exile is later called a "return to Egypt" and the promised restoration a "second" exodus (Hosea 9:3; Isaiah 11:11). Thomas Richard Wood, "Exile and Exodus," Carson, *NIV Study Bible*, 2659.

2. Elisa Morgan, *The Prayer Coin* (Grand Rapids, MI: Discovery House, 2018), 9.

3. Ken Nichols, "Always Living In View of Eternity,*"Alive Ministries, May 7, 2017 http://www.aliveministries.net/firstpost/.

4. Stephen R. Miller, *Daniel: An Exegetical and Theological Exposition of Holy Scripture*, ed. E. Ray Clendenen, New American Commentary (Nashville, TN: Broadman & Holman, 1994), 18:58, WORD*search* CROSS e-book.

5. "The city of Babylon was not only bisected by the Euphrates but was also penetrated by many canals. The height of the Euphrates would have been at its lowest level at this time of the year, normally about twelve feet deep. If the famine (mentioned in more than one text) was caused by a dry year, the level would have been even lower." Edwin M. Yamauchi, *Persia and the Bible* (Grand Rapids: BakerBooks, 1996), 86.

6. Ibid., 87.

7. James M. Hamilton, Jr., *With the Clouds of Heaven*, ed. D.A. Carson, New Studies in Biblical Theology (Downers Grove, IL: InterVarsity, 2014), 32:86.

8. Carson, *NIV Study Bible*, s.v. "Daniel 2:36-45."

9. Hamilton, *Clouds of Heaven*, 181.

10. Ibid., 150.

11. Ibid., 181.

12. Poythress, *Theophany*, 67-68.

13. James A. Brooks writes, "Both Jesus and Mark may have intended 'I am' to be more than an affirmative answer. It may be an allusion to the divine name in Exod 3:14." But this isn't certain." James A. Brooks, *Mark: An Exegetical and Theological Exposition of Holy Scripture*, ed. David S. Dockery, New American Commentary (Nashville, TN: Broadman Press, 1991), 23:242, WORD*search* CROSS e-book.

14. Carson, *NIV Study Bible*, s.v. "Mark 14:62."

15. Hamilton, *Clouds of Heaven*, 150.

16. Ibid., 190.

17. Poythress, *Theophany*, 402-03.

18. Alexander, *Eden to New Jerusalem*, 17-18.

19. Ibid., 18-19.

## Chapter 12—Zechariah 2: Jesus the Kingdom Deliverer

1. Isabel Kershner, "Iran Fires Rockets Into Golan Heights From Syria, Israelis Say," *New York Times*, March 9, 2018, https://www.nytimes.com/2018/05/09/world/middleeast/israel-iran-attack.html.

2. "It is preferable to understand the phrase in 2:9 to mean 'the latter glory of this house' rather than 'the glory of this latter house.' This understanding is confirmed by v. 3, which speaks of 'his house in its former glory.'" Richard A. Taylor, *Haggai, Malachi: An Exegetical and Theological Exposition of Holy Scripture*, ed. E. Ray Clendenen, New American Commentary (Nashville, TN: Broadman & Holman, 2004), 21a:167, WORD*search* CROSS e-book.

3. Carson, *NIV Study Bible*, s.v. "Ezra 1:1-11."

4. Gerald L. Borchert, *John 1–11: An Exegetical and Theological Exposition of Holy Scripture*, ed. E. Ray Clendenen, New American Commentary (Nashville, TN: Broadman & Holman, 1996), 25a:118, WORD*search* CROSS e-book.

5. Carson, *NIV Study Bible*, s.v. "John 1:14."

6. Poythress, *Theophany*, 382.

7. Carson, *NIV Study Bible*, s.v. "Zechariah 12:1–14:21."

8. "Peter, however, possessed as he was by a nationalistic concept of the Messiah, contradicted Jesus." Brooks, *Mark*, 135.

9. Alexander, *Eden to New Jerusalem*, 20.

## Acknowledgments

### All of Us

To our *Discovering Hope in the Psalms* and *Discovering Joy in Philippians* readers, thank you for being our traveling companions on this creative Bible study devotional journey. May we sojourn together on more biblical expeditions.

### Pam Farrel

Karla, your amazing art continues to inspire me to walk in the footsteps of Christ with my eye on heaven and all God's glory. To Jean, thank you for this labor of love. We owe you a day at the spa and a life's supply of sticky notes. To Hope, our steadfast editor, your life is an expression of the power of Christ. To Bob Hawkins and the Harvest House team, thank you for faithfully standing strong on the truth of Scripture and believing in this creative Discovering the Bible series. To my kids and grandkids, watching you each walk with Jesus is a delight! To our Living Love-Wise Community, thank you for your prayers and support, may God lavish you with love.

### Jean E. Jones

To God, thank you for revealing to us your great love. To Clay, thank you for reading the manuscript and offering so many valuable suggestions, for taking over chores, and for being the best husband ever. To Pam, thank you for pouring your considerable talents and exuberance into this project. To Karla, your incredible, worshipful art astounds me. To Angie Wright, Jean Strand, Kerrie Parlett, and Virginia Thompson, thank you for timing the lessons, my amazing friends. To Hope Lyda, our editor, thank you for your patience, insights, and encouragement—you're a joy to work with. To Kathleen Kerr and the Harvest House team, thank you for taking on this project and for embracing the vision so enthusiastically.

### Karla Dornacher

Pam...thank you again for asking and encouraging me to join you on this Discovering Jesus journey. It's been a beautiful ride! Jean...your skills make my head spin and your love for the Lord and knowledge of His Word inspire me. Thank you to the Harvest House team for walking with us through every step of this journey. And as always to my beautiful family...you are the most loving supporters a girl could ask for.

*About the Authors*

## Pam Farrel

Pam Farrel is an international speaker, author of 45 books including *7 Simple Skills for Every Woman* and bestselling *Men Are Like Waffles, Women Are Like Spaghetti*. Pam has loved studying and teaching the Bible for over 40 years, and is wife to Bill Farrel, and together they enrich relationships through their ministry, **Love-Wise.** She and her husband enjoy the beach near their California home, often making family memories with their three sons, three daughters-in-law, and four grandchildren.

www.Love-Wise.com | Twitter: @pamfarrel |Facebook: billandpamfarrel & Creative Biblical Expressions

## Jean E. Jones

Jean E. Jones started teaching the Bible in high school and has served on women's ministry leadership teams for 20 years. She enjoys writing Bible study guides that help people put God's words into actions. With Pam and Karla, she wrote *Discovering Hope in the Psalms* and *Discovering Joy in Philippians*. Jean is a contributing writer for Crosswalk.com and has written for *Today's Christian Woman* and *Home Life*. She is a member of Women in Apologetics. Her husband, Dr. Clay Jones, is an associate professor of Christian apologetics at Talbot Seminary.

www.JeanEJones.net | Twitter: @JeanEstherJones | Facebook: JeanEJonesAuthor

## Karla Dornacher

Karla Dornacher is an artist, bestselling author, and encourager. She has written and illustrated 16 books including *Down a Garden Path* and *Love in Every Room*. Her art has been licensed for home decor and gift items including fabric, flags, cards, calendars, and most recently, coloring books and Bible journaling bookmarks. Working in her home studio in the Pacific NW, where she lives with her husband and two cats, makes her heart happy and she finds her inspiration in her walk with God, the beauty of his creation, and time spent with family and friends!

www.karladornacher.com | Facebook: karladornacher

He
WILL CRUSH
YOUR head, and
you WILL STRIKE
his heel.

genesis 3:15 niv

I WILL SURELY MULTIPLY
your offspring
as the stars
of
heaven...

and in your offspring
SHALL ALL the nations
of the earth be
blessed.

Genesis 22:16-18

The Lord...
WILL SEE THE BLOOD
ON THE TOP and SIDES
OF THE doorframe
and
will pass over
THAT doorway,

and

he WILL NOT
PERMIT
THE DESTROYER
TO ENTER.

EXODUS 12:23 NIV

for he has
NOT despised
or scorned the
SUFFERING
of the
afflicted
ONE

Psalm 22:24 niv

Y·O·U·R THRONE shall be established FOREVER

2 Samuel 7:16

YOU ARE A PRIEST FOREVER after the order of MELCHIZEDEK

Psalm 110:4

His name shall be called WONDERFUL counselor, Mighty God, everlasting FATHER, prince of PEACE.

Isaiah 9:6

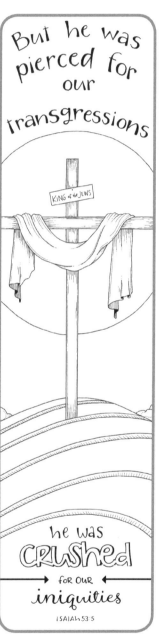

But he was pierced for our transgressions

KING of the JEWS

he was CRUSHED for our iniquities

Isaiah 53:5

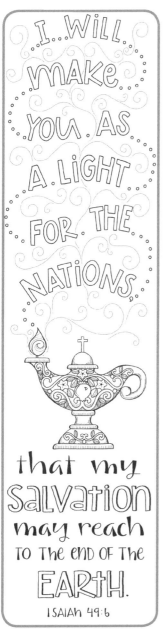

I WILL MAKE YOU AS A LIGHT FOR THE NATIONS, that my SALVATION may reach TO THE END OF THE EARTH.

ISAIAH 49:6

behold the days are coming, declares the LORD when I will make a new covenant

Jeremiah 31:31

with the clouds of heaven there came one like a SON of MAN

-DANIEL 7:13-

He shall speak PEACE to the nations his RULE shall be from Sea to Sea

Zechariah 9:10

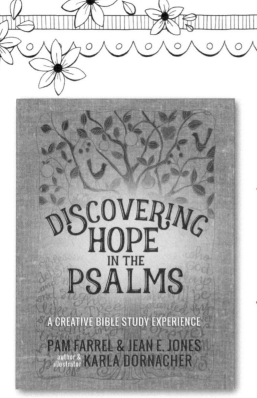

"What an incredibly unique and creative Bible study! It's multilayered, dimensional, theologically rich, touching the senses—enlightening the mind, capturing the heart."

—Kay Arthur,
cofounder of Precept Ministries International

"I love the encouragement, inspiration, and delightful details woven throughout."

—Darlene Schacht,
Time-Warp Wife and bestselling author of
*Messy Beautiful Love*

## This Isn't Your Average Bible Study

Explore God's Word on a deeper level and engage with his truth in fresh ways! This study of 10 psalms of hope invites you to discover the incredible design and purpose of inspired Hebrew poetry.

Perfect for group discussion or personal reflection, *Discovering Hope in the Psalms* offers compelling teachings, motivating devotions, and plenty of creative options for interacting with the psalms—including beautiful artwork to color. This discovery book will show you how to...

- rejoice in God's mercy when sin knocks you down
- request help with hope when troubles surround
- respond with thanksgiving for each answered prayer

Immerse your mind, heart, and soul in the hope flowing through the Psalms.

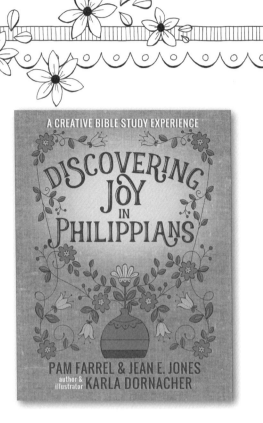

## Share the Joy

If difficult days have ever left you discouraged, this interactive 11-week journey will help you engage creatively with God's Word and establish habits that lead to greater joy and peace. Refresh your delight in the Lord through:

**Daily Lessons** with an introduction and key questions for each chapter to help you dive deeper into the heart of Scripture and incorporate it into your life with *joy builder* activities

**Choosing Joy Devotions** and inspirational quotes to stir hope even in difficult times as you learn to trust God's faithfulness and rest in his strength no matter what circumstance you find yourself in

**Creative Connections** including bookmarks and coloring pages that provide an outlet to knit your heart to God and explore your faith through artistic expression

"…that your joy may be full." John 15:11

This unique discovery book includes ideas for group studies, verse-inspired artwork to color, fascinating details about the Bible, and online connections and communities so you can build up your joy and build up others!

To find out more about the complete series, explore many creative resources, and connect with the authors and other readers, visit www.DiscoveringTheBibleSeries.com.

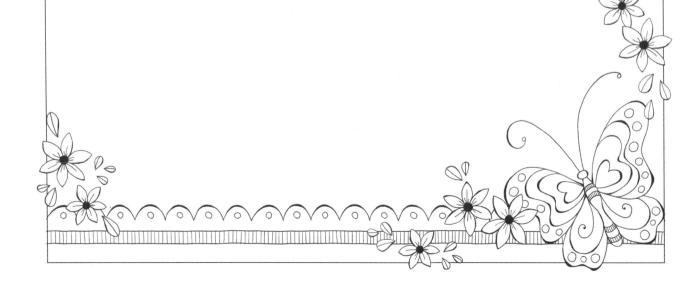